Above the Fray

AFTER THE BATTLE OF GRAVELOTTE   NACH DER SCHLACHT BEI GRAVELOTTE

Sisters of Mercy arriving on the Battle -field   die Barmherzigen Schwestern kamen aufs Schlactfeld um

to Succor the Wounded.   den Verwundeten Beizustehen.

Above the Fray

The Red Cross and the Making of the Humanitarian NGO Sector

SHAI M. DROMI

The University of Chicago Press
Chicago and London

The University of Chicago Press, Chicago 60637
The University of Chicago Press, Ltd., London
© 2020 by The University of Chicago
All rights reserved. No part of this book may be used or reproduced in any
manner whatsoever without written permission, except in the case of brief
quotations in critical articles and reviews. For more information, contact the
University of Chicago Press, 1427 E. 60th St., Chicago, IL 60637.
Published 2020
Printed in the United States of America

29 28 27 26 25 24 23 22 21 20   1 2 3 4 5

ISBN-13: 978-0-226-68010-1 (cloth)
ISBN-13: 978-0-226-68024-8 (paper)
ISBN-13: 978-0-226-68038-5 (e-book)
DOI: https://doi.org/10.7208/chicago/9780226680385.001.0001

Library of Congress Cataloging-in-Publication Data

Names: Dromi, Shai M., author.
Title: Above the fray : the Red Cross and the making of the humanitarian NGO
    sector / Shai M. Dromi.
Description: Chicago ; London : University of Chicago Press, 2020. | Includes
    bibliographical references and index.
Identifiers: LCCN 2019024405 | ISBN 9780226680101 (cloth) |
    ISBN 9780226680248 (paperback) | ISBN 9780226680385 (ebook)
Subjects: LCSH: International Committee of the Red Cross—History. |
    Humanitarianism—History—19th century. | Humanitarianism—
    History—20th century. | International relief—History. | Non-governmental
    organizations—History. | Humanitarianism—Religious aspects. |
    Calvinism—Influence.
Classification: LCC HV568 .D74 2020 | DDC 361.7/72—dc23
LC record available at https://lccn.loc.gov/2019024405

CONTENTS

Preface / vii

Introduction / The Humanitarian Space / 1

ONE / Inter Arma Caritas: The Cultural Origins of Humanitarian
NGOs / 14

TWO / The Réveil and the Founding of the Red Cross / 35

THREE / The Spread of Humanitarian Culture Across Borders / 61

FOUR / The Spread of Humanitarian Logics into New Domains / 88

FIVE / *Sans-Frontiérisme* and the Rise of "New Humanitarianism" / 116

Conclusion / Reconsidering the Culture of the Humanitarian Field / 132

Acknowledgments / 139
Appendix: Sources and methodology / 141
Notes / 143
Bibliography / 181
Index / 207

A series of explosions rocked the Afghan city of Kunduz on the night of October 3, 2015. Over the course of an hour, a U.S. Air Force gunship fired 211 shells at a building its crew identified, at the time, as a Taliban stronghold. However, far from being a terrorist base, the small building housed the Kunduz Trauma Centre—a hospital providing free, high-quality medical care to trauma victims. The hospital housed 140 beds, three operating rooms, an intensive care unit, an X-ray facility, a pharmacy, and physiotherapy practitioners—rare commodities in northeastern Afghanistan. The facility made no political distinctions among its patients, treating wounded Taliban and Afghan government personnel side by side. At least forty-two people died in the attack, including fourteen staff members, twenty-four patients, and four patient family members.[1] The hospital, large parts of which were destroyed, was permanently shut down, cutting locals off from their main source of medical support.

The Kunduz hospital airstrike sparked international outrage. Within hours of the attack, United Nations Secretary-General Ban Ki-moon issued a strong condemnation, and called for an impartial investigation into the events of that night. UN High Commissioner for Human Rights Zeid Ra'ad Al Hussein called the event "tragic, inexcusable, and possibly even criminal."[2] Photographs of the ruins circulated widely in international media, and demonstrations occurred in Geneva, Washington, D.C., and elsewhere.[3] However, similarly deadly—and considerably deadlier—incidents had occurred in Afghanistan prior to the Kunduz attack and had received far less international exposure: a 2009 U.S. airstrike in the village of Granai—among the casualties, ninety-three children dead;[4] a 2010 NATO attack on Sangin village—fifty-two civilians dead;[5] U.S. warplanes bombing of a wedding party in

Wech Baghtu in 2008—among the casualties, twenty-three children dead;[6] an attack on a wedding celebration in Haska Meyna later in the same year— forty-seven were reportedly killed.[7] Despite the staggering noncombatant death tolls in these and other incidents, few of them received nearly the same international attention as the Kunduz hospital airstrike.

Part of the international anger over the hospital bombing certainly stems from the fact that Westerners were killed in Kunduz, when Afghan deaths sadly receive far less notice outside of Afghanistan, but numerous Western- ers have previously died in the cross-fires and have not received such atten- tion. However, the Kunduz Trauma Centre was different because it was oper- ated by the international nongovernmental organization (NGO) Médecins sans Frontières (MSF), renowned for its volunteer medical humanitarian projects in the harshest conflict zones. Like many of its peer organizations, MSF prides itself on being *impartial* by treating all those in need without discriminating among them; being *independent* of all constraints not relating directly to humanitarian work; and being *neutral*, and thus not taking a side in hostilities or political controversies. The MSF flags that were placed on the roof of the Kunduz Trauma Centre demarcated the hospital as neutral terri- tory. By striking this building, the U.S. Air Force did not simply contravene international humanitarian law, which designates such spaces inviolable. It violated a sacred international norm—that humanitarian NGOs occupy a special position outside of all routine conflict considerations and should thus be protected from all harm. As an international organization, MSF was able to communicate its censure of this violation across boundaries and to draw international outrage unlike any other type of actor in Afghanistan.

But while the work MSF does in Afghanistan and elsewhere is commend- able, the idea that volunteer societies ought to do it is remarkably new. In fact, critical voices in scholarly and policy conversations have raised ques- tions about whether NGO work ultimately displaces local state and civil society institutions. However, the question of *how* humanitarian NGOs have come to possess such extraordinary prestige and international authority in the first place is rarely asked. In this book, I investigate how organizations like MSF, Oxfam International, the International Rescue Committee, and other international humanitarian NGOs came to be sanctified in interna- tional law, politics, society, and culture. To do so, I examine the history of the oldest and largest network of humanitarian organizations in existence today, the International Red Cross and Red Crescent Movement, and in par- ticular its founding committee, the International Committee of the Red Cross (ICRC). While normally Red Cross societies in different countries are at least partially supported by their national governments (and are thus not entirely "nongovernmental"), the Red Cross movement provided the template and the institutional infrastructure that have supported humanitarian NGOs in the past 150 years. The ICRC specifically is behind the Geneva Convention, which provides the legal protections that allow humanitarian NGOs to work in conflict zones.

When I first visited the archive of the ICRC in Geneva in 2012, my research interests revolved around the ways the Red Cross worked to elicit sympathy across borders in the nineteenth century. Since the ICRC emerged through the private initiative of five Genevans in the 1860s, I started by examining their early professional correspondences. Looking at the diaries, personal correspondences, and meeting protocols, I was struck by the ways these early activists employed theological reasonings as they grappled with organizational and ethical issues relating to humanitarian work. To better understand the religious context in which they were operating, I turned to the teachings, writings, and sermons of the clergy working in Geneva at the time—especially those belonging to the Réveil movement, to which the ICRC founders belonged. The Réveil was a nineteenth-century conservative Calvinist movement that emphasized, among other things, the active involvement of private charity in addressing public problems. Before I knew it, my research had turned to the role of religion in shaping civil society organization.

This book does not use these archival findings to provide an exhaustive retelling of the history of humanitarian NGOs or to identify the overall historical origins of humanitarian practices and sentiments. Instead, it asks how the idea that humanitarian work is best provided by nongovernmental organizations—impartial, neutral, and independent ones—became so prevalent among practitioners and policy makers alike. It argues, in brief, that the Réveil provided the founders of the Red Cross movement with the logics that shaped their ideas about how good relief work ought to be waged. Based on their religious beliefs, the founders of the Red Cross became convinced that humanitarian work is a unique endeavor that must be conducted under its own ethical code, free of any political consideration. The framework the Red Cross propagated was at once malleable enough to transverse political and professional boundaries with ease and durable enough to withstand considerable challenges from competitors to the Red Cross's hegemony. The ethical underpinnings that inform contemporary humanitarian work today thus emerged from a specific strand of Swiss Calvinism. The unique standing of the international humanitarian NGOs we know today, then, is the result of a century-and-a-half-old cultural project that has bridged religion, politics, professions, and social movements.

While much of its analysis is historical, the book has widespread implications for twenty-first-century public policy and international development programs. For one thing, understanding contemporary humanitarian policies as historically and culturally specific (rather than universally valid) helps identify alternate options for providing international aid, which—as chapter 1 will show—have been marginalized. Historicizing current beliefs about humanitarian work can and should further contemporary conversations on international aid ethics. In addition, understanding the dominance of a religious movement in establishing the still-existing infrastructure of the humanitarian NGO sector is doubly important in this day and age. Numerous contemporary aid organizations highlight their secular identity and draw boundaries between themselves and their religious counterparts, believing religion to be primarily a source of violence. In contrast, this book demonstrates the capacity of religious frameworks to voice grievances, conceive of solutions, and mobilize for their execution—a point that should be taken into account in future discussions of humanitarian policy.

In order to interpret the historical findings, I draw on Bourdieusian field analysis and on the Strong Program in Cultural Sociology. By bringing cultural sociology into field analysis, I draw attention to the role of religious beliefs in generating the field of transnational humanitarian work, where many contemporary applications of field theory see beliefs as emerging from already-existing economic, political, or organizational social structures. In this, I claim that the appearance of a new social field requires a preexisting belief system (religious or otherwise) that orients actors to believe that specific endeavors are so unique and essential that they require an independent social space, a field, where they can be waged according to their own internal logic. In the interest of accessibility, I have relegated much of the theoretical metacommentary to the notes. Similarly, while the International Committee of the Red Cross only adopted its current name in 1876, I refer to it as ICRC for continuity throughout the text, except where the name change was of particular importance. Similarly, I left commentary on sources and methods to the appendix. I focused the text on those aspects of the history of the Red Cross movement that show the cultural dynamics of the nascent humanitarian field, and thus demonstrate my theoretical intervention in action.

Although much of the story ahead took place in the nineteenth century, there are numerous equivalences between the challenges the founders of the International Committee of the Red Cross faced and those with which humanitarian NGOs grapple today. Indeed, as the last two chapters of the book will demonstrate, the tensions inherent to the moral framework the founders laid down remain germane to the humanitarian field today, across its different organs and divisions.

The Humanitarian Space

Humanitarian nongovernmental organizations (NGOs) have become so ubiquitous that few today can imagine a global world order without them, and their legitimacy is often taken for granted. With the expanding reach of humanitarian NGOs, entire nations now rely on charitable humanitarian aid. Haiti, otherwise known as the "NGO Republic," is a case in point.[1] While 2009 reports already estimated the number of NGOs working in Haiti at between three thousand and ten thousand,[2] a series of natural disasters, disease, and mass population displacement over the following seven years made foreign aid agencies the de facto provider for the nation, pushing aside the incapacitated Haitian government. Due to discoordination among NGOs, poor planning, unfulfilled donor promises, and an overall lack of accountability, only a fraction of the allocated humanitarian aid funds reached the Haitians who needed them the most. Many NGOs attempted to dispense humanitarian aid directly, rather than bolstering existing Haitian institutions, and thus further weakened state organizations. As relief organizations became the only providers of food, supplies, and medicine, Haitians learned to look to them, instead of their own government, for basic necessities. But unlike governments, NGOs have no formal obligation to serve a community beyond what their funding schemes and organizational priorities dictate.[3] Thus, rather than receive access to basic necessities as a political right, Haitian citizens were left at the mercy of international donors and organizations that are unaccountable to them.[4]

Humanitarian NGOs have been able to intervene so profoundly in Haiti and in sites like Ethiopia, Rwanda, and Puerto Rico because they present themselves as servants of the most longstanding and universal human values, which transcend all political considerations and should be given complete latitude in the field. Indeed, international NGOs (INGOs) have been gradually increasing their scope and operational reach. In 2017, staff members of the International Committee of the Red Cross (ICRC) alone worked in eighty countries around the world. Their tasks ranged from providing immediate humanitarian assistance to millions of endangered and displaced people in conflict-torn areas like the Lake Chad basin and Iraq, to helping families affected by the Yugoslav wars and the Iran-Iraq War in continuing attempts to locate their loved ones, to promoting international humanitarian law in international policy forums. Humanitarian NGOs like Médecins sans Frontières (Doctors without Borders), Oxfam, and World Vision delivered aid to Syrians who have been facing extremely difficult conditions because of the conflict in their country, as well as the hundreds of thousands of Syrian refugees in neighboring countries and those making their way into Europe. In the Horn of Africa and in other drought- and famine-stricken areas, humanitarian NGOs have delivered emergency supplies and have worked to restore a level of public health and self-reliance. In 2015–2016 alone, Oxfam International directly impacted 22,200,000 beneficiaries, Médecins sans Frontières conducted 9,792,200 outpatient consultations worldwide, and CARE International helped 11.6 million people through humanitarian response, with all three organizations recording an increase in the number of beneficiaries served over the previous year.[5]

Representatives and supporters of the humanitarian community routinely demand that NGOs be given autonomy from political and military institutions because they are willing to offer relief in the harshest conflict and disaster zones. Policy reports have claimed that "humanitarian actors [hold] a special place in the international political scene, occupying a special area at the margin of state geostrategic and political considerations," where they have "acted independently and . . . pushed against state boundaries."[6] Former Médecins sans Frontières president Rony Brauman similarly claimed that this neutral "space" defends humanitarian nongovernmental organizations' freedom "to evaluate needs, . . . to monitor the delivery and use of assistance, . . . [and] to have dialogue with the people."[7] For many advocates, the best possible way to intervene where war or disaster strike is through humanitarian NGOs, despite considerable disagreement between relief organizations, operational failures, and occasional scandals within the humanitarian community.[8]

And yet, while the values humanitarian NGOs ascribe to their work—impartiality, neutrality, universality—are certainly ageless, the idea that nonprofit, nongovernmental, and apolitical voluntary associations are the ones that manifest such ethics is astonishingly new.[9] When the forerunners of the ICRC began spreading these ideas and advocating for recognition of volunteer humanitarian organizations as an autonomous sector in the 1860s—independent of political, economic, or any other consideration and committed solely to saving lives—they caused considerable controversy.[10] The nascent Red Cross faced competition for public attention from other parties with radically different ideas about how to address social suffering, and some gained better traction in certain circles. Late-nineteenth-century peace activists, for example, denounced volunteer-based battlefield relief because they believed attention should focus on achieving permanent peace and disarmament rather than simply cleaning up the messes national governments create. For many such activists, investing efforts in organized relief projects for the wounded in war was tantamount to accepting war as an inevitable part of social life, and was therefore irreconcilable with the aspiration for a perpetual peace.[11] In a different way, health care professionals opposed assigning humanitarian care to volunteer movements on ethical grounds, since doing so absolved states from responsibility toward those harmed by their actions and thus made war an easier affair to conduct.[12] On the other hand, some religious reformers saw permanent aid associations as unnecessary, believing that news of war would spontaneously move Christians across Europe and the United States to travel to battle sites and provide help to the needy.

Nevertheless, within two short decades, the ICRC managed to convince activists, professionals, and statesmen across three continents that humanitarian NGOs embody the most efficient, desirable, and ethical way of organizing help to those in need. By the late 1870s, Red Cross societies had appeared across Europe and beyond, gaining such prestige that local parties now struggled over ownership of the Red Cross "brand." The humanitarian NGO model, controversial only a decade earlier, became increasingly accepted and rapidly disseminated into new national contexts and new areas of relief work.[13] The notion of a humanitarian space on a battlefield, marked as neutral by a white flag bearing a red cross, evoked romanticized ideas about battlefield medical aid in the harshest of conditions and bolstered the appeal of volunteer relief work. The painting *After the Battle of Gravelotte* (1870/1871; see frontispiece) provides a compelling example, rendered less than a decade after the 1864 Geneva Convention was first ratified. In the painting, nuns arrive on the battle scene to help the wounded even as the village still burns and the armies are reassembling behind them. Under a hanging Red Cross flag, they find an island of civility: a courteous soldier helps them disembark from the wagon; the militaries leave the neutralized area untouched (back left); Prussian medics, wearing red cross armbands, provide medical relief and carry their patient on a stretcher; locals offer assistance (center left) and even take wounded soldiers into their homes to recuperate (top right, in the window); and French and Prussian soldiers await treatment together with their weapons seemingly forgotten. As they wait, they exhibit some cordiality toward their would-be enemies (bottom right), even as they quietly despair side by side (bottom left). In visual representation, news reporting and literature, and legislation, the values the founders of the Red Cross movement propagated became *the* metric to evaluate what constitutes good humanitarian work. As a result, other emerging late-nineteenth-century humanitarian organizations adopted Red Cross criteria to justify their own work. How did an organizational model that met such initial ethical criticism become the gold standard for humanitarian work? And how did it persevere over the last 150 years?

For some scholars, the virtuous work that humanitarian NGOs undertake is itself the natural explanation for their extraordinary international success and continuing influence over global affairs.[14] For example, Canadian public intellectual Michael Ignatieff has claimed that the humanitarian sector—broadly defined to include relief NGOs, diplomats, reporters, and other supporters—offers the international community excellent means to resolve global social problems.[15] For Ignatieff and others, humanitarian NGOs represent a broad historical arc of recovery from the ravages of World War II and a surge in global consciousness that is gradually overcoming primordial social divisions.[16] Other scholars have claimed that the latent interests humanitarian NGOs serve explain their international prominence.[17] Authors have shown how humanitarian justifications provide power holders—usually states—the appearance of legitimacy and selfless concern for global human suffering under which to pursue their own interests.[18] While some see these interests as benign ones—such as creating a cosmopolitan world order or restricting the freedom of nations to fight[19]—more critical scholars claim that humanitarian projects ultimately subject populations to power-laden rules and categories.[20]

Despite their divergence on the nature of humanitarian NGOs, enthusiasts and critics agree that humanitarian NGOs possess a remarkably persuasive system of moral justifications. And yet, the burgeoning literature on the emergence of humanitarian institutions, laws, movements, philosophies, and sentiments has said little about the origins and spread of the cultural structures that make humanitarian NGOs so persuasive. In this book, I argue that the humanitarian NGO sector gained its social, cultural, and political eminence through a cultural project spanning the second half of the nineteenth century. Through an intertwined set of cultural processes, actors within the humanitarian NGO sector came to attach a specific set of meanings to relief work, thereby demarcating "true" humanitarian organizations as autonomous, impartial, neutral, and permanent rather than ad hoc. The book explains why and how the specific values the early Red Cross movement propagated captivated so many parties, where those values originated, how they were disseminated and embedded into preexistent social sites, and what lasting institutional effects they have had on the humanitarian community and other social spheres. The nineteenth-century origins of the humanitarian sector have deeply affected the character of humanitarian work for the following century and a half.[21]

The historical analysis will show that the founders of the Red Cross movement drew their organizational model from the theology of the early-nineteenth-century orthodox Calvinist movement, the Réveil. They intended the Red Cross project to counter secular modernity through a revitalization of Christian charity. As the book will demonstrate, the foundational assumptions of the humanitarian community—that humanitarian NGOs ought to be a permanent fixture in civil society; that they must be impartial; and that they must be considered neutral—emerged specifically from a renewed nineteenth-century Swiss Reformed Protestant emphasis on the separation of church, state, and charity institutions, as well as an accompanying intensified interest in battlefields as a site for Christian charity. These notions resonated deeply with the concerns and interests of multiple late-nineteenth-century parties, and were translated into patriotic terms that compelled activists in numerous countries. The language and imagery of humanitarianism the Red Cross presented also appealed to professional communities such as nurses, international lawyers, and journalists, who employed them in their own work and simultaneously conferred prestige back onto the humanitarian community. These processes facilitated the spread and institutionalization not only of the Red Cross movement, but also of an ethos consecrating humanitarianism across Europe and beyond.[22] Despite significant developments that have occurred within the humanitarian sector since the mid-nineteenth century, contemporary NGOs continue to carry the imprint of the Reformed Protestantism that inspired the founders of their field.

Understanding that the ethical justifications on which humanitarian organizations rely trace back to one particular tradition rather than to more vaguely defined and ostensibly "universal" human values helps broaden conversations about intervention ethics.[23] Although humanitarian organizations often claim that their work relies on foundational, universally valid ethics, critics have noted that their well-intentioned intervention often depoliticizes social suffering.[24] In this view, since humanitarian organizations by and large seek to represent themselves as neutral, they frame suffering as "complex humanitarian emergencies" rather than as the result of crimes that should be punished. However, over the past twenty years, advocates of the "human-rights approach" to humanitarian action have raised serious questions about the ethics of international NGO (INGO) humanitarian intervention and have emphasized the need for aid agencies to empower the recipients of aid and to ensure a speedy transition back to state-sponsored aid programs.[25] Nevertheless, such discussions have largely remained within academic circles, and have carried little weight in policy circles. This book contributes to such debates with an account of how contemporary humanitarian ethics took shape in relation to the competing views on humanitarian aid that have historically coexisted with them, and thus explains the enduring trust the global community places in humanitarian NGOs.

The Emergence of the Humanitarian Sector

Despite considerable sociological and historical interest in the origins of humanitarianism, existing work has paid little attention to the cultural processes in play in the late nineteenth century. Such work has thus looked either to earlier periods or to the twentieth-century for the origins of the humanitarian sector.

One set of scholars has examined the long history of humanitarian work that preceded the Red Cross, with particular emphasis on the eighteenth-century efflorescence of transnational empathy, manifested both in philosophical writings and in abolitionist initiatives. Scholars like Abram de Swaan and Thomas Haskell have ascribed the growth of humanitarian sentiments over the eighteenth century to the growing interconnectedness of humankind as it transitioned to modernity, as social and economic networks gradually made actors in different countries feel morally responsible to act on behalf of distant others.[26] Other authors have seen the Enlightenment era as marking a general cultural shift toward new values and practices oriented toward helping those who suffer in distant locations.[27] Yet other studies of antislavery abolitionism have examined the spreading capitalist logics of the eighteenth century and its interaction with specific faith communities, claiming that they were key to the rise of international activism.[28] Other authors like Michael Barnett have linked the emergence of humanitarianism to imperialism, and have shown how humanitarian projects infused eighteenth-century expansionist projects.[29] In addition, scholars like Steven Pinker have described the growth of humanitarian work as part of the broader development of human empathetic faculties over history and a gradual decrease in human violence.[30]

In contrast to these longue durée approaches, a different group of scholars have seen transnational humanitarian activism as a late-twentieth-century phenomenon (emerging as late as the 1980s for some).[31] Authors like anthropologist Didier Fassin and philosopher Étienne Balibar have suggested that humanitarianism predating the post–World War II era, for one reason or another, is not "true" humanitarianism. According to Fassin, until the mid-twentieth century, humanitarianism amounted to "moral sentiments in philosophical reflection, and subsequently in common sense," which the abolitionist movement epitomized in politics. At the same time, claims Fassin, "emotional pleas and even military interventions to defend endangered populations . . . have received little attention until recently." By contrast, Fassin points to the end of the twentieth century as a period characterized by "the articulation of these moral sentiments in the public space, and . . . in political action" along with "the creation of humanitarian organizations (which invoke a right or duty to intervene), the establishment of ministries of humanitarian assistance . . . , the description of conflicts as humanitarian crises . . . and the proliferation of measures and initiatives designed to aid the poor, the unemployed, the homeless, [and] the sick without social protection."[32]

However, the Red Cross and the Geneva Convention—two of the most important markers of humanitarian work of our time—appeared in the mid- to late nineteenth century, a period to which neither camp pays particular attention. While transnational humanitarian organizations like the International Shipwreck Society were already in existence, the International Red Cross and Red Crescent movement remains the largest and oldest extant network of humanitarian organizations.[33] Its late-nineteenth-century establishment was central in disseminating the organizational model of the international relief NGO.[34] The Geneva Convention of 1864 was the first international treaty specifying the minimum protections required for relief workers, ambulances, field hospitals, and victims of armed conflicts. And, I argue, accompanying the appearance of the Red Cross and the Geneva Convention was a novel discursive framework, now ubiquitous among contemporary NGOs, that demarcates impartial and neutral relief work as a unique endeavor that must be elevated from all political or economic considerations and waged under its own system of ethics. The Red Cross movement played a particularly important role in the dissemination of this new cultural structure, on several different levels.

First, the Red Cross was the first large-scale transnational operation that advocated for humanitarian activities to be recognized as independent (rather than being in service of the military or of religious organizations). Unlike previous humanitarian advocates, the Red Cross worked to separate aid workers legally, operationally, and culturally from other actors on the battlefield. The movement was established in 1863, when five Genevan philanthropists—a businessman, a jurist, two physicians, and an army officer—created the International Aid Committee for Wounded Soldiers with the intention of improving medical care on the battlefield. The committee organized an international conference concerned with the medical provisions for the wounded in battlefields in October of the same year. It presented to the attendees—official emissaries of fourteen European states as well as unofficial delegates of charitable associations—a plan to boost the level of care for the wounded. According to the plan, volunteer aid societies would be organized in each nation. They would train personnel, collect supplies, work to secure the cooperation of their respective governments and militaries, and—should war erupt—travel to the battlefield to care for the wounded alongside the official military medical corps. These aid societies would provide medical care impartially, regardless of the nationality, race, or religion of their beneficiaries, and would be afforded protection and neutral status by all belligerents. The committee objected to the view that its ends could be achieved by reinforcing existing military medical facilities. It insisted instead that an autonomous volunteer sector to care for the wounded was an absolute necessity. It similarly made significant publication efforts to popularize the notion that humanitarian work—especially during war—is an independent and unique endeavor, which is open to any charitable volunteer. A spokesperson for the Belgian Red Cross wrote as early as 1871 that "since the invention of the Red Cross, battles are no longer simply opportunities to practice the military profession, but they have become major sites of charity."[35] While many of the national aid societies have rarely been truly free from state interests, the movement as a whole instilled the ethical injunction that volunteer aid organizations ought to be autonomous, which still guides the humanitarian sector today.

Second, the Red Cross was responsible for the widespread ratification of the 1864 Geneva Convention, which—for the first time—formulated a universally binding designation of aid workers, volunteers, and wounded soldiers as neutral (and therefore protected) individuals. The convention thereby established the legal infrastructure that provides humanitarians in conflict zones with the inviolability indispensable for their type of work.[36] But more notably, the Geneva Convention carries international prestige that few other legal documents possess. While it has seen three revisions and additional articles since its introduction, the Geneva Convention remains "the most nearly universally known and seemingly accepted statements about what is due to man from man," as historian Geoffrey Best put it.[37] As an early instance of international humanitarian law, the Geneva Convention facilitated mutual recognition among actors working in different national contexts and articulated one of the key problems humanitarians face—that of neutrality.[38]

Third, the Red Cross has long advocated for volunteer humanitarian aid on the battlefield through conferences, expositions, museums, and publications, bringing considerable donor and legislator attention to their work, and simultaneously endeavoring to create a growing sense of collective identity within the humanitarian community. In doing this, it also popularized an image of courageous relief workers who put their lives at risk to save others. Thus, the movement simultaneously offered an institutionalized pathway for interested individuals to volunteer and rendered intervention in distant suffering imaginable for wide populations in the metropole.[39] The Red Cross (and in particular the International Committee of the Red Cross) has also exerted unusual influence on world leaders and decision makers for an organization of its type, and has been central in convincing them of the uniqueness of the humanitarian field.

Finally, the proposals the Red Cross put forth subsequently served as the basis for competition and hierarchies in national and international humanitarian communities. As the Red Cross gained momentum, various national Red Cross societies emerged across Europe (and later globally), and intra-national struggles often erupted between aid societies over which best represented impartial humanitarianism (thus meriting the favor of the aristocracy and international acclaim). The emergence of new humanitarian organizations in the 1970s exacerbated the dispute over which movement best adhered to the ideal of impartial humanitarianism and on the effectiveness and ethical standing of the Red Cross.[40] The nature of the debate remained tied to the value of saving lives impartially, from a neutral and permanent position, as the Red Cross advocated more than a century earlier.[41] As a former director of research at Médecins sans Frontières—an organization that has historically been critical of the Red Cross—claimed, the Red Cross doctrines "provide the most broadly accepted principles to guide humanitarian action and form the basis of the various codes of conduct."[42]

Religion and Humanitarianism

What happened in the mid-nineteenth century that led to the formation of the Red Cross and its powerful advocacy for a new program for relief work? The answer lies in the religious processes that were at work in Central Europe at that time. In fact, although the late eighteenth century saw numerous philosophical treatises calling for universal compassion based on secular humanistic principles,[43] religion has been key in motivating concrete intervention and advocacy projects on behalf of suffering populations since early modernity. Peter Stamatov has shown that transnational advocacy networks on behalf of exploited groups began in the sixteenth century, when radicalized missionaries became convinced that the subjugation of indigenous Hispaniolans was a sin affecting the entire Spanish Empire. Appalled by the atrocities they witnessed in the Caribbean Islands, missionaries like Bartolomé de las Casas began advocating passionately on their behalf to the Spanish Crown, thereby forming the first transnational advocacy network. In a similar fashion, eighteenth-century Pennsylvania Quaker reformers became convinced that the wars the colony experienced with surrounding Native American tribes were punishments for the sin of slavery, and—after their abolitionist efforts within the colony failed—they appealed to the Society of Friends in London to exert pressure on Pennsylvania to abolish slavery.[44] Michael Young has similarly highlighted the role of new religious movements in the explosion of abolitionist activism in the early-nineteenth-century United States during the Second Great Awakening. The accompanying notion of "national sin"—novel for its time—enabled religious reformers to convince others both of the immorality of slaveholding and of the personal responsibility all Americans held to fight it.[45] Across these and other cases, religious denominations possess both the critical worldview by which to problematize human suffering and the institutional means to organize volunteers and support to combat it.[46]

As this book will show, the ethical, organizational, and economic logic of the humanitarian NGO sector originated in the teachings of the staunchly conservative nineteenth-century Réveil movement.[47] This movement was anything but a humanistic movement in religious disguise: it emerged in the 1810s in opposition to the gradual modernization of the Swiss Reformed Church and to the influence of French Revolutionary ideals on the religious world. Through its influence on the nascent Red Cross movement of the 1860s, the Réveil provided a logic that continues to guide contemporary humanitarian NGOs: an insistence that the most ethical way to address social suffering—especially conflict-related suffering—is through impartial, nonstate, volunteer- and donation-based intervention. Although scholars have resisted claims about the rootedness of human rights or humanitarian ethics in one religious tradition or another (in particular Christianity),[48] I argue that the humanitarian sector continues until the present day to rely on ethical principles inherited from the Réveil.

The Humanitarian Field

To capture how the logics of the Réveil formed the basis for the humanitarian NGO sector, I conceptualize the humanitarian sector as a *field* and examine how the central values that underpin it emerged and became institutionalized. At its most basic, a field is a "domain of relative autonomy marked off from others by its distinctive hierarchy, values, struggles, styles of improvising action, and forms of capital."[49] It is populated by actors who believe they are engaged in the same type of social action and therefore work in relation to each other. Those actors collectively identify a limited set of hierarchical positions and largely agree on who occupies which one. They implicitly agree on a certain set of logics that dictate the norms by which action within the field ought to be conducted, and share a belief in specific stakes that orient their work.[50] Whether those stakes are artistic purity in the art world, excellence in the field of sports, or innovativeness in the field of science, all social fields are organized around some form of "field-specific capital," which "orients practice relatively independently of other stakes, such as money and power."[51] A field-specific capital provides a metric to hierarchically position field actors and serves as an indicator of worth and prestige.[52]

The genesis of a new field is indicated by the appearance of a new type of capital—essentially a new way of evaluating worth—along with a new elite that possesses it.[53] French sociologist Pierre Bourdieu's classic example was the mid-nineteenth-century field of French avant-garde literature: once a growing group of readers, critics, and writers began evaluating literature based on its own independent value, and not based on its market success, and once they began identifying figures such as Flaubert and Baudelaire as exemplary authors—an elite—based on this logic, the literary field emerged. Subsequently, new authors would begin to struggle with each other over the relative worth of their work and to position themselves differentially within the field based on the template Flaubert and his contemporaries imprinted in the literary field.[54] Similarly, I examine how the notion that the best humanitarian organizations are those that demonstrate impartiality and are independent of state interests emerged as a form of field-specific capital, and how the Red Cross came to be the first elite of the nascent humanitarian field of the mid-nineteenth century.

Most studies of the genesis of new fields begin by examining how their structural features appeared—their objective positions, their boundaries vis-à-vis other fields, and their economic and political underpinnings. In this approach the cultural, meaning-laden aspects of fields are seen as emerging only after this objective infrastructure is established.[55] In fact, Bourdieu cautioned students of fields not to begin their explanations from the ideas and preferences of actors, since those are "too directly dependent on the particular dispositions and virtues of individuals and no doubt too easily reversed or overturned."[56] Practices that are relatively autonomous from political pressures, Bourdieu continued, cannot rely on "the fluctuating inclinations of moods or the voluntarist revolutions of morality." Instead, Bourdieu saw their origins "in the very necessity of a social universe which has as a fundamental law, as a *nomos*, independence with respect to economic and political power."[57] By contrast, this book examines what caused mid-nineteenth-century activists to identify humanitarian work as requiring its own metric of worth *before* humanitarianism became a "social universe," and how their set of beliefs about what constitutes good relief work—drawn from the Réveil—subsequently shaped the organizational structure of the humanitarian field.[58]

To this end, I begin by turning to the early work of advocates of the Red Cross. I trace the social and cultural conditions that made multiple parties in late-nineteenth-century Europe and elsewhere particularly receptive to the idea of organized volunteer relief work. Chapter 1 shows that the early advocates of the Red Cross were successful in articulating an intersecting set of inchoate anxieties prevalent among their contemporaries, especially surrounding the neglect of wounded soldiers on the battlefields of Europe. By drawing on these specific concerns, the Red Cross gained the necessary leverage to advocate for volunteer humanitarianism in broader terms. Chapter 2 delves into the early genesis of the Red Cross in the 1860s and presents the theological origins of its proposal to organize a humanitarian sector. It focuses on the nineteenth-century Réveil movement and the social conditions in Geneva that led to the establishment and success of the movement there. The claim here is that the principles the movement espoused—impartiality, neutrality, permanence—were rooted in the religious convictions of its founding members about the nature of war, the agency of humankind in alleviating its effects, and the proper relationship between the state and civil associations. I show how those principles became embedded in the legal and organizational structures of the humanitarian field.

Chapter 3 turns to the international dissemination of the cultural structures and the organizational logics of the Red Cross from the 1860s to the 1890s. It shows that processes of cultural production and of translation of meanings across national contexts mediated the transition from social movement to a broad social field. In particular, the first large-scale achievement of the movement, the Geneva Convention, gave numerous parties in different nations the language to problematize and criticize belligerents' conduct, to classify specific populations as neutral or vulnerable, and to formalize the role of volunteer humanitarians. The chapter demonstrates that the growth of the transnational humanitarian field was facilitated by the resonance of its meaning structures with patriotic sentiments that were prevalent across late-nineteenth-century Europe and beyond.

The emergence of the transnational humanitarian field also had considerable reverberations in adjacent fields. Chapter 4 traces the relationships between the humanitarian field and the fields of nursing, journalism, religion, and international law in the late nineteenth century. It shows that a symbiotic relationship emerged between the transnational humanitarian field and each of these other fields. The affiliation with humanitarian agents helped actors in these other fields reimagine their own undertakings as aligning with a universal common good. And it provided the language to confer distinction and prestige upon their undertakings.

But from here, the question remains: to what extent does the contemporary transnational humanitarian field continue to bear the mark of the religious faith of its founders? Chapter 5 shows that even though the field has seen significant upheavals, its core identity and logics have persevered. However, humanitarians have continuously disagreed about the ways in which they believed core field values should be realized. By studying the rise of Médecins sans Frontières, a movement critical of the Red Cross that emerged in the 1970s, this chapter shows that despite the multiple aspirations for revolution, the new movement had to rely on the existing moral infrastructure the Red Cross had laid in place to gain a prominent standing in the civil sphere.

———————————

The history of the transnational humanitarian field has direct implications for present-day humanitarian NGO policies, particularly regarding relations between faith-based and secular humanitarian work and regarding the tensions between traditional humanitarian work and social and political change. The last chapter will highlight the implications of this study for contemporary humanitarian organizations, for policy makers, and for scholars who study them. It will similarly draw out the theoretical implications for scholars studying how institutional and ethical systems of belief emerge and how they persevere over time.

ONE

Inter Arma Caritas: The Cultural Origins of Humanitarian NGOs

The roots of the International Committee of the Red Cross (ICRC) in one Central European battlefield are enshrined in its longstanding motto *inter arma caritas*— "in war, charity."[1] This battlefield is in northern Italy—part of the former Lombardo-Venetian Kingdom—and was the site of a decisive episode of the Second Italian War of Independence in 1859. The combined French-Piedmontese armies defeated the Austrian forces here and made key advances toward the unification of Italy under the rule of Victor Emmanuel II. In this one-day battle, approximately 14,000 Austrian and 15,000 Franco-Piedmontese soldiers were killed or wounded, and the meager medical facilities of the warring sides were incapacitated.[2] As a result, the dead bodies were left unburied for loved ones to retrieve in person, for local clergy or charitable individuals to bury on site, or for wildlife to consume. Those wounded soldiers who did not immediately die faced the sad fate of many other fighters in mid-nineteenth-century battlefields, which was remaining on the battlefield and seeking help from locals.

Henry Dunant (born Jean-Henri Dunant; 1828–1910), a Swiss merchant traveling to seek audience with Napoleon III, incidentally reached the Solferino battle site and witnessed the scores of wounded soldiers—Sardinian, French, and Austrian alike—left on the battlefield together to fend for themselves. Dunant was from Geneva, born to an upper-class, devoutly Calvinist family. His father was a merchant, and a member of the Grand Council of Geneva. Dunant was sent to the Collège Calvin, one of the oldest and most prestigious secondary schools in Geneva, but was ultimately expelled for poor performance. However, he developed a strong fascination with religious education and remained active in informal Christian study initiatives. Dunant helped found the Geneva chapter of the YMCA in 1852 and became involved in various charitable associations as well. He worked at a bank and became acquainted with the Geneva Company of the Swiss Colonies of Sétif, which managed Swiss acquisitions in Algeria. Dunant set up his own business in Algeria through this company, but encountered difficulties dealing with the local French officials soon after. As a result of these setbacks, Dunant was on his way to seek the aid of Napoleon III in facilitating his business when he came across the site of the Battle of Solferino.

Shocked by the carnage, Dunant approached the citizens of the nearest town and managed to organize a makeshift relief force for all wounded soldiers (regardless of their nationality), helped establish a field hospital, and paid for much of the required supplies himself. In the surrounding towns, he visited the bedsides of wounded soldiers of both sides, offered consolation, and helped some of the patients mail letters to their families at home. Upon returning to Switzerland, Dunant testified to his church about the suffering he had witnessed and the efforts he and the local volunteers had taken to alleviate them. He highlighted the impartiality of the local volunteers, the desperate need for trained medical staff and for supplies on the front, and the dangers aid workers face without a neutral designation.

Dunant reported on his experience in Lombardy in a book called *A Memory of Solferino*, published in French in 1862.[3] The book described the hardships wounded soldiers faced due to lack of treatment, praised the efforts volunteer aid workers took to ameliorate the suffering of the soldiers, and pleaded for the organization of neutral standing aid committees for wounded soldiers in each country. *A Memory of Solferino* outlined in general terms the organizing principles for the Red Cross societies that would start appearing later in the decade. Dunant printed 1,600 copies (which he labeled "not for sale") at his own expense, and sent them to leading European intellectuals, military leaders, and statesmen. He traveled extensively to promote the book, using his wide social network to advocate the ideas presented in it. The book was translated into Dutch, English, German, and Italian within five years of its appearance.[4] It circulated among European elites and professional circles, who commended it both for its poignancy and for its cogent proposals. Nobles such as Prince Friedrich Karl of Prussia and King John of Saxony read the book and praised Dunant's effort.

A Memory of Solferino caught the attention of the young Genevan jurist Gustave Moynier (1826–1910), who approached Dunant with an idea to turn his proposals into reality.[5] Dunant and Moynier recruited Swiss general Guillaume Henri Dufour (1787–1875) and surgeons Louis Appia (1818–1898) and Théodore Maunoir (1806–1869) to form what they called the Committee of Five, and renamed shortly after as the International Committee for Aid to the Wounded. After an initial attempt to organize through the Geneva Society for Public Utility was unsuccessful, the five founding members organized a conference on the state of the sick and wounded in the battlefields in 1863. Delegates of eighteen states and several others in nonofficial capacities attended the meeting. Their historic resolutions laid the groundwork for the establishment of aid societies in each nation that would provide relief for wounded soldiers and would rely on volunteer work (rather than military medical facilities), the neutrality of all medical personnel in the battlefield, established protections for wounded soldiers, and the future succession of conventions that would start building the body of international humanitarian laws.[6] The early endeavors of the International Committee for Aid to the Wounded—which would become the International Committee of the Red Cross—laid down the legal, organizational, and cultural infrastructure for humanitarian work to be waged on its own terms.

Scholars and activists tend to praise Dunant as the "inventor" of organized volunteer-based humanitarian relief work, thereby forming the basis for humanitarian NGO work and for international humanitarian law.[7] But even though some scholars have claimed that A Memory of Solferino "stirred the conscience of Europe" by alerting diplomats, philanthropists, and aristocrats to the conditions on the battlefield, of which most metropolitans were supposedly unaware,[8] the state of the wounded on the front had already been a matter of public concern in the 1850s. The development of critical long-distance reporting gave rise to iconic early reporters such as Januarius MacGahan, and reports of the suffering wrought by the Irish Potato Famine had already traveled internationally in the late 1840s.[9] As European armies gradually adopted mass conscription schemes,[10] and as soldiers served for longer periods of time (compared to pre-Napoleonic soldiers), civilians were taking particular interest in the conditions on the battlefield.[11] Many actors in the European diplomatic, medical, military, and religious spheres were already interested in new and better arrangements for the care of the wounded in the preceding century by the time A Memory of Solferino appeared and were writing about this subject. As historian John Hutchinson notes, while the book was widely read and well received, few of its 1860s readers saw it as particularly new, or as a straightforward call for action.[12]

If A Memory of Solferino was not particularly new for its time, how did this book propel Dunant (and, by extension, his Genevan colleagues) to international fame? What made Dunant, rather than any of the other authors proposing reforms in the world of battlefield medicine that preceded him, one of the founders of the humanitarian field?[13] As this chapter will show, European activists and decision makers were conflicted over whether improving battlefield medical conditions required an autonomous sector of volunteer aid workers, whether boosting military medical facilities would be more efficient and ethical, or whether efforts should be directed toward eliminating warfare altogether. When Dunant began advocating for independent humanitarian societies to be organized as a sector, other ideas about how to improve medical conditions on the battlefield were already circulating. To understand how the ethics of the humanitarian field emerged, we need to examine what made the idea of an autonomous humanitarian field appealing enough for a wide range of activists to support the establishment of independent volunteer aid societies at a time when other popular ideas on the topic were also circulating.

Cultural sociologists have shown that texts that achieve widespread success are those that articulate previously inchoate social tensions and circulate through existing social networks. In particular, texts that resonate widely are those that offer possible ways to resolve such tensions, either through concrete action or through emotional, social, or cultural strategies.[14] Even though *A Memory of Solferino* may not have directly *caused* the Red Cross to come into existence, it came to be widely discussed in 1860s European cities because it addressed the common cognitive and emotional challenges presented by the almost continuous sequence of armed conflicts that plagued Europe in the second half of the century. Unlike other treatises suggesting military medical reforms, *Solferino* embedded its proposal in a dramatized narrative of suffering and charity on the battlefield, and unlike other sentimentalist war literature of its time, the book offered specific "recipes" for individuals to involve themselves in helping those in need on the front.

Battlefield Relief in the Nineteenth Century

Mid-nineteenth-century battlefield practices were significantly more ferocious than eighteenth-century ones, as previously held customs prescribing civility and restraint on the battlefield were largely cast away during the Napoleonic Wars. Until Napoleon, the eighteenth-century battlefield was gradually becoming less violent and more civil, with belligerents often meeting before the battle to discuss the rules of the battle and its limitations. By contrast, the wars of the nineteenth century brought back practices such as starving populations to death, attacking medical facilities, and targeting civilians alongside soldiers.[15] Technological innovations similarly affected midcentury warfare, with the introduction of the machine gun in the early 1860s particularly increasing the death toll.[16]

At the same time, the series of wars and civil conflict that occurred in midcentury Europe, alongside disasters like the Potato Famine in Ireland

(1845–1852), gave rise to a host of humanitarian initiatives and proposals for medical reforms well before the Red Cross materialized. Public attention and activity (e.g., advocacy, donation, volunteering) had turned toward the battlefield in the preceding decades, scrutinizing existing medical arrangements and grappling with their perceived ineffectiveness. Although many of these initiatives had parallels to the volunteer humanitarian societies that Dunant would propose in the 1860s, none of them showed much interest in transforming volunteer relief work into an international program and dissociating it from the existing institutions that supported them. A brief review of the other parties interested in the conditions on the battlefield shows that Dunant's proposals were not entirely new for their time, and in some respects unusual and relatively unpopular.

Nurses and military medical facilities

The British, French, and Prussian militaries had gradually improved the care they provided to the wounded over first half of the nineteenth century. After the conditions on the Crimean front caused public outcry in the 1850s, militaries boosted their efforts at medical reforms. At the same time, military medical facilities remained understaffed and largely disorganized. Unsanitary conditions and lack of awareness regarding sanitation caused outbreaks of cholera and typhus that, at times, decimated entire camps before they even reached the battlefield.[17] Scarce supplies and working hands made death sentences out of relatively minor gunshot wounds. A general lack of preparedness among military corps in the wars of the 1850s left thousands of wounded soldiers virtually unattended. The lack of internationally agreed-upon conventions of neutrality for medical staff placed field surgeons in danger of imprisonment by enemy forces, and disorganized state bureaucracy occasionally thwarted attempts to deliver medical supplies.

While welcoming additional working hands from outside the armed forces, discussion within medical circles revolved around improving intramilitary care rather than allowing volunteers independent access to the battlefield. However, news from the Crimea, and then from Lombardy, had aroused professional interest in battlefield medicine reforms, and several proposals for reforming military medical care preceded *A Memory of Solferino*. In fact, some publications of that era named Dunant as simply one among many philanthropists of their time who called for concerted efforts to ameliorate the suffering of wounded soldiers.[18] Professionals had similarly published proposals to regulate the treatment of the wounded in the 1950s, for example French pharmacist Henri Arrault, Italian surgeon Ferdinando Palasciano, Russian philanthropist Anatoli Demidov, and Prussian military doctor August Wasserführ.[19]

A significant midcentury advance was the introduction of nurses to battle-field medical facilities. Although British nurse Florence Nightingale rose to fame as the pioneer in battlefield nursing, Sisters of Mercy had already tended to the wounded French and Russian soldiers in the early 1850s.[20] *The Times* reported in 1854 that about fifty French nurses had been sent to Crimea to take care of patients in field hospitals.[21] The alarm raised by news reports in *The Times* about the conditions of British soldiers helped Night-ingale convince the War Office to send her and a group of nurses to work in Scutari. Through this work Nightingale established military nursing as an institutionalized profession.[22]

The United States saw its own advances with the establishment of the United States Sanitary Commission as an auxiliary unit in 1861. The com-mission, established through federal legislation at the urging of Rev. Henry Whitney Bellows, raised millions of dollars and enlisted thousands of vol-unteers. Its aim was to support the care of wounded soldiers on the front, both by sending supplies to field hospitals and by training volunteers. The nurses the commission employed were known to have cared for Union and Confederate soldiers alike, garnering praise in America and Europe. Com-mission administrators and activists such as Mary Ann Bickerdyke and Mary Livermore wrote about their experiences and highlighted the need for fur-ther improvements in military medical care.[23] Although the commission was dismantled after the war, news of its endeavors and its impartiality reached Europe and was covered enthusiastically in newspapers.[24]

Dunant, then, was certainly not the only person urging stakeholders to improve medical conditions on the battlefield. But unlike Dunant, military medical reformers were not calling for volunteer societies to be established— they were working to improve the medical services the militaries themselves provided.

Faith-based groups

Medical aid came not only from groups affiliated with the militaries, but also from religious orders and from ad hoc faith-based societies. Among the Christian orders providing aid on European battlefields, the Order of St. John of Jerusalem was one of the best known in the 1850s and 1860s. Tracing its heritage to the Knights Hospitaller, this order was reconstituted in 1852 under the patronage of the Prussian royal house after a hiatus of forty years. As a Protestant faith-based order, it combined spiritual evangelism with charitable work, in hospitals during peacetime and on the battlefield during war. While the Sovereign Order of St. John and the Sovereign Military Order of Malta conducted similar work elsewhere, the Prussian order reached considerable prominence through its direct relief efforts during the German Unification Wars of the 1860s, thanks to its well-organized (and internationally publicized) assistance to wounded soldiers, which included relatively efficient ambulance transport under fire.[25] Early Red Cross advocates like Louis Appia approvingly cited the Order of St. John of Jerusalem, along with the Field Deacons of Rauhe Haus, aid workers from the Deacon House of Duisburg, and members of related orders, as demonstrating the efficiency and courage the Red Cross should emulate.[26]

These orders were joined by women's groups that traveled to battlefields independently to offer help.[27] During the Crimean War, Irish Sisters of Mercy, coming from a Roman Catholic order founded in Dublin that cared primarily for the poor and sick, traveled to Anatolia to work with the British nurses.[28] On the Russian side, a faith-based group of women organized and traveled to the front to offer help (Tolstoy mentioned them appreciatively in his *Sebastopol Sketches*). The United States Christian Society conducted similar work during the American Civil War, and news of its successful endeavors traveled to Europe and garnered praise as a clear demonstration of "the power of the simple gospel of Christ to meet the needs of broken hearts and dying men."[29]

Religious "hospitaller" orders were, for the most part, closed off from the public, which diluted their effects on broader cultural dynamics except in setting a clear—if distant—example of humanitarianism and Christian courage. Such orders showed little interest in advocating for a clear international program that would make permanent a set of humanitarian institutions across Europe. Women's societies were often organized around one specific war, and disbanded shortly after warfare ended. Dunant differed from these groups in his proposal that volunteer societies exist permanently, in order to prepare for action during wartime, and in his view that those groups needed to be independent, rather than subordinated to militaries, church organizations, or economic interests.

Legislating neutrality

In *Governing the World: The History of an Idea*, historian Mark Mazower shows how nineteenth-century European powers turned from the notion of the "Concert of Europe" to international treaties as the preferred form of governance.[30] This shift was evident in the area of military conduct, and Dunant's call for neutrality to be established for relief workers on the battlefield also had precedents in the legal field. Neutrality was not a new ideal for those advocating for medical reforms, and the concept already existed in some forms in international law.[31]

For example, the French pharmacist Henri Arrault (1799–1887) won some attention in his home country for proposing establishing medical workers, wounded soldiers, and hospitals as inviolable. In 1861, a year before Dunant published *A Memory of Solferino*, Arrault published a pamphlet petitioning the French government to enter a "synallagmatic contract" with other states ensuring the neutrality of the wounded and medical care providers on the battlefield. Arrault proposed that black flags, which were the customary marker for hospitals in besieged cities, designate field hospitals as neutral territories. He also proposed various practical measures to improve the care for the wounded soldiers on the battlefield.[32] However, due to Arrault's republican sympathies, the imperial government did not include him in its engagement with the Red Cross project or the Geneva Convention. Arrault attempted on numerous occasions to claim that he had already promoted the project before the Red Cross did, appearing in conferences on the subject and even enlisting his friend, author George Sand, for this purpose.[33]

Ferdinando Palasciano (1815–1891) was another predecessor to Dunant in proposing neutrality for medical staff on the battlefield. Palasciano, a medical officer in the army of the Kingdom of Two Sicilies, served in Messina during the 1848 revolutions in the Italian States. Messina had rebelled against the reigning Bourbons, and the Royal Army was sent in with strict orders not to offer any medical assistance to wounded insurgents. Openly defying this order, Palasciano had treated wounded rebels alongside soldiers and was threatened with execution for insubordination. This sentence was commuted to a one-year imprisonment thanks to the intervention of King Ferdinand II.[34] After his release, he reported on his experiences to the Academy Pontaniana in Naples and pleaded for neutrality for medical staff to be adopted by all belligerents. He printed his address to the academy, as well as a follow-up treatise on this subject, in 1861.[35] Palasciano posited that "it should be that all belligerents, in their declaration of war, mutually recognize the neutrality of the wounded soldiers."[36] Like Arrault, Palasciano continued to try to claim his status as one of the forebears of the Geneva Convention well into the 1870s.[37]

In addition, at least one international agreement on neutrality already existed in Dunant's time. Preceding the Geneva Convention by almost a decade, the 1856 Paris Declaration Respecting Maritime Law had already established neutrality for certain transported goods during warfare. The participants of the Congress of Paris, which settled the Crimean War, drafted and signed the declaration primarily to abolish privateering. Privateering, the state practice of commissioning private vessels in order to wage maritime warfare, was becoming increasingly difficult to regulate. The parties agreed at the Congress of Paris that states should abandon this practice. But in the process, neutrality rules were also included in the declaration: ships were now prohibited from seizing goods belonging to a neutral party transported on an enemy vessel or goods belonging to an enemy party transported on a neutral vessel. Although such arrangements had already existed as bilateral wartime agreements between states, the declaration was the first multilateral treaty specifying wartime neutrality conventions, ultimately ratified by fifty-five states. Although this treaty only applied between its signees and had no universal application, it remains a predecessor to the Geneva Convention in international humanitarian law with regards to neutrality.

The Instructions for the Government of Armies of the United States in the Field of 1863, better known as the "Lieber Code," was another legalistic measure aimed at civilizing warfare by designating some parties inviolable. These instructions were commissioned by Abraham Lincoln and written by Columbia law professor Francis Lieber. The Lieber Code instructed Union soldiers about humane treatment of civilian populations and prisoners of war during armed conflict. The code forbade the use of certain weapons as well as practices such as retribution against prisoners of war, with some exceptions. The norms the Lieber Code specified served as the basis for much of the Hague Convention of 1899, and thus made their way into international humanitarian law.[38] The Lieber Code developed independently from the 1864 Geneva Convention, which the United States would only ratify in 1882, and was unrelated to Dunant's advocacy.[39]

In short, many readers of *A Memory of Solferino* were already familiar with previous calls for the establishment of neutrality on the battlefield, in the form of both treatises advocating for such arrangements and actual legislature to its effect.

Peace societies

Peace activism drew many activists in European and American civil societies and served as an additional way to express concern about the consequences of war.[40] Peace advocacy had been a staple of Quaker activism before the nineteenth century,[41] but the 1810s saw increasing organization and expansion of this activism, and the creation of the Society for the Promotion of Universal and Permanent Peace (commonly known as the London Peace

Society).[42] The intent was to "print and circulate Tracts and to diffuse information tending to show that War is inconsistent with the spirit of Christianity, and the true interests of mankind; and to point out the means best calculated to maintain permanent and universal Peace, upon the basis of Christian principles."[43] The society grew to become part of the International Christian Peace Fellowship, and peace congresses were held in different locations in Europe starting in the 1840s. Prominent societies were also established in the United States. While the societies—predominantly Protestant but also socialist groups—were diverse, they shared the view that widespread peace was an achievable goal. For some of those societies, peace was a condition they believed could materialize in the lifetimes of their members.[44] A public letter from the London Peace Society demonstrates the utopian ideas about the future of international relations these societies harbored:

> For indeed Your Majesties have been pleased to consider your own and other Christian states as only forming one great Christian nation; to acknowledge yourselves as delegated by Providence to govern the several great branches as fathers of this one family; and to confess, "that in reality there is no other sovereign than Him, to whom alone belongs all power, because in Him alone are found all the treasures of love, science, and infinite wisdom."[45]

Although a Quaker initiative to provide humanitarian help to civilian victims of war emerged in the late 1850s, it was part of a wider project aimed at eradicating war altogether. Much like late-century socialists, the peace societies were interested in promoting a new world order, but at the same time did little to address the very immediate concerns of the families of the soldiers at the front. Given the assumption these societies held, that war can—and will!—soon come to a permanent end, they saw little sense in establishing infrastructure to prepare for future wars.

All of these initiatives—the peace societies, the calls for reform of military relief work, legislative initiatives—articulated some universal aspiration. But while they enjoyed some level of public attention, they did reach the same level of international success as the Red Cross would. The various proposals to bolster military medical practices and to establish neutrality on the battlefields were confined to government and military circles, and did not gain much traction with the wider public. The peace societies' radical edge similarly limited their outreach. The nursing professionals were largely uninterested in pursuing a transnational reform project that would require wide public support. But by the late 1860s, the Red Cross had subscribers in most Western and Central European states, and by the early 1880s it had made important inroads into Asia and America. Dunant's book had opened many doors for the founders of the Red Cross, and was crucial in establishing humanitarian work as an independent field. This is because, unlike other initiatives, A Memory of Solferino spoke directly to a general preoccupation with the medical conditions on the battlefield and at the same time offered solutions that individuals could take to directly help alleviate the suffering of the wounded.

A Memory of Solferino Revisited

A Memory of Solferino can be broadly split into three sections. The first section describes the battle itself; the longer second section describes the suffering of the wounded soldiers and the efforts to provide relief; and the short third section lays out Dunant's proposal for the establishment of volunteer societies that would care for those wounded in war, regardless of their nationality. Examining the key themes A Memory of Solferino raises and the conjunctures between them will unpack the context for the emergence of the Red Cross.[46] The following section will then tie these themes to the concrete proceedings of the early Red Cross movement.

From glory to misery

Although A Memory of Solferino is dedicated to humanitarianism, its first quarter contains a praiseful description of the militaries involved in the battle for their maneuvers under fire. Specific generals are celebrated for their bravery: "General Desvaux, brave and imperturbable as ever, met the fierce onslaught of the Hungarian Infantry at the head of his cavalry in a fearful encounter" (26). Broader praises are given to the French military: "mention cannot be omitted of the glorious deeds of the brave Brigadiers, the brilliant Colonels, the fearless Majors and valiant Captains, who did so much to bring about the victory of that famous day" (29). In this, Dunant specifically notes moments of compassion, for example when an officer "saw one of his [wounded] men aiming at [a] boy; the officer stopped him, and then, going up to the wounded man, wrung his hand compassionately and gave orders for him to be carried to a safer place" (31–32). (Dunant himself was not present during the battle and did not witness these events himself, but rather reconstructed them retrospectively.) While some condemning tones are interspersed with this narration (e.g., describing the soldiers as men "of whom many had been made into murderers at the age of twenty!" [31]), Dunant depicts the battle in excited tones. However, when Dunant turns to the condition of the wounded and the scarcity of medical personnel, his tones dramatically change:

> What now has become of that deep intoxicating spirit by which the brave combatants were electrified, which stirred them so strongly, so mysteriously, to the very depths of their being, when the campaign began, and on the day of Solferino when they were risking their lives, and when their valour craved for the blood of men like themselves which they went forth raging to shed? . . . In those Lombardy hospitals it could be seen and realized how dearly bought and how abundantly paid for is that commodity which men pompously call Glory! (105)

The fall of night exacerbated the conditions on the battlefield for the remaining soldiers:

> When the shades of night began to cover this immense field of slaughter, many a French officer and soldier went searching high and low for a comrade, a countryman or a friend. If he came across someone he knew, he would kneel at his side trying to bring him back to life, press his hand, staunch the bleeding, or bind the broken limb with a handkerchief. But there was no water to be had for the poor sufferer. How many silent tears were shed that miserable night when all false pride, all human decency even, were forgotten! (38)

The following day saw the conditions deteriorate even further:

> Old General Le Breton went to and fro in search of his wounded son-in-law, General Douay. He had left his daughter, Mme Douay, amid the scenes of wild confusion a few miles away, in a state of fearful anxiety. . . . Colonel de Maleville, who had been wounded fighting heroically at Casa Nova, now breathed his last; . . . They found the body of the young Count de Saint Paër, who had risen to the command of his battalion only a week earlier. Second Lieutenant Fournier, of the Light Infantry of the Guard, had been gravely wounded the previous day, and now his military career was ended. (46)

The ambivalent stance toward the battlefield—on the one hand described as magnificent and on the other as brutal—reflected a common thread in mid-nineteenth-century English, French, and German writings about warfare. Many authors romanticized the battlefield and numerous intellectuals preoccupied themselves with the study of battle tactics and military organization.[47] Newspapers were central in popularizing this interest, as glorifying reports of battle victories (which the generals themselves recounted) were common. The discourse on medical welfare on the battlefield and volunteer relief work showed similar enchantment with the battlefield, as reflected in *A Memory of Solferino*. Indeed, philanthropists, much like their military counterparts, saw the battlefield as the most honorable site in which to realize their own charitable aspirations. Traveling individuals and societies were thus appearing unannounced at battle sites in order to care for the wounded, and later enthralling Victorian-era readers with their reports of courage and charity. Rather than simply conveying horrific descriptions of the state of the wounded, these stories tended to depict the battlefield as exciting and exotic, sparking popular imagination and moving others to follow.

For example, in the tellingly titled 1857 book *The Wonderful Adventures of Mrs. Seacole in Many Lands*, Mary Seacole, of Kingston, recounted her long years of service in health care in her native Jamaica, and of her desire to aid the wounded elsewhere, especially in war: "no sooner had I heard of war somewhere, than I longed to witness it; and when I was told that many of the regiments I had known so well in Jamaica had left England for the scene of action, the desire to join them became stronger than ever."[48] Having traveled to Crimea, she describes her first view of the battlefield as "pleasant enough," writing that it was "very pretty to see [armies] advance, and to watch how every now and then little clouds of white smoke puffed up from behind bushes and the crests of hills, and were answered by similar puffs from the long line of busy skirmishers that preceded the main body." This was, in her words, quite an emotional experience: "I felt that strange excitement which I do not remember on future occasions, coupled with an earnest longing to see more of warfare, and to share its hazards."[49] Seacole's account joined a growing number of such glowing autobiographic accounts of the excitement of the battlefield.[50] American novelist Louisa May Alcott expressed similar sentiments about her work as an army nurse during the American Civil War: "I've often longed to see a war, and now I have my wish. I long to be a man, but as I can't fight, I will contend myself with working for those who can."[51]

Dunant's admiration of the military maneuvers in Solferino thus spoke directly to the two opposing views of war. On the one hand, Dunant expressed the same enchantment that absorbed Mary Seacole by presenting the battlefield as an exciting site where both war and charity can be undertaken, and where strong human virtues such as bravery, dignity, and humaneness can be expressed. On the other hand, Dunant juxtaposed these positive views of the battle with the horrors of the aftermath of war, described in gory details, and spoke to the concerns of the disarmament movement of his time about the horrific consequences of war.

Inefficiency of existing arrangements

Interspersed with Dunant's depiction of the misery of those wounded soldiers were more direct criticisms of the existing arrangements for the protection of medical staff on the battlefield, the understaffing of existing facilities, and the inefficiency of the well-intentioned volunteers who attempted to help.

Although various preexisting traditions had established that medical facilities ought to be left out of the battle, this was not the case in many battlefields, Solferino included.

> During a battle, a black flag floating from a high place is the usual means of showing the location of first-aid posts of field ambulances, and it is tacitly agreed that no one shall fire in their direction. But sometimes shells reach these nevertheless, and their quartermaster and ambulance men are no more spared than are the wagons loaded with bread, wine, and meat to make soup for the wounded. (39)

The homes of those locals who took in some of the wounded soldiers in order to care for them were not exempt either. When mistaken news of the Austrian army making its way back to Castiglione spread in town,

> immediately houses were shut, their inmates barricaded themselves in, burned the tricolor flags that had decorated their windows, and hid in their cellars or attics . . . [others] took in the first Austrian wounded they found lying in the streets, and suddenly began lavishing thoughtfulness and care upon them. . . . Many wounded men, deaf to all remonstrances, tore off their bandages and staggered out of the churches into the streets, with no clear idea where they could go. (60)

Dunant highlighted the distrust between the parties since impartiality in care for the wounded was not established:

> a French rifleman saw an Austrian lying on the ground in a pitiful state, and went to him with a flask of water to give him a drink. The Austrian could not believe that he meant well by him and, seizing the musket lying beside him, he struck at the Frenchman with the butt with all the strength he had left. (50)

Dunant reaffirmed the already-existing concern that the military medical facilities are in no shape to handle the volume of wounded soldiers through his long descriptions of the understaffed field hospitals.

> All the French surgeons showed tireless devotion to duty; several took no rest at all for more than twenty-four hours. Two of them, working in the ambulance directed by Doctor Méry, Surgeon-in-Chief of the Guard, had so many amputations to make and so many dressings to apply that they fainted away. In another ambulance, one of their colleagues was so exhausted that he had to have his arms steadied by two soldiers as he went about his work. (38–39)

Despite the praises Dunant heaped on the Lombardy locals who volunteered to assist, he also noted the disorganization their lack of training caused. "The crowding in Castiglione became something unspeakable. The town was completely transformed into a vast improvised hospital for French and Austrians." Despite the donations of linen and mattresses, the local hospitals and churches "were all filled with wounded men, piled on one another and with nothing but straw to lie on," and straw was also spread in the streets "so that the wounded pouring in from all directions might have a little shelter from the sun" (55). Having brought some of the wounded into their own homes, some of the locals "ran wildly through the streets, looking for a doctor for their guests. Others went to and fro in the town distraught, begging to have the dead taken from their houses" (55). Disorganization and overwhelm took its toll, as "there was water and food, but even so, men died of hunger and thirst; there was plenty of lint, but there were not enough hands to dress wounds" (58). Dunant wondered:

> Oh, how valuable it would have been in those Lombardy towns to have had a hundred experienced and qualified voluntary orderlies and nurses! Such a group would have formed a nucleus around which could have been rallied the scanty help and dispersed efforts which needed competent guidance. (102)

Although charitable, the townspeople and foreign visitors had little experience in medical care.

> Selected and competent volunteers, sent by societies sanctioned and approved by the authorities, would easily have overcome all these difficulties, and would have done infinitely more good. (103)

The emerging picture, then, was that of multiple well-intentioned parties—physicians, locals, philanthropists, merciful soldiers—but of a lack of trained personnel and of organization. Without established neutrality conventions, the deep mutual suspicion the belligerent parties harbored not only prevented cooperation, but also hindered attempts at humane conduct toward one another.

Senseless death

A Memory of Solferino not only depicted the lack of compassion between militaries, but also highlighted the senseless and inglorious deaths of soldiers of both sides; that is, rather than dying heroically in the battlefield, they died in terrible suffering, lying in poorly equipped hospitals (if not in the ditches), often without final rites. As Dunant lamented,

> How much better it would have been for thee, poor sufferer, hadst thou met a sudden death from a bullet on the field of carnage, amid the splendid horrors which men call glory! Thy name at least had then been surrounded by a little honour, if thou hadst fallen beside thy Colonel, fighting for thy flag! (104)

A common belief among many nineteenth-century Europeans and Americans was that dying properly—in one's own bed, in a calm state of mind, with one's loved ones present—ensured one's soul safe passage to Heaven. Dying a heroic death in the battlefield constituted one alternate way to die rightly, but the increasingly available news about the conditions in which most conscripted men died in reality challenged the notion of such a noble exit. Historian Drew Gilpin Faust demonstrated that news reports from the Civil War front provoked anxiety in Union and Confederate home fronts, as families of the deceased sought some confirmation that their loved one died gloriously. Secular Western European attempts to prevent clergy from entering hospitals and visiting the dying contributed to similar anxieties about where the souls of those who perished without their last rites were destined.[52]

Dunant spent many pages illustrating how the deaths in Solferino were anything but glorious. Many of the dead "were disfigured by the torments of the death-struggle, their limbs stiffened, their bodies blotched with ghastly spots, their hands clawing at the ground, their eyes staring widely, their moustaches bristling above clenched teeth that were bared in a sinister convulsive grin" (48). The way to the hospital brought further misery:

The poor wounded men that were being picked up all day long were ghastly pale and exhausted. Some, who had been the most badly hurt, had a stupefied look as though they could not grasp what was said to them; they stared at one out of haggard eyes, but their apparent prostration did not prevent them from feeling their pain. Others were anxious and excited by nervous strain and shaken by spasmodic trembling. Some, who had gaping wounds already beginning to show infection, were almost crazed with suffering. They begged to be put out of their misery, and writhed with faces distorted in the grip of the death struggle. (44)

Even in the hospitals, death was often tormented and lacked even a final sense of humanity.

A man might be dying in a bed next to that of a companion of misfortune who had himself just died, and he was obliged, while he felt his own strength ebbing, to watch his dead comrade so obscenely handled that he could readily see the kind of thing which was in store for himself. Such a man was still lucky if his eyes did not light on certain people who, knowing him on the verge of death, took advantage of his weakness to search his haversack and rob it of anything in it that took their fancy. (104)

Dunant also found that letters awaiting soldiers in the hospital were often not delivered and many of them died without having such last comfort.

A chief concern was that some of the casualties were not brought to proper burial, and if they did, they often lay in unmarked graves.

It took three days and three nights to bury the dead on the battlefield, but in such a wide area many bodies which lay hidden in ditches, in trenches, or concealed under bush or mounds of earth, were found only much later; they, and the dead horses, gave forth a fearful stench . . . because of [the] haste . . . there is every reason to believe that more than one live man was buried with the dead. . . . The wounded man agonizes, dies, and his dear body, blackened, swollen and hideous, will soon be thrown just as it is into a half-dug grave, with only a few shovelfuls of lime and earth over it! The birds of prey will have no pity for those hands and feet when they protrude, as the wet earth dries, from the mound of dirt that is his tomb. (48–49)

At the time of the Battle of Solferino (and, to great extent, until World War I), the state bureaucracy and ideology that might render a military death heroic by virtue of its imagined service to the nation that many states presently espouse was barely developed.[53] Mid-nineteenth-century European armies were ill-equipped to bring the bodies of the dead to burial and provided little in terms of consolation to the bereaved aside from a brief visit by local officials announcing the death. Dunant reported a young corporal asking "with tears in his eyes: 'Oh, Sir, if you could write to my father to comfort my mother!'" Dunant, who contacted the parents, noted that he was the parents' sole source of information about their son's fate. Many soldiers spoke of "the fear of the grief their mothers would feel when they heard what had become of them" (66). With little in terms of national commemoration of the deaths of "ordinary" soldiers (rather than heroic national figures), many family members had to confront the notion that their loved ones may have died ingloriously and senselessly. Since mass burial of war casualties was common in the nineteenth century, families were often left without clear information about what became of their sons or husbands, raising great concern about dependable communication between the field hospitals and the metropole.[54]

The poor treatment the soldiers received, and the excruciating pain they suffered, stood in sharp contrast to the "civilized" manner in which the war was depicted in the beginning of the book. A large part of the concern *A Memory of Solferino* raised was not only about the numbers of dead and wounded soldiers, but also about their loss of *dignity*.

The role of the volunteer

The book aimed, however, not to condemn war as such but to propose solutions to care better for those the war affected. "In an age when we hear so much of progress and civilization, is it not a matter of urgency, since unhappily we cannot always avoid wars, to press forward in a human and truly civilized spirit the attempt to prevent, or at least to alleviate, *the horrors of war?*" (127, emphasis added). This, Dunant posits, can be best achieved through volunteer work. The book both highlights at various points the merits of volunteer work and concludes by proposing that volunteer societies should be organized to undertake such tasks more efficiently in the future.

> For work of this kind, paid help is not what is wanted. Only too often hospital orderlies working for hire grow harsh, or give up their work in disgust or become tired and lazy. On the other hand, immediate action is essential, for help which will save a wounded man today will not save him tomorrow, and if time is lost gangrene takes hold and carries off the patient. There is need, therefore, for voluntary orderlies and volunteer nurses, zealous, trained

and experienced, whose position would be recognized by the commanders or armies in the field, and their mission facilitated and supported. The personnel of military field hospitals is always inadequate, and would still be inadequate if the number of aids were two or three times as many, and this will always be the case. The only possible way is to turn to the public. (124–125)

Dunant highlighted that volunteers are more inclined to act impartially toward the wounded, conationals and enemy soldiers alike. The Castiglione volunteers, "seeing that I made no distinction between nationalities, followed my example, showing the same kindness to all these men whose origins were so different, and all of whom were foreigners to them. 'Tutti fratelli', they repeated feelingly." A Frenchman, "who had also come three hundred leagues to look after his compatriots . . . saw that the Austrian wounded were left practically to themselves, and he devoted himself more especially to them, trying to help them in every possible way, thus returning good for the evil he had suffered forty-five years before at the hands of an Austrian officer" (113). French, Swiss, and Belgian volunteers joined the local efforts, having traveled to Solferino after hearing about the situation. "Geneva and other Swiss towns, and certain towns in Savoy also, sent very large consignments of linen and lint. . . . Fairly large sums of money were devoted to providing the wounded, without distinction of nationality, with all kinds of small comforts" (111).

In particular, Dunant emphasized what he believed to be the positive effects of charitable conduct on the volunteer.

> The moral sense of the importance of human life; the humane desire to lighten a little the torments of all these poor wretches, or restore their shattered courage; the furious and relentless activity which a man summons up at such moments: all these combine to create a kind of energy which gives one a positive craving to relieve as many as one can. (73)

He quoted a Milanese woman, having lost her own son in war eight months earlier, telling him: "When I heard that French wounded were coming to Milan and that I could help to care for them, I felt that God was sending me his best consolation" (111). Such instances helped Dunant make a case for what he believed is a natural human zeal for charity, which is ignited at the battlefield:

> Spontaneous devotion of this kind is more easily to be found than one is inclined to think. There are plenty of people who, once they were sure they

could be useful and convinced that they could do real good, with the encouragement and facilities given by the administrative authorities, would certainly be prepared to go, even at their own expense, and undertake for a limited time such an eminently philanthropic task. In this age, which is often called selfish and cold, what an attraction it would be for noble and compassionate hearts and for chivalrous spirits, to confront the same dangers as the warrior, of their own free will, in a spirit of peace, for a purpose of comfort, from a motive of self-sacrifice! (118)

To summarize, Dunant's book invoked four themes that directly touched preexisting preoccupations that were prevalent among his readers at the time. It conjoined the glory of the battlefield with the misery that the battle causes, thereby touching an already-open nerve brought on by news reports from previous battle sites that revealed similar atrocities; it demonstrated—through Dunant's own "participant observation"—the lack of working hands and the chaos in field hospitals, joining an already-existing public discussion about the quality of medical care on the battlefield; it highlighted the dishonorable state in which many of those retrieved from the battlefield ended their lives, and the careless way the dead were buried, thus touching on prevalent concerns about death and what comes after; and it glorified the role of the volunteer, tying it to an innate human passion for charity. The book's "best-seller" status and the prestige it conferred on Dunant himself were due to its direct expression of a locus of tensions between idealized views of the battlefield and concrete war realities that was felt across civil societies.

The Success of *Solferino*

The publication of the book provided Dunant with renown within philanthropic and charitable circles, and provided him and his collaborators—Moynier, Appia, Maunoir, and Dufour—with leverage to organize international conferences and to extend invitations to all the governments of Europe, as well as select nations from other parts and international organizations. The book received praise from figures such as Victor Hugo, Ernest Renan, the Goncourt brothers, and Charles Dickens. Dunant was well received at the Berlin International Statistical Congress, where he presented his ideas about neutrality. He was also received by King John of Saxony, the Archduke Rainer, and the Bavarian minister of war.[55] The excitement Dunant generated with *A Memory of Solferino*, and the specific meaning systems it activated across its audiences, was crucial in convincing a wide circle of advocates that humanitarian work requires an autonomous space in the first place. As the responses from pacifists, military leaders, and medical professionals show, the idea that humanitarian aid societies—prototypes of today's NGOs—should offer assistance to the wounded (and be organized as a sector independent from extraneous considerations) was far from a consensus.[56]

While *A Memory of Solferino* was central in expressing the problems with nineteenth-century battlefield norms and medical care, its proposals for improvement were articulated in a speculative and rudimentary manner in the last few pages of the book. The system of justifications for a standing sector of charitable societies that would intervene once wars erupt was certainly not elucidated clearly in this work. The origins of this idea was precipitated by the Calvinist faith of the founding members of the Red Cross. The next chapter will examine in detail how the relatively abstract proposals of the last pages of *A Memory of Solferino* transformed into coherent field logics.

Despite the central role Dunant played in the establishment of the Red Cross movement, his tenure in it was very short. In 1867, at the age of thirty-nine, Dunant declared bankruptcy and left Geneva, leaving unpaid creditors and suppliers behind. The Geneva courts condemned his business malpractices and he was dismissed from his post as secretary of the ICRC and from the YMCA in 1868. Dunant was devastated: "I was barely entering my thirty-ninth year when everything collapsed around me. . . . I lost that elasticity, that spring, that confidence, which I had possessed until then, to fall into a black grief."[57] Although he continued to advocate for the Red Cross from France during the Franco-Prussian War (1870–71) and later pursued other wartime relief initiatives, by the mid-1870s he was living in abject poverty and relative anonymity. From 1887 until his death, Dunant resided in the Swiss village of Heiden. In 1895, Swiss journalist Georg Baumberger contacted Dunant and publicized his poor living conditions, compared to his legacy in the world of humanitarian aid. Newspapers in numerous countries reported on this, and Dunant received donations to pay for his expenses. Thanks to this renewed attention, Dunant received the 1901 Nobel Peace Prize alongside French pacifist Frédéric Passy. Nevertheless, Dunant spent his last years lonely and embittered. He died in a Heiden hospice in 1910 at the age of eighty-two.

TWO

The Réveil and the Founding of the Red Cross

The idea of impartial humanitarian aid societies on the battlefield, as Henry Dunant proposed it, was the initial inspiration for the Red Cross movement: the first large-scale operation identifying humanitarian work as fundamentally different from other endeavors and advocating for relief workers to be given complete latitude in the battlefield. The founders of the Red Cross depicted the ideal humanitarian society as indifferent to the militaries' hierarchies, as enjoying protection from harm in the battlefield, as politically independent, and as occupying a permanent position in civil society from which to monitor military affairs for humanitarian emergencies. Although new and controversial, the position of the modern humanitarian was adopted astonishingly fast, not only within humanitarian circles but also among diplomatic, professional, and popular audiences. The true success of the Red Cross was its differentiation of the humanitarian sector from the social structures that had traditionally sponsored it—particularly the church and the state—and its formulation of humanitarian work as an independent type of work. In a series of conferences in the 1860s, the Red Cross established the relative autonomy of humanitarian work, which humanitarian NGOs still profess today.

The founding members of the Red Cross proposed a relatively limited project, involving merely the treatment of the wounded on the battlefield, when other activist groups had far grander plans in mind. The peace societies, as well as socialist pacifist circles, were advocating disarmament as the solution for the carnage war causes and saw humanitarian initiative as futile since it did not seek to eliminate warfare. As the previous chapter shows, disarmament initiatives gained appeal in religious circles (especially Quaker), but also in nonreligious ones. What caused the founders of the Red Cross, who were so deeply committed to alleviate the suffering on the battlefield, to pursue the far more modest route of volunteer humanitarian work? Why did their project, which was crucial for the establishment of the humanitarian field, succeed so well at a time when Europe was saturated with proposals on alleviating wartime suffering?

Scholars such as Martha Finnemore and John Hutchinson have claimed that the reason for the unusual success of the Red Cross was precisely its relatively modest aims, which did not impinge on state sovereignty and state leaders' need for legitimacy in the eyes of their constituents.[1] However, while the Red Cross was certainly far more palatable for rulers than peace societies, it also enjoyed massive grassroots success in Europe and beyond, including in states where governments were initially suspicious of this project, such as France and Austria.

To answer these questions, then, we need to first understand the origins of the unusual proposals the Red Cross made, and then to examine why they were adopted so rapidly internationally. This chapter examines the roots of the organizational ideas the early Red Cross advocated in the 1860s. As the chapter will show, the Red Cross emerged from a nineteenth-century Calvinist revival, whose theological home was Geneva, and whose teachings instilled in the founders of the movement the conviction that the world can and ought to be civilized by bringing all human endeavors—political, philosophical, diplomatic, scientific—under the aegis of a Christian ethic. The aspiration to establish an independent humanitarian sector, which would permanently stand watch and intervene where relief was needed, was not simply the venting of the founding members' charitable spirit, but part of a wider program to realize a Godly community on earth. The chapter will focus on Geneva, the birthplace of the Red Cross, and provide the social background as well as the religious framework from which the movement emerged. It will then analyze in detail the core proposals the Red Cross put forth in relation to the religious justifications the members of the movement offered and the links they made between the work of the proposed aid societies and a wider program to civilize the world. The following chapters will address the ways in which the movement turned into a worldwide network of societies and specifically demonstrate that, despite its subsequent downplaying of its religious origins, transnational support for movement was boosted by its continuing perception as a religious movement.

Cultural sociologists and social historians have repeatedly shown that new types of discourse consecrating one value or the other emerge out of historical circumstances and cultural dynamics.[2] In particular, scholars have highlighted how religious belief has influenced the ways actors have thought about social problems and conceived of solutions, and how those solutions gave rise to permanent social institutions.[3] Since the logics of social fields are embedded in a discourse of ultimate value, this chapter investigates the anterior system of belief that gave rise to the ultimate value the early Red Cross activists endorsed. The chapter demonstrates how the humanitarian field founders become convinced that certain logics are indispensable for the true fulfillment of this value.

The Réveil and the Origins of the Logics of the Humanitarian Field

Four years after the establishment of the ICRC, two of its founding members—Gustave Moynier and Louis Appia—published a treatise for the national relief societies, outlining the ways in which they understood their project. This work sheds much light on the ways the founding members conceived of the movement and justified its existence:

> We have shown that it is to the influence of Christianity on civilization that armies owe, in a great measure, the assiduous care bestowed upon wounded soldiers. The sentiments of that kind of philanthropy which is called humanizing, those more particularly of honour and patriotism, can do much, and we should be very unwilling to depreciate their value. Patriotism is, among others, one of the most powerful levers. To prove this, we have only to recall the admirable labours of the Sanitary Commission of the United States, which were carried on chiefly by the impulse of patriotism and sympathy with the success of the army of the North. Yet, we frankly declare that we see in Christian sentiments the wisest and most energetic motive for every philanthropic enterprise. We consider this most powerful force as the best means to regulate human actions, and to sustain the devotion of man at a moment when all his faculties are to be exerted; in short, we find in it the true expression of that international bond which ought to unite all nations upon the common ground we have indicated.[4]

The authors cite Christianity not only as a worthy motivation for charitable undertakings on the level of the individual (i.e., in providing the proper character for devoting oneself to the philanthropic mission), but more importantly as pertaining to interpersonal relations and social arrangements. The authors view Christianity as a guiding ethic that civilizes nations, and they ascribe the cosmopolitan stance crucial for transnational humanitarianism to its tenets. The authors refer repeatedly to the "Christian spirit which ought to preside over every part of the work" in which

they engaged.[5] While scholars have certainly identified the influence of religious motivation on humanitarianism, they have made little mention of the
public role of religion in establishing its precise mechanics.[6] In what follows,
I examine the religious context from which the Red Cross emerged and highlight the Calvinist significance its founders found in the logics they sought to
promote (permanence, independence, and neutrality).[7] In particular, I look
at how the unique position Geneva held in European history propelled the
ideas that shaped the Red Cross.

Geneva: a Calvinist theological center

Despite its central role in housing diplomatic, humanitarian, and human
rights organizations in the twentieth century, mid-nineteenth-century Geneva was unremarkable. In 1860, Geneva had an estimated population of
only 31,000 inhabitants, compared to London's 3,227,000, Paris's 1,696,000,
Berlin's 548,000, and Vienna's 476,000.[8] Even among Swiss cities, Geneva
did not stand out as particularly important or populous.[9] Having been
walled for much of its history,[10] Geneva had little agriculture, and special-
ized in textiles, jewelry, and—famously—clock making. The demolition of
the walls surrounding the city in the 1840s helped set in motion a process
of modernization and economic prosperity, but Basel and Zurich preceded
Geneva in terms of economic development. Although the city was, since
1815, the capital of its namesake canton, Geneva did not bear extraordinary
diplomatic importance.

However, Geneva stood out on one dimension: its significance in the
nineteenth-century Reformed Protestant world was close to unparalleled.
Its history as home to John Calvin for most of his working life is certainly
one reason for its prominence, but political and theological developments
in the early nineteenth century amplified its international religious sway.
Geneva had begun converting to Protestantism in the 1520s, when French
Protestants—fleeing religious conflict in their homeland—began arriving
in the city. Relations between the Grand Council of Geneva and the local
Catholic diocese had already soured by then, given the former's push for
independence from its rulers, the House of Savoy, and the latter's enduring
loyalism. By the time the council adopted Lutheranism as its religion in
1528, Catholic priests had been expelled from the city. Protestantism gained
considerable support among the locals, and violent clashes often erupted
between religious groups in the late 1520s and 1530s. The city converted
officially to Lutheranism in 1536.

John Calvin arrived in Geneva in the same year, shortly after having published his 1536 *Institutes of the Christian Religion*, to escape religious oppression in his native France. The Grand Council appointed him to be a public lecturer. After a heated controversy and near-riot over the proper bread for Eucharist, Calvin was exiled from the city. He was reappointed, however, in 1541 and began to work in earnest to bring life in the city in line with his vision of a Christian polity. This was, in particular, through the creation of Reformed institutions, which exist in Geneva to this day. Calvin organized what came to be called the Venerable Company or the Company of Pastors, a formal church institution composed of ministers from the city's churches, professors from the Academy of Geneva, and pastors from the smaller churches in the surrounding villages. The Venerable Company governed both theological and practical church matters in Geneva and evaluated candidates for ministry. The company took an interest not only in local matters but also in international church affairs and gained wide international esteem.[11] In the same year, Calvin also organized the Genevan Consistory, the ecclesiastical disciplinary institution of the church, which was reproduced in other Calvinist communities and was key to the spread of Calvinism.[12] Calvin founded the Academy of Geneva in 1559 to train Reformed pastors. The academy trained Calvinist ministers from much of the Protestant world, and their movement back and forth forged international ties between Geneva and other locations.

As Reformed Christianity expanded across, and then beyond, Europe, Geneva became not only an important theological hub, but also a safe haven for persecuted Protestants. French Protestants, first fleeing the French Wars of Religion (1562–1598) and then the Huguenot rebellions of the 1620s and the ensuing persecution of Protestants, arrived as refugees in the city. English Puritans also came to Geneva to escape persecution during the reign of Queen Mary I, and established a temporary home in the city. This group, which included Scottish reformer John Knox, the future bishop of Durham James Pilkington, and English translator of the Geneva Bible Anthony Gilby, was a politically and theologically radical Puritan faction. Even though Heinrich Bullinger and Pierre Martyr influenced English reformers of this era more directly than Swiss reformers, they were welcomed in Geneva.[13] Knox carried Calvin's Presbyterian theory of church governance back to Scotland during his exile. Ecclesiastical institutions in Geneva maintained strong connections with their counterparts in English-, French-, German-, Dutch-, Hungarian-, and Polish-speaking Reformed communities.

The French Directory annexed Geneva to France in 1798. While some rise in the Catholic population occurred as French civil servants and their families migrated to the city,[14] Napoleonic rule increased Geneva's centrality for

Reformed Christianity exponentially. As part of a broader Napoleonic program to centralize religions under state administration, the French Consulate published the *Articles organiques des cultes protestants*, which dealt with the reorganization of the Church of the Augsburg Confession and the Reformed Church in the French Empire. The French Reformed Church itself did not have a central organ that the Consulate could coopt. It was organized in presbyteries of no more than six thousand persons as part of an *Articles* requirement. However, the Reformed Church was required to organize one single academy for the training of pastors—the Academy of Geneva—in which the training of pastors could be tightly controlled. Although the Consulate allowed a second academy to be opened in Montauban in 1810, Geneva remained *the* center of Reformed theological education in the empire.[15] The increased reliance of French Protestants on Geneva amplified the theological eminence of the city.

After French troops withdrew from the city, Geneva delegates appealed to the Congress of Vienna to reestablish the city as an independent Calvinist republic, and were denied. Geneva, however, was accepted as the twenty-second canton of the Swiss Confederation in 1815, allowing the city to regain at least some of its past independence. At the same time, the transition to a canton involved admitting some sixteen thousand Catholics into Geneva's political borders. Anticipating friction between the Calvinist majority and the Catholic minority, the 1816 Treaty of Turin stipulated that Catholic rights were to be protected in Geneva Canton.[16]

The Réveil and the inspiration for the Red Cross

The position Geneva-born Red Cross founders Moynier and Appia expressed in their writings, that religious morality—once publicly established—would have a strong civilizing effect, was a common one amongst the myriad European Protestant revivals of the nineteenth century. In this era, revival movements sought to reinvigorate Christian doctrine and worship in parishes across Europe and to claim independence from state powers. These movements counteracted a widespread turn-of-the-century marginalization of the role of religion to the private sphere. Among the chief concerns for these movements was an increased state involvement in church affairs. In the Reformed world in particular, "free churches" broke away from the established churches in Scotland, Switzerland, and the Netherlands, among others, in protest of their submission to state influence. It was similarly felt as Lutherans and Methodists traveled internationally and organized conventicles in order to revitalize local parishes and to spread their beliefs in new regions.

Both in Europe and the United States, such revivals were often connected with ecumenicism and social reforms. Since awakening movements typically went along with a more emotional and activist understanding of religion (as opposed to a doctrinal or devotional one), it was easier for such movements to work across confessional lines for social reforms.[17] While many of these religious movements espoused a strong sense of reformist social activism, few were as determined to instill Christian morality through public order as those belonging to the Calvinist Réveil movement ("the Awakening"), which originated in Geneva.

Origins of the Réveil

Although Geneva's lateral influence on Reformed Protestantism skyrocketed under French rule, some of the doctrines circulating within the Academy of Geneva and the Church of Geneva were controversial. Under Napoleonic rule, the Church of Geneva had adopted the rationalizing intellectual currents of its time and acquiesced to state regulation of religious affairs. After France withdrew in 1814, the Church of Geneva—seeking to counteract the spreading atheism of French Revolutionary ideals—published a new catechism that further subdued their theology to Enlightenment principles. As a result, most pastors in the city were reluctant to preach on topics such as the incarnation or the atonement, and restricted their theology to abstract, conservative values.[18]

Moravian evangelists visiting the city met with a group of students, the Société des Amis, who convened regularly in 1810–1814 to discuss theology. Members of this group would grow up to be some of the most prominent leaders of the Réveil, including theologians such as Henri-Louis Empaytaz (1790–1853), Émile Guers (1794–1882), and Ami Bost (1790–1874). Church leadership and the Academy of Geneva frowned upon the unsupervised activities of the Société, and the group ceased its official meetings in 1814. However, its members retained a zealous objection to the quietist church, and both Empaytaz and Guers were denied the ministry for refusing to yield to the Venerable Company's rules regarding doctrinal teaching.

In 1816, Empaytaz published a treatise in which he criticized harshly the silence of the Church of Geneva on the matter of Christ's divinity. Bost, too, described his exasperation with what he saw as a cowardice among the pastors of Geneva, who he thought feared public reaction and were reluctant to proclaim the Gospel in public:

You ask them, "do you believe in the divinity of Christ? Yes or no?"; "That," they say, "is a subject too obscure for me to explain right now." "Do you believe in the Redemption?"; "Maybe not in the same sense that you do"; "Then in what sense?"; "I cannot, in a simple conversation, improvise a response to a question so grave." Do they acknowledge the multitude of passages from the Scripture that tell us "that salvation is granted to the believer through the blood of Christ, that Jesus died for our sins—both for the just and for the unjust among us—and that we have been redeemed by his precious blood, the blood that cleanses us from all sin and has washed away our iniquities"—in a word, that it is through the death of the Savior, and only through his death, that we have been reconciled with God? "Those," they say, "are figurative expressions."[19]

The Scottish minister Robert Haldane visited the city in 1816. He met with several divinity students—members of the Société des Amis—and, surprised by their lack of biblical education, began a series of lectures, starting with Paul's Epistle to the Romans. Future pastor Jean-Henri Merle d'Aubigné—a key influence on the Red Cross—was one of the students in this forum. Through the activist theology Haldane introduced, the movement developed stout ideas about the need for reformation of individual beliefs and practices in the Calvinist polity. Reinvigorating Calvinist identity this way appealed to many Genevans in part because of a rising local concern about the migration of Catholics into the city, which was already home to contentious relations between the Calvinist majority and Catholic minority.[20] Viewing with worry the growing audience at Haldane's lectures and the publication of Empaytaz's treatise, the Venerable Company instructed that ministers and ordinands in the city refrain from promulgating their views on the divinity of Christ, on original sin, on grace, and on predestination—core elements in Protestant Christianity—and to refrain from public debate with other ministers on such issues.[21] These rules, if anything, increased the fervor of Haldane's teachings as well as his students' eagerness.

Between the late 1810s and the middle of the century, the Réveil became influential in Francophone parishes beyond Geneva (especially among the Huguenot diaspora), as well as in Dutch- and German-speaking congregations. Réveil theologians such as Henri-Louis Empaytaz, François Louis Gaussen, César Malan, and Jean-Henri Merle d'Aubigné gained significant international prestige. Merle d'Aubigné, for example, served as pastor at the Brussels Protestant Church between 1823 and 1830. His preaching influenced Guillaume Groen van Prinsterer, who was to become a leading figure in the Dutch offshoot of the Réveil. William II of the Netherlands, as crown prince and the representative of the United Kingdom of the Netherlands in

Brussels, was also one of Merle d'Aubigné's congregants.[22] The Réveil had connections elsewhere as well. Empaytaz, among the earliest Réveil theologians, was a close advisor to Czar Alexander I and a friend of theologian and author Madame de Krüdener. Malan visited England and Scotland and was warmly received. The Réveil also impacted the more radical factions within British evangelicalism, including Lewis Way, Henry Drummond, and Edward Irving.[23]

From religious to humanitarian principles

While Réveil theology was not uniform across these different locations (or, for that matter, within Geneva itself), several of its common doctrinal points were particularly salient for the founders of the nascent Red Cross movement:

1. The Réveil strongly opposed the view that one should understand that Calvin's texts were written in a sixteenth-century context and that nineteenth-century theology should be made to fit the spirit of its own time (i.e., be modernized, rationalized, and less confrontational with other faiths or with secularism). Réveil ministers saw Calvin's sixteenth-century writings as speaking directly to their time, and preached strict and literal orthodoxy (Haldane's stance was that they should "adopt no rule in anything other than the Word of God"). Notably, two Réveil preachers republished the Second Helvetic Confession, the 1566 statement of belief of the Swiss Reformed Church, with a new introduction explicating the direct verbatim relevance of this document to the nineteenth-century church.[24]

2. In tandem with their objection to modernizing Calvinist theology, numerous Réveil spiritual leaders criticized the self-assured tones in which nineteenth-century Europeans described progress and modernity. They highlighted the poverty, moral corruption, and in particular the wars the century was seeing. Speaking to the Evangelical Society of Geneva in 1859, Merle d'Aubigné exclaimed:

> The scourge of war, armed with untold hardships . . . these terrible battles in the middle of a surprised Europe, which have let streams of blood flow just as the century boasted of its progress and dreamed of the brotherhood of peoples, have filled us with sadness and compassion. In the midst of our isolated mountains, on the peaceful banks, facing a lake that smiles upon us . . . in these beautiful days of June . . . we hear through the Alps and the glaciers the thunder of war, and we receive, trembling, the heart-wrenching cries of the wounded.[25]

Merle d'Aubigné particularly objected to claims about religion being a cause of conflict, and emphasized instead that wars were, without question, the outcome of an intrinsic human impurity. While Christianity is inherently peacemaking, humankind is incapable of truly receiving the goods religion had to offer. Elsewhere, Merle d'Aubigné wrote:

> Christianity is divine and therefore perfectly pure. Everything that emanates from it is good. But upon descending from heaven to earth, from God into man, it becomes impure. Christianity in man, and even in the holiest of men, is still not Christianity in God, that is, in Jesus Christ. Do not impute to God that of which man alone is guilty . . . those irreligious so-called wars of religion have not come from Christianity, but from the influence of that very power of evil which Christianity has come to destroy.[26]

Thus, while Merle d'Aubigné and his colleagues affirmed emphatically that peace was the ultimate goal of Christianity, they also viewed human passions and sinfulness as a permanent barrier in its way. Réveil leaders therefore saw opposing war as a cardinal Christian endeavor, but at the same time voiced few aspirations to literally end warfare within their lifetimes.

3. The Réveil placed great emphasis on making an impression not only on the beliefs of its adherents, but also on every sphere of human activity—the familial, the social, the economic, and the political, among others. Réveil theologians called for a return to one of the key features of Calvinism, namely its encouragement of engaged social activism, and highlighted Calvin's role as a social reformer and not only as a theologian.[27] As Michael Walzer described, "The resigned passivity and quietism which predestination might induce were dangers of which Calvinist divines and preachers were nervously aware. God's command sought out not only pious acquiescence, but a kind of eager consent, a response registered, so to speak, not in the mind or the heart so much as in the conscience and the will."[28] For nineteenth-century Reformed theologians like Abraham Kuyper,[29] this was a point of distinction with Lutheranism, which Kuyper thought "restricted itself to an exclusively ecclesiastical and theological character."[30]

Key here was the drive to ensure that everyone in the polity adhere to Calvinist law. Traditionally, almost every Calvinist polity had some form of communal ecclesiastical disciplinary body—specifically focused on moral conduct (rather than witchcraft or blasphemy). Thus, Calvinist communities far surpassed Lutheran and Catholic polities in the rigidity of their ecclesiastic disciplinary institutions and their focus not only on self-discipline but on communal discipline as well.[31] The movement was critical of the Church of Geneva for its reserved and nonconfrontational character, and saw the reinvigoration of Calvinist social activism as emulating the principles of the Swiss Reformation—specifically the belief that "the godly community was not only possible, but imperative . . . [and that it] would reconcile within itself all human endeavor by subordinating it to and directing it towards the fulfillment of God's will."[32] In this spirit, movement members also established charitable voluntary societies focusing on temperance, poverty relief, and other social causes.

4. While role differentiation between church and state is a staple of numerous Reformed Protestant strands, the Réveil espoused a particularly suspicious view of the state and saw charity as belonging outside of its purview.[33] Few were as outspoken on this issue as Kuyper. The state itself, he explained, originated in human sinfulness: while the division of the world into states, along with the installment of magistrates and the legislation of secular laws, is meant to preserve humanity from perishing in its own unavoidable sinfulness (and is thus Godly), the power invested in the state constricts human liberty and—if left unchecked—may constrain the work of Christianity in the world.[34] Kuyper took issue with the state taking responsibility for what ought to be acts of individual Christian charity:

> The fact that the government needs a safety net to catch those who would slip between the cracks of our economic system is evidence that I have failed to do God's work. The government cannot take the place of Christian charity. . . . The face of our Creator can't be seen on a welfare voucher. What the poor need is not another government program; what they need is for Christians like me to honor our savior.[35]

We see, then, the combination of adamant orthodoxy, a sharp critique of modernity (and especially of modern warfare), a strong drive for social activism and for communal discipline, and a suspicious stance toward the state and its unchecked power. These were principles that the young Henry Dunant heard as he attended the sermons of prominent Réveil theologians, such as Jean-Henri Merle d'Aubigné and François Louis Gaussen, in the 1840s. Their passionate evangelism deeply affected Dunant.[36] Both Dunant and Louis Appia—fellow founder of the Red Cross movement—were members of the Committee for the Wounded of the Evangelical Society of Geneva, which sought to provide relief to wounded soldiers in the late 1850s and was associated with the Réveil.[37] Like their British counterparts—such as pioneer nurses Agnes Jones and Florence Nightingale—they recounted in their memoirs epiphanic experiences and a strong sense of a calling from

God to serve humanity.[38] Dunant wrote in his memoires: "I was no more than an instrument in the hand of God and had never considered my role in other terms . . . this invisible hand forced my mind and spirit to write my book and to go on from there."[39] The religiously inspired relief and social reform culture of midcentury Geneva similarly brought together jurist Gustave Moynier and physician Théodore Maunoir—central ICRC figures and devout Calvinists—at the Geneva Society for Public Welfare, which was concerned with social issues such as prison conditions, alcoholism, and orphan care.[40] As a result of the economic boom Geneva had enjoyed since the 1810s, these men were raised with both professional and theological education, and with the wealth and connections to act upon their charitable aspirations.

Like many other European philanthropists of their generation, the early Red Cross activists were the children of professionals, military men, or clergy, who profited from a general upward mobility of the previous generation. Their wealth and education firmly situated them in the upper echelons of the bourgeoisie. The generation coming to age in Geneva in the 1840s (especially Genevans claiming some Huguenot heritage) prided itself on its Calvinist identity and saw public activism as part and parcel of their culture.

The Founding Conferences of 1863–1864

How did these beliefs inform the specific organizational proposals the founding members of the movement made? The two first international conferences that the Red Cross convened demonstrate just how pervasive the principles outlined in the preceding section were in the genesis of the transnational humanitarian field.[41]

These conferences were organized in a relatively short time and were an unexpected success. When Moynier first presented Dunant's ideas to the Society for Public Utility in Geneva in 1862 and suggested that the society act to promote them, his program was rejected outright. Society members admired the spirit of the proposal, but were skeptical of their small society's ability to intervene in international affairs. His second attempt, several months later, was successful because it merely asked for himself, Dunant, and three of their colleagues to be sent to an international welfare conference in Berlin to present these ideas. When the Berlin conference was canceled several months later, Moynier and his colleagues decided to hold their own conference instead.[42]

The first conference took place in October 1863. It included delegates from eighteen states. The committee members were pleased with the turn-out and with the positive reception of their proposal. Moynier said in his opening remarks, "Your presence here testifies . . . that your hearts are filled with compassion for the unfortunate victims, and that you sense the urgency of a remedy. We have assembled here to look for that remedy, and we will find it with the help of God."[43] Its resolutions mandated the establishment of an impartial aid society in each nation, which would provide care to wounded soldiers regardless of nationality. The Geneva-based International Committee of the Red Cross (ICRC) (then called the International Committee for Relief to the Wounded) would coordinate these aid societies. This conference marked the official inauguration of the movement. The second conference took place in August 1864. It culminated in the signing of the Convention for the Amelioration of the Condition of the Wounded in Armies in the Field, better known as the Geneva Convention. The convention provided the legal groundwork for the neutrality of medical facilities on the battlefield and established minimal requirements for the humane treatment of enemy wounded soldiers. Newspapers covered its ratification extensively. It also spoke directly to the growing appeal of international law as a means to influence state conduct in the international arena.[44]

Three aspects of the proposals raised in 1863 (and again in 1864) became central themes in future debates in the humanitarian community. First was that the network of aid societies they proposed to establish should occupy a *permanent* position in each country where it operates, rather than being war-specific. Second was that these societies should be impartial and therefore *independent* from state (or any other) influence, being mainly staffed by volunteers rather than military personnel. Third was that those societies would be considered *neutral* due their humanitarian activities and that such neutrality be similarly conferred upon their chief beneficiaries—the wounded. These features of the Red Cross proposal were rooted in a wider worldview espoused by the ICRC founders about the nature of war and charity, drawn directly from the Réveil.

The permanence of charity

Toward the end of his life, Henry Dunant claimed that he (or, more precisely, his movement) "created the permanence of charity."[45] This was no exaggeration. Since in most locations aid societies emerged only once a war broke out and were disbanded once war ended, establishing that aid societies must be a standing feature in most civil societies was an achievement for the ICRC. The committee cited this often as its crucial intervention in the philanthropic world, as the introduction to the inaugural issue of its official bulletin boasted: "what distinguishes our societies from their predecessors . . . is their permanence even at times of peace."[46]

The establishment of permanence as a key logic of the humanitarian field was also an achievement because the idea of a permanent relief sector clashed with the views of the peace societies, as chapter 1 has shown. Other parties in the diplomatic and philanthropic communities saw this idea as admirable but impractical. Several of the international delegates to the 1863 founding meeting claimed that keeping in place a large-scale volunteer society at times of peace was infeasible because volunteer societies had been, until then, motivated by a sense of urgency the delegates thought only war could provide. Once the war would end, so they believed, the passion would die out and these activists would lose interest in their charitable activities. This problem plagued national Red Cross societies in their early years, as they often lost traction once war has ended (as an Austrian philanthropist complained in a letter to the ICRC, "each armistice sees an end to our work's efficiency").[47] In fact, the American national relief society (founded originally in 1866) and several other local societies failed to gather public attention and, with the absence of war, disbanded.[48] In short, the idea of a permanent humanitarian sector was far from readily acceptable.

And yet, the ICRC insisted in the inaugural international conference that a permanently standing committee should be established "in each of the capitals of Europe." It would recruit the "most honorable" volunteers, and it would "come to an agreement with its government that, if a war were to erupt, its offer of services would be accepted." But crucially, such committees would "exist before the eruption of those conflicts that make their intervention necessary, so as not to be caught unprepared." At times of peace, committees would "study service of the field and the most effective use of resources . . . prepare instructions for inexperienced volunteer nurses . . . [and] support the invention . . . [of] medical supplies or ways of transportation."[49] Thus, these were not to be simply ad hoc societies, but they were to be stable institutions in their respective societies. What made this so pertinent for the ICRC?

The ICRC delegates—Dufour and Moynier in particular—reasoned that the world would truly supply humanitarian emergencies for a very long time, necessitating the permanent humanitarian INGO presence in world society. This idea derived from the theology of its members, who were pessimistic about the notion of perpetual peace. ICRC president Guillaume-Henri Dufour expressed this view as he opened the 1863 inaugural conference:

Despite the philanthropic efforts of the Peace Congress—efforts that deserve
our respect and sympathy without a fair bit of illusion about their chances of
success—as long as human passions remain (and they will surely endure for
a very long time) there will be wars in this world. Thus, rather than to pursue
the fantasy of their eradication, it would be truly useful to mankind to focus
on making their consequences less terrible.[50]

At the same time, the committee rejected the idea that war was a natural
element of the world order "as established by God" as such a view, in their
opinion, would "lend to Providence views that are incompatible with its essential attributes." Resonating with the Calvinist belief in the unavoidable
nature of sin (demonstrated by Réveil theologians), committee members
subscribed to the view that war originates in unavoidable human sinfulness;
that it is a "calamity of human origin from which our race seeks to recover,
albeit slowly," as Moynier claimed.[51] Thus, committee members did not see
their project as bringing an *end* to war in itself but rather as civilizing war
by mellowing its atrocities and by soliciting the help of volunteers, thereby
bringing it under the permanent aegis of religious scrutiny. Their commentary on the aims and successes of the project clarified that the mission for
them was far from confined to wartime alone, but was rather a long-term
involvement in international relations:

> The Red Cross is the fruit of Christianity. It is the morality of the Gospel that
> has . . . inspired in men an active pity toward fellow men in pain . . . [and has]
> made them practice en masse the highest of virtues: the love of their enemies.
> The breach this has caused in the egoism of nations is irreparable, and the
> consequences of this victory are infinite: slowly but surely, all social relations,
> so often entrenched in animosity and hatred, will become affected by the
> infusion of new blood in the veins of the civilized races.[52]

Moynier himself was closely acquainted with the short-lived Ligue internationale et permanente de la paix (1867–1871) and with its president, Frédéric Passy. But while sharing the aspiration for peace with Passy, Moynier
believed that wars were going to continue for the foreseeable future and that
imposing regulations through positive law would do more to subdue it than
any passionate political activism might achieve.[53]

The question of what the aid societies were to do between wars was subject to some debate in the 1863 conference. On the one side, Prussian representatives supported broadening Red Cross activities from the battlefield
to various additional fields of charity—helping the poor and sick, helping

victims of natural disasters, or assisting hospitals—and thus keeping the passion for humanitarian work alive in the volunteers. On the other side, the Russian delegates claimed that the attempt to do everything will ultimately achieve nothing: if donations were to be expended on arbitrary causes, the committee would eventually alienate both donors and recipients. While delegates revisited the question in subsequent meetings, they ultimately accepted the need for the permanent presence of aid societies, with the understanding that those societies would be intended primarily for wartime relief and would devote their resources at peacetime mainly for preparation and training.[54] The argumentation chiefly focused on pragmatics and operationality in case war erupted, with the ICRC representatives claiming that the high probability of recurring wars requires aid societies to prepare supplies and train themselves to be always ready for intervention.

The succession of wars in Central Europe in the 1860s–1870s and in the Balkans in the 1870s–1890s helped convince wider publics of the necessity of a permanent humanitarian sector. The aid societies established after the 1863 conference received international acclaim once newspapers reported their work, leading to increased donations and support. The question of whether the societies ought to exist permanently was de facto answered by their continued involvement in wars and, once specific national Red Cross societies took matters into their own hands, in additional peacetime crises. Furthermore, while the ICRC posited that the aid societies should work only in international conflict, realities in 1870s Spain quickly expanded the humanitarian mission onto civil wars as well. Writing to Geneva, the Spanish Red Cross reasoned that while "some claim that, since our association is rooted in an international act, and is undergird by a diplomatic convention, its purpose must be limited to the relief of misfortunes arising from major international conflicts [but not in civil wars] . . . Christian charity cannot distinguish between the wounded based on their national origin."[55]

In this, the committee's sensibility that war is unavoidable and should be anticipated spread beyond Geneva into other religious, national, and operational contexts. For example, in the aftermath of the Franco-Prussian War, the newly unified German-speaking relief societies convened for their first pan-German general assembly in Nuremberg. The elected president of the Central German Committee, the Baron Rudolf von Sydow, emphasized "that the German relief societies had, above all, to return thanks to God for the good work He had allowed them to perform during the last war."[56] But he immediately added that "their task was far from finished once peace had been achieved" and that—on the contrary—they had to "return to the work with renewed courage and redoubled zeal in order to maintain, improve, develop the emergency means, and be always ready for the outbreak of a new war (which, God willing, will be as far away as possible!)."[57] In fact, much of the German assembly's business during its three-day meeting dealt with peacetime activities. The establishment of the Red Cross as a permanent fixture in a growing number of nations was augmented by Red Cross periodicals, reports, international conferences, and even a museum that boosted the visibility of the movement, for itself and for others, thereby contributing to a shared sense of enduring collective identity. While the question of the proper peacetime activities for the societies remained under debate for future conferences,[58] the understanding that the societies were intended to maintain a permanent presence was no longer challenged in the movement. Offshoots of the movement (many of which were unauthorized) also appeared and participated in the efforts to alleviate distant suffering. In short, if volunteer humanitarian aid in the 1850s tended to be organized sporadically, the 1870s saw the emergence of large-scale, internationally recognized humanitarian arrangements that continued to exist beyond the specific wars in which they were employed.

The ICRC, then, pushed forward the controversial proposal to establish a standing humanitarian sector because its members distrusted the ability of human progress to achieve a lasting peace and were pessimistic about humankind's power to overcome its passions. Because ICRC founders believed war could not be eradicated, they saw the mission of their organization as establishing aid societies that would make wars a more civil affair through subordination to Christian ethics.

The independence of humanitarianism

The same vision of the Red Cross as a permanent civilizing agent inspired by transcendent Christian morality gave rise to an intertwined notion, namely that humanitarians should not only have a permanent position in civil societies but also be independent from all extraneous influences and completely impartial in their interventions.

Although philanthropists and commentators found the notion that humanitarian volunteer and medical forces ought to serve neither side of a conflict admirable as an abstract ideal, the idea that humanitarian societies must be separated from other institutions—particularly the state—in order to provide proper care was controversial. Objectors (with Florence Nightingale chief among them) claimed that the militaries themselves should reinforce their medical facilities. British and Dutch statesmen, for example, asserted that their medical care and ethics had sufficiently improved so as not to require additional volunteers. A letter from the War Office in London to the ICRC explained:

> The introduction of the conflicting element of a purely voluntary agency with parallel duties would create confusion in the organisation of the Hospital Department, and moreover it could probably not be obtained even if otherwise unobjectionable in those distant colonies where most of the Field Service of the British Army is performed.[59]

The French delegate to the 1863 conference, Dr. Boudier, elaborated on the unreliable nature of a volunteer-based society and, instead, discussed the multiple improvements the French army has seen in its medical corps—in terms of staff, treatment, and means of transportation—and suggested that such investments would be a better service to wounded soldiers.

Beyond the conference itself, the committee also faced an ethical objection to the Red Cross idea, which was that states are obliged to care for their wounded rather than relegate them to volunteer relief workers.[60] The claim was that in moving responsibility away from the state and toward volunteer societies, these well-intentioned activists would make war an easier affair for the state to conduct. The ironic result would be that the benign intentions of the Red Cross would simply make wars longer and deadlier. The great support the Red Cross received from small states such as Switzerland and Baden, which have "not known war," was not lost on these detractors.[61] Pacifist circles pointed further ideological criticisms, claiming that by not condemning war, the Red Cross was in fact endorsing it. Military leaders had their own set of objections, which ranged from seeing war as a site for cultivating noble virtues of courage and self-denial that should not be sullied by humanitarian workers, to claiming that the shortest wars are the most humane and that humanitarian intervention would unnecessarily lengthen them.[62]

And yet, despite these objections, ICRC representatives insisted in 1863 and at follow-up meetings that simply enhancing the existing military medical facilities would be insufficient. Representatives contended that medical force subordinated to military decision makers would likely be influenced by war-related financial considerations, and thus be blind to the true medical needs of the wounded. Moynier reasoned that, at times of war, military staff may be unwilling to offer impartial care to wounded enemy soldiers (or be prevented from doing so). He envisioned the role of the aid societies as inherently independent of the military, and staffed by charitable volunteers (unaffiliated with the warring militaries) who could be trusted to provide such help:

We would like the wounded who are scattered across the battlefield to be rescued by nurses from either side of the battle; this would require that . . . [these nurses] would wear a distinct sign that would be recognized and would command the same respect as the robes of a priest or a nun. Army leaders would also . . . officially inform their troops about the existence of volunteer corps, about the insignia that marks them out, and of their peaceful and beneficent mission.[63]

Appia and Moynier's commentary on the proceedings of the conference provide further insights into the reasons for this insistence. Subordination to any external authority, according to them, would "completely denaturalize the work of the [aid] committees." In the battlefield, committee members reasoned, "men who, from motives of pure charity, devote themselves to the relief of their brethren, have no need for any other restraint other than moral law."[64] In the international arena, co-optation by state interests would stand in the way of the project of moving belligerents "to take the solemn commitment . . . to renounce . . . the most revolting of practices to be found at times of war." The aim was to move belligerents to "care for the enemy wounded like those of their own army, as this imperative is directly derived from the love of one's neighbor, as presented by Jesus Christ himself as the compendium of divine law."[65] The differentiation between social institutions was thus seen as a key condition for humanitarianism to thrive.

The notion of independent relief associations received support from several growing professions that espoused an ethos of disinterestedness. The new profession of nursing was directly relevant to the Red Cross, but international lawyers, physicians, and reporters were also significantly involved in its development. (This will be elaborated in chapter 4.) Once news of the first battles of the Franco-Prussian War were made public in 1870, and the inability of the French military medical facilities to cope with the sheer masses of the wounded became apparent, support in philanthropic circles for an impartial aid society increased dramatically.[66] Reports arriving in Geneva from battlefields were thus particularly praiseful of sights of volunteers providing impartial help on the battlefield, rather than serving as auxiliaries to their national forces. Physician Louis Appia, the ICRC delegate to the Schleswig War of 1864, described the work of the aid societies during the war in glowing terms, where wounded Danes and Prussians were treated side by side with no discrimination.[67]

Through its religiously inspired insistence that volunteer corps should be employed alongside military forces, the ICRC opened the way for a far-reaching involvement of the public in warfare: by making war the concern not only of politicians, state bureaucrats, and military personnel, these endeavors dislocated war from the battlefield and made it into a general public concern in which ordinary men and women could take part. Especially for women's philanthropic associations, which had been forming for several decades and traveling independently to war-ridden areas to provide relief, such a project was certainly appealing, as it was to create an institutionalized way for such associations to mobilize themselves and to gain legitimacy. As national Red Cross societies were forming in an increasing number of states, it became common for volunteers to be dispatched to provide relief in wars in which their home countries were not involved (e.g., the Second Boer War [1899–1902] drew to Africa activists from numerous European countries), garnering further public praise for independent volunteer relief work. Thus, women's volunteer associations were mobilized to new sites. Altogether, the idea of widely organized volunteer activism touched precisely upon the flourishing popularity of philanthropy in the late nineteenth century, popularizing the view that activists can and should become personally involved in alleviating suffering in distant lands and providing the institutional resources to act upon these notions.

Another implication of the independence principle was that the Red Cross made considerable efforts to present itself as an impartial and (at least in its public capacity) nonjudgmental actor to avoid upsetting relations with state leaderships. The Geneva Convention endowed no person with the power to arbitrate or to determine fault at times of war, and Red Cross activists were cautious about taking on such efforts. American Red Cross founder Clara Barton, for instance, commented thus on her experiences in the Spanish-American War: "There were unpleasant incidents to relate, and unfortunate conditions to describe, but I have neither said nor written that any particular person, or persons, were to blame. It is not my duty, nor is it within my power, to analyze and criticize all the intricate workings of a government and its armies in the field."[68] Likewise, the ICRC itself declined invitations to directly evaluate the conduct of other nations. At the outbreak of the Serbo-Bulgarian War (1885), the two belligerents reportedly proposed that the ICRC serve as witness to their conduct in war and be "a jury of honor" that would attest to their adherence to the Geneva Convention. The committee declined, "not wanting to exercise such an authority without having been officially invested with it."[69] (However, the ICRC negotiated the release of wounded prisoners in accordance with the Geneva Convention as early as the Franco-Prussian War, thereby further accentuating its role as a nonpartisan agent between belligerents.)

Red Cross agents have tended to "remind all belligerents" of their obligation to international humanitarian law rather than to directly accuse one party or the other of breaking it. Direct communication with state powers in the early decades of the movement was similarly understated. When Dunant wrote to French empress Eugénie during the Franco-Prussian War in response to news of French indifference to the convention on the front, he asked her to merely turn her attention to "the [Geneva] Convention of 1864 . . . which was ratified by all European states," and to advise her that the foreign press has been extremely critical of France for failing to comply with it.[70]

The notion of independence—drawn from the aspiration to subordinate war to a Christian moral code and the Calvinist objection to state-sponsored charity—was thus a central contributor to the growing perception that relief societies ought to answer only to universal values and to be solely concerned with saving human lives (rather than furthering the military interest of their state or providing care only to their own compatriots).

The neutrality of humanitarians and beneficiaries

Finally, the designation of aid societies as standing outside the mundane workings of the military and the battlefield was also accomplished through the principle of neutrality, which requires belligerents to protect both volunteers and wounded soldiers. Until the mid-nineteenth century, physicians, nurses, and wounded soldiers were very much at risk of attacks or imprisonment by enemy forces (aside from some protection that local agreements between belligerent sides provided). Unlike the previous two logics, neutralization of actors on the battlefield requires the active restriction of acceptable practices on the battlefield, making it a particularly sensitive topic with some belligerents. But while greeted with some doubt about its practicality in 1863 (both within and outside of the committee), neutralization became the main concern of the 1864 Geneva Convention—less than a year later—as six of its ten articles dealt with neutrality directly. This third principle further differentiated the humanitarian world from other social domains.

The convention established that all medical staff, volunteers, ambulances, and chaplains remain untouched and be allowed to care for the wounded of all nations. It further extended neutrality onto the wounded, specifying that "wounded or sick combatants, to whatever nation they may belong, shall be collected and cared for" and be repatriated once fit for travel, rather than imprisoned, tortured, or killed. The convention went as far as to require military officials to notify local civilians "of the neutrality which humane conduct will confer," and to assure them that no action will be taken against those tending the wounded of either side of a battle. The idea proved far less controversial than other details discussed at the 1863 conference, and the delegates approved it in principle. In fact, in response to this proposal, the Prussian delegate recalled with pride that "the neutralization of ambulances already existed between Prussia and France" in a 1759 treaty, which convinced him that the Geneva Convention was a feasible and desirable arrangement.[71]

Dunant and the Dutch physician J. H. C. Basting were among the key proponents of including the issue of neutrality in the 1863 conference agenda to address this concern. They believed that news of war and suffering would spontaneously ignite a sense of Christian charity in civilians of all localities, and that an agreement of neutrality for volunteers would prevent belligerents from standing in the way of this work. While Moynier thought the proposal would raise state objections, the delegates unanimously approved the principle at the convention in 1864.

The ratification of the Geneva Convention and the agreement by a growing number of nations to the principle of neutrality aligned directly with the religious convictions of the ICRC members because to them it signified an important step toward subduing the uncontrolled passions and violence of the battlefield—as Moynier put it, this was a step in "advancing the Kingdom of God in this world."[72] In the eyes of ICRC leadership, divine inspiration had made this proposal a success, despite the fact that not all other actors saw it as a religious act:

> rulers who endorse [the principles of the Geneva Convention] do so as an act of faith . . . the motives they obey are purely religious, regardless of what they say; they are simply too little accustomed to see religion play such a role in the relations between peoples.[73]

In spite of the practical doubts some ICRC members initially raised, the widespread approval and enthusiasm with which the proposal was greeted served the leaders as further proof of their own religious superiority:

> The [Geneva Convention's] design is eminently Christian. It pleases us to take note . . . that [by ratifying it] people of all faiths agree to pay respect to our religion . . . [and] to a group of men firmly attached to the Evangelical faith.[74]

The Geneva Convention not only protected military medical staff but also paved the way to the battlefield for more civilian volunteers, who were already involving themselves in the battle through ad hoc aid relief societies. The Convention codified, for the first time, the role of the volunteer on the battlefield as well as the neutrality of both relief staff and their beneficiaries, and the wars of the late 1860s and 1870s were fertile grounds in which to popularize its provisions. For the Spanish Red Cross, the "painful circumstances" of the 1872–1875 Third Carlist War "have served. . . . to make known and popularize the Geneva Convention." A medical worker wrote from Pamplona:

> My main goal has been to establish the neutrality of the wounded, even during the civil war, and I had the good fortune to succeed. In this, I looked . . . for the wounded insurgents and I cared for them while ensuring their protection.

When insurgents occupied the village where the Red Cross was operating, they behaved "in the most humane way," offering medical services and transportation to the remaining wounded Spanish army soldiers and allowing the Red Cross to continue to operate.[75]

The promise of neutrality inspired volunteers to travel to the front. During the Franco-Prussian War, the ICRC was surprised by the appearance of uninvited civilians (Clara Barton among them) who believed that the committee would confer neutrality upon them and send them to the front (when, in fact, only their role as aid providers on the battlefield itself and the local military authorities that recognize them could confer it).[76] In response to their plea for neutrality, ICRC staff "had to answer them, the Geneva Convention in hand, that . . . the International Committee has not standing to provide it," since this was a law to be observed by the belligerents themselves.[77] At the same time, the transformation of neutrality from an ad hoc, temporary state into a condition grounded in universal principles endowed the category of the "defenseless" with new moral value. Since wounded soldiers, according to the convention, are no longer to be considered combatants, they were recodified as the prime beneficiaries of humanitarian aid societies.[78] Responses to the occasional violation of the principle of neutrality by military forces became increasingly scathing toward the end of the century. The Balkan Wars of the late 1870s saw new usage of the Geneva Convention in journalistic discourse to evaluate civil conduct in warfare. For example, a report of Russian fire on an Ottoman hospital was "expose[d] to the indignation of the whole of Europe" as a "cruel act . . . which is not only contrary to humanity, but is another blow to the obligations imposed on all the signatories of [the] Geneva Convention."[79]

The new arrangement of humanitarian activism on the battlefield thus spread the assumption that humanitarian societies (Red Cross and others) must to be afforded a safe space at times of war, to allow Christian charity to thrive. By doing so, it allowed volunteer relief forces to integrate operationally into conflict zones and marked humanitarian activities as outside the control of the state and as such, at least in principle, safeguarded within a protected space. It was thus a crucial element in the differentiation of the humanitarian field as a unique professional and social domain.

The controversy around the proper role of humanitarians on the battlefield never died out completely. But the ethical framework the ICRC promoted convinced many of contemporaries that humanitarian work should be waged autonomously, under its own logics. Clara Barton, while differing from her Swiss counterparts in many ways in her views about relief work, articulated the same ethics the ICRC espoused in 1881. On the one hand, she addressed the ethical concerns about volunteers unwittingly making wars easier to wage:

> Among these hard facts [of war] appears a conscientious theorist and asks, Is not war a great sin and wrong? Ought we to provide for it, to make it easy, to lessen its horrors, to mitigate its sufferings? Shall we not in this way encourage rulers and peoples to engage in war for slight and fancied grievances?
>
> We provide for the victims of the great wrong and sin of intemperance. These are for the most part voluntary victims, each in a measure the arbiter of his own fate. The soldier has generally no part, no voice, in creating the war in which he fights. He simply obeys as he must his superiors and the laws of his country. Yes, it is a great wrong and sin, and for that reason I would provide not only for, but also against it.[80]

On the other hand, Barton responded to the pacifists who saw humanitarian initiatives as a distraction from the superior project of promoting world peace:

> But here comes the speculative theorist! Isn't it encouraging a bad principle; wouldn't it be better to do away with all war? Wouldn't peace societies be better? Oh, yes, my friend, as much better as the millennium would be better than this, but it is not here. Hard facts are here; war is here; war is the outgrowth indicator and relic of barbarism. Civilization alone will do away with it, and scarcely a quarter of the earth is yet civilized, and that quarter not beyond the possibilities of war. It is a long step yet to permanent peace. We cannot cross a stream until we reach it. The sober truth is, we are called to deal with facts, not theories; we must practice if we would teach. And be assured,

my friends, there is not a peace society on the face of the earth to-day, nor ever will be, so potent, so effectual against war as the Red Cross of Geneva.[81]

From Religious Values to a Nascent Social Field

The Red Cross was the first to translate the charitable concern of its founding members into a systematic program that operates according to logics that are irreducible to those of state medical institutions or the religious field per se. But while much of the historiography presents the Red Cross as the product of the ingenuity of its founders, the movement articulated the values of a much broader religious movement, and its proposals "worked" because they resonated with the concerns of many of the Red Cross's contemporaries. As this chapter showed, the interaction between the Calvinist Réveil movement—which had been present for almost half a century by the time the Red Cross appeared—and the conditions surrounding mid-nineteenth-century battlefield relief moved the founders of the Red Cross to advocate for its principles of humanitarianism. The role of the ICRC as founder of the humanitarian field remained inscribed into contemporary humanitarian institutions, and the committee is the only humanitarian international non-governmental organization recognized in international humanitarian law.

For the genesis of the humanitarian field, the organizing principles established in the 1860s were key because they removed battlefield relief work from the sole purview of the militaries or religious orders, and redefined them as acting under their own logic. Even though neutrality and impartiality were not always observed in practice in subsequent decades, and many humanitarian societies remained ad hoc rather than permanent, establishing permanence, independence, and neutrality as the core principles of the Red Cross movement set them as the gold standard definition of good humanitarian work, making a humanitarian field possible.

The next two chapters will show how the proposals the Red Cross founders put forth resonated with social and political concerns that preoccupied actors of its time. Chapter 4 in particular will show that the Christian ethos that the Red Cross espoused resonated in other religious circles and contributed to the circulation of humanitarian ideas and imagery. In other words, the conjuncture of the preexisting cultural framework on which the early Red Cross actors grew and the specific circumstances they faced was the prerequisite for the emergence of a humanitarian field.

The analysis highlighted the role of religion in giving rise to what numerous scholars assume is a secular endeavor,[82] namely impartial humanitarianism that presents itself as the natural expression of universal human values.

The early organizers and supporters of the new movement saw themselves as making an active intervention in a depraved social reality, with the aim of reinstating a religious moral code they believed applies universally and was lost with modernity. The early Red Cross actors thus rejected the subdued role assigned to religion by modernizing theological currents and sought to reclaim its public role in social life. Notably, the Red Cross grew not from the rationalized, humanistic state church but from the revivalist movement that countered such modernized theology. This has been a recurrent phenomenon in the history of humanitarian projects. Peter Stamatov, for example, has demonstrated that radicalized religious actors have been historically the ones to advocate globally on behalf of mistreated peoples and were the ones who put into place the infrastructure for contemporary long-distance activism.[83]

Existing studies in cultural sociology have highlighted the relatively autonomous effects that belief exerts on "noncultural" realms, such as economic and political structures.[84] Despite the lack of attention to belief systems that give rise to social fields among field studies, the humanitarian field is a prime example of such a cultural process. Having been convinced that humanitarianism is an independent task that carries transcendent value and must be pursued at all costs, and after benefitting from the international success of Dunant's book, the early Red Cross activists propagated this notion across Europe and managed to organize the institutional means to realize such a vision. This new institutional arrangement caused new actors to emerge and to lay claim to the humanitarian "capital" that the Red Cross espoused.

THREE

The Spread of Humanitarian Culture Across Borders

The late-nineteenth-century expansion of the Red Cross and the wide-scale ratification of the Geneva Convention far surpassed the expectations of the movement's founders. The model of volunteer humanitarianism that the International Committee of the Red Cross (ICRC) advocated crossed political, cultural, and religious divides with unexpected ease, and the Red Cross established a presence in most European states within a mere decade of its 1863 inception. By the end of the century, it had become the largest international popular movement of its time, spanned three continents, and swept up thousands of volunteers, donors, and state officials. The work of Red Cross volunteers on the battlefield—celebrated in newspaper coverage, volunteer biographies, and expositions—modeled a transnational identity for humanitarian workers that was at once rooted in their local national context and oriented toward a shared global mission to reduce suffering. ICRC president Gustave Moynier wrote in 1899 that although the Geneva Convention was "inaugurated at the heart of Christianity," their "unexpected good fortune is now a fait accompli, and among the signatories to the Convention are two Muslim states (Turkey and Persia), and two Buddhist ones (Japan and Siam), who have joined of their free will and without expressing any reservation as to its content."[1]

Despite Moynier's delight at the international success of his humanitarian project, aggressive nationalism and xenophobia were also on the rise, especially in the newly formed Italy and Germany, as well as in France after its defeat in the Franco-Prussian War in 1871.[2] Why would a transnational movement like the Red Cross enjoy such success at a period when national boundaries were being fortified? Historians like David Forsythe have claimed that the Red Cross succeeded in large part because it spoke to the interests of state leaderships, even as the movement worked to create international

humanitarian provisions that would require states to moderate their conduct during warfare.[3] A project like the Red Cross thus appealed to state leaders because it helped mollify public concern about the medical conditions
on the battlefield, and at the same time involved more citizens in prepara-
tions for war.[4] John Hutchinson has shown how Red Cross societies (inten-
tionally or not) bolstered militaries during wartime by providing them with
medical services and public legitimacy.[5] For such scholars, the spread of the
Red Cross across borders occurred primarily on the diplomatic level.

However, while some states recognized the establishment of a Red Cross
society as serving their own interests, others were reluctant to join in. Austrian and French Red Cross activists, for example, had tense and occasionally mistrustful relationships with their governments and were at times
suspected of promoting foreign agendas in their home countries. In other
locations such as Serbia and Romania, local Red Cross societies preceded
the establishment of an independent state and appeared as an assertion of
national moral robustness in face of the Ottoman imperial rulers. While
state leadership interests were certainly at play in the international adoption
of the Red Cross project, their influence varied dramatically across locales.

However, the Red Cross enjoyed unprecedented popularity among volunteers, as well as health care professionals, across borders. In many ways,
the attractiveness of the movement in different circles was crucial to its international dissemination and its effect on the humanitarian sector as a
whole. As this chapter will show, the model of humanitarian work the Red
Cross proposed traversed boundaries with such ease because its decentralized nature resonated directly with the nationalist cultural currents of the
late nineteenth century. The Red Cross project unfolded in a way that afforded nation-level parties with considerable autonomy to adapt the norms
blueprinted in Geneva in ways that fit local culture. This country-level focus
allowed each national Red Cross society (NRC) to draw from a domestic rep-
ertoire of images and myths to represent humanitarian work as aligning with
national character. At the same time, the continuing association of each NRC
with the international movement contributed to the transnational spread of
humanitarian norms, organizational models, and ethics—as developed by
the ICRC in the 1860s. While establishing an NRC certainly served the interests of many states, the ICRC's appeal to national cultures was crucial to its
international success, and the national-level success of ideas about restraint
on the battlefield and humane treatment of enemy nationals created the
infrastructure for a transnational field of humanitarian activism.

Decentralization was part of the overall vision for the Red Cross that the
movement founders harbored. One of the key ecclesiastical principles of

the Calvinist Réveil movement to which they belonged was an emphasis on the independent organization and governance of each parish, with relatively loose overarching church organizations to coordinate. This feature had helped Reformed Protestantism expand into new linguistic and cultural contexts with considerable ease. Historically, the internationalism of the Reformed Church was significant ideologically for many Calvinists.[6] The ICRC founders envisioned a loosely federated set of organizations, each organized by local activists dedicated to a central mission that promotes Christian values globally.

Cultural sociologists have demonstrated that the processes that assign texts and ideas new meanings as they travel internationally are crucial for their reception in new cultural contexts.[7] Since meaning systems are largely nationally defined,[8] and given the patriotic (and often xenophobic) upsurge that washed across North Atlantic nations in the late nineteenth century, projects that resonated with notions of national responsibility and superiority had greater leverage than movements that emphasized globalism and advocated for global disarmament.[9] This chapter examines the meanings nationally situated actors assigned to the universal mission of the Red Cross and looks at how those meanings shaped the nascent transnational humanitarian field.[10]

After providing a brief historical context for the rapid growth of the movement in the late nineteenth century, this chapter will proceed in four parts. First, it will demonstrate that the ICRC worked in multiple ways to create an internationally shared identity for humanitarian workers, thus increasing the global prestige of this new profession. Second, the chapter will show that the ICRC simultaneously deemphasized its centrality and encouraged national-level actors to take the lead in their own countries. The analysis will show how NRCs took on a decidedly patriotic form as activists and volunteers identified humanitarian work as an expression of national values. Third, the chapter will show that, as a result of these dynamics, engaging in relief work—and particularly emulating Red Cross ideals—gained prestige and drew actors to the humanitarian sector. Finally, the chapter will show how the growing prestige of the Red Cross also drew parties eager to exploit the symbolic power it affords.

Historical Context: Expansion from a Movement to a Transnational Field

Although much of the ICRC's diplomatic work had taken place in peacetime, the various outposts of the movement came into action during the late-nineteenth-century wars. The NRCs, which began appearing in both core and periphery states, shared with Geneva and with other NRCs knowledge, procedures, principles, and symbols. At the same time, they enjoyed considerable operational and cultural autonomy. In many states, provincial volunteer societies joined the national society, which coordinated them (with varying levels of success), and additional unaffiliated societies often worked closely with the NRC (or competed against it for funding and prestige).[11] NRCs worked primarily within national boundaries—establishing hospitals, training, and accumulating funds and resources—but during wartime also provided aid to foreign nationals. In the first decade of the movement, aid societies had been established in most independent European states. In the second decade, Eastern European countries, the United States, Peru, and Argentina joined in. By the end of the century, thirty-three NRCs had been established, each with its own constellation of local donors, activists, administrators, supporters, and detractors. The 1864 Geneva Convention, which established neutrality for aid workers and was thus fundamental to the work of the Red Cross, was ratified at a similar pace.

The movement saw its baptism by fire soon after its inauguration. The 1864 Second Schleswig War between Denmark and the combined forces of Prussia and Austria was the first war in which NRCs existed on both sides. The 1866 Seven Weeks War soon followed, with the Austrian-led southern segment of the German Confederation fighting the Prussian-led northern German states and their Italian allies. While both wars carried considerable historical significance, both wars (as well as the role of Red Cross personnel therein) were perceived at the time as local and limited in scope. The 1864 war had very few casualties, estimated at 2,500 altogether (compared to an estimated 356,000–410,000 in the Crimean War), and was confined to Jutland. Although the 1866 war had a higher death toll—a total estimate of 79,000—it was widely considered to be an intra-German affair, and was at times referred to as the "German Civil War." The Red Cross was active throughout both wars, but the longer and deadlier 1870–71 Franco-Prussian War provided it with significant international public attention, since it involved volunteers and NRCs from across Europe and beyond.

The Franco-Prussian War exacted a devastating toll on both sides. France lost an estimated 140,000 soldiers and saw its civil society torn in continuing battles between militias during the Paris Commune period and beyond. In addition, by January 1871, almost 20,000 French civilians had perished under the Siege of Paris.[12] Although victorious and unified, Germany lost approximately 45,000 to 47,500 soldiers.[13] Civilian deaths from retaliation and disease outbreak were common on both sides. At the same time, the humanitarian communities of France and the German states flourished during the war and, for the first time, the Red Cross could demonstrate its plans for international humanitarian cooperation in real time. Württemberg, Prussia, Hesse, Saxony, Baden, and Bavaria already had active NRCs in their capitals, formed in the mid-1860s. France had made a more reluctant entry into the Red Cross project but it, too, featured a lively Red Cross presence at the eve of the war. The war also spilled over into neighboring Switzerland in 1871, when approximately 87,000 French soldiers crossed the border close to Pontarlier in search of food, shelter, and medical assistance. News of their condition elicited volunteers and donations from across Europe and from America as well.[14]

The 1870s also brought the Red Cross into new domains. First, Red Cross personnel deployed during civil wars such as the Third Carlist War in Spain (1872–1876), in spite of the ICRC plan for Red Cross volunteers to intervene solely in *international* wars. Geneva Convention protections did not strictly apply to domestic disputes, and thus the extent of protection aid providers could expect was unclear. Second, the Great Eastern Crisis of 1875–1878, which included the Serbo-Turkish War (1876–78), the Montenegrin-Ottoman War (1876–78), and the Russo-Turkish War (1877–78), brought European NRCs for the first time into contact with Ottoman forces. Although Constantinople had ratified the Geneva Convention in 1865, the extent to which the empire intended to respect its provisions remained in question for Western European observers.

The Red Cross diversifies

Throughout this violent first decade, the Red Cross saw uneven growth. In some countries, NRCs were successfully installed, but in other locations the new societies could not gain traction and disappeared. The ICRC reported in 1870, for example, that the "death or the dispersion of most of the members" of the Portuguese society "made its maintenance impossible and in fact, at least for the time being, it no longer exists."[15] Some NRCs, like the early Italian society, consisted of a small group of activists, whereas others, such as the German and Japanese NRCs, had thousands of trained workers on their staffs. In addition, some of the NRCs expanded from the battlefield relief mission that was discussed in the founding conferences of the movement, and took upon themselves many of the domestic tasks that became state responsibility in the twentieth century: locating missing soldiers, notifying families of prisoners of war, consoling the bereaved, and other such duties.

As the movement grew, disagreement emerged between international organs of the Red Cross and NRCs over the proper ways of conducting humanitarian work. In particular, while the ICRC limited its view of Red Cross activities to war-related matters, the American National Red Cross (ANRC) provided famine relief in Russia and parts of Asia in the 1880s and 1890s without seeking ICRC approval and became an internationally influential organization on its own right.[16]

However, despite the growing fragmentation of the movement, the role of the ICRC in establishing the legal, organizational, and cultural infrastructure necessary for any of these struggles to take place was crucial. On the one hand, the ICRC supported the NRCs and their dominance in their local context by maintaining global recognition of the Red Cross as an elite movement and establishing its ethical framework as the standard for humanitarian organizations. On the other hand, NRCs drew upon the growing international reputation of the ICRC to gain symbolic distinction in their home countries, while at the same time being influenced by local dynamics, competition, and cultural contexts. Local actors became carrier groups for the transnational humanitarian cultural framework, while interlacing it with their own views of charity.

Creating a Humanitarian Character

The ICRC, from its early years, invested considerable effort in producing a shared identity among its national chapters and drawing outside attention to its work. Red Cross officials placed importance on publicizing the aims and achievements of the movement internationally. The explanation Red Cross officials gave to infringements of humanitarian norms on the battlefield was often "insufficient publicity given to the philanthropic ideas that are the basis of the [Geneva] Convention and to its provisions," as the Baden committee concluded after the Franco-Prussian War.[17] Aside from publishing reports about its endeavors and achievements in newspapers, Red Cross actors formed their own media to spread knowledge and respect for its mission. The ICRC and many of the NRCs were producing considerable numbers of papers, some hundreds of pages long and some no longer than brochures. This type of publishing was in addition to the numerous personal accounts individual humanitarian activists wrote and published, which they intended for wide readership.[18]

In 1869, the ICRC established a periodical dedicated to the movement, *Bulletin international des sociétés de secours aux militaries blesses*, which was published in French in Geneva.[19] Its purpose was first and foremost procedural, to help coordinate activities between the various NRCs, to update them about developments at the Geneva committee, and to appeal for donations for societies in formation or in financial difficulties. But another function of the journal was the exchange of NRC stories of heroic successes, often recounted by the volunteers themselves, which helped those societies receive recognition of their work by the international community. By the mid-1880s, domestic Red Cross periodicals resembling the *Bulletin* had appeared in Berlin, St. Petersburg, Madrid, Stockholm, and Zurich.[20] Various expositions were also dedicated exclusively to the work of the Red Cross, as this was a common way for organizations to draw attention to themselves and to present volunteers with tangible representations of their causes.[21]

In 1872, as part of the efforts to increase identifiability, the ICRC proposed that all movement organs adopt the "Red Cross" as their name.[22] Since the establishment of the movement each society had been free to choose its own name, and—as the ICRC emphasized—remained free to do so. Newspapers had occasionally referred to movement organizations as "red cross" societies because of their use of the cross armband to identify themselves on the battlefield. However, the ICRC "strongly urged the national societies to adopt the name Red Cross Society or, better still, Austrian, Russian, English, etc.,"[23] to achieve coherence in the eyes of diplomatic powers. As the ICRC explained, given that NRCs

> do not hold monopoly over the assistance to the wounded . . . it is highly necessary that there be an easy way to differentiate between permanent societies, united by international relations, from those who—free from such attachment—form at the moment of need, moved by their own inspiration and not always able to offer the same guarantees.[24]

The gradual adoption of the Red Cross name over the 1870s helped the movement gain more concentrated public attention. Figure 3.1 presents the number of appearances of "Red Cross," "Croix-Rouge," "Croce Rossa," and "Cruz Roja" in books published between 1850 and 1898. The figure shows a steady rise in the mentions of the terms starting in the mid-1860s and increasing the 1870s, primarily in the aftermath of the Franco-Prussian War and with the Third Carlist War. English mentions of "Red Cross" had multiplied twenty-five times and French mentions multiplied by sixteen between 1863 and 1898.[25]

Another ICRC activity aimed to build a shared identity and to draw attention to humanitarian work was the international meetings it organized

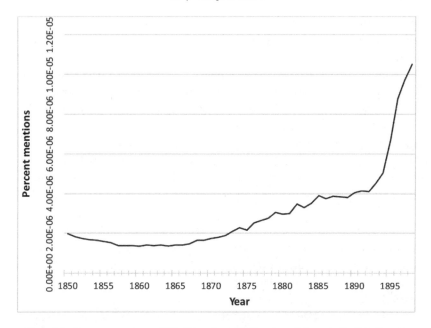

Figure 3.1. Percent occurrence of "Red Cross" out of all two-word terms in English, French, Spanish, and Italian publications in these respective languages, 1850–1900. Based on Google Ngram. For technical details, see Jean-Baptiste Michel et al., "Quantitative Analysis of Culture Using Millions of Digitized Books," *Science* 331 (2011): 176–182.

for NRC representatives. These meetings served in part to exchange information, but they were also explicitly designed to maintain morale and belief in the importance of their joint mission, as well as form friendships and collaborations between delegates, especially during prolonged periods of peace.[26] Some similar identity work was facilitated through direct cooperation between societies during war. After the Franco-Prussian War, the *Bulletin* saw numerous societies praise one another for their mutual help. The president of the French committee, the Count de Falvigny, demonstrated the cohesiveness of the Red Cross network:

> We considered it our duty to send members of our office to express our thanks to the relief societies, our sisters in neighboring countries: I was charged to go for this purpose to London and Dublin. The Count Sérurier and Count de Beaufort, and Mr. Vernes de Arlandes and Mr. de Gazenove were charged with the same mission for Switzerland, Belgium, the Netherlands, and the Grand Duchy of Luxembourg.[27]

Making Transnational Humanitarianism into a National Mission

Alongside its efforts to create a shared cross-national identity, the ICRC initially made efforts to minimize its public role and to downplay its centrality in the movement, encouraging national actors to take the lead instead. In the inaugural Red Cross conference, Moynier was apologetic about the ICRC's presenting itself as the leader of the movement, and explained this as the result of its being the *only* Red Cross society at the time of its formation.[28] Elsewhere, he expressed some regret about the use of the term "international" in the committee name, explaining that at the time he and his colleagues preferred it to "central" because they believed the committee would centralize nothing.[29] Their original plans for the ICRC, according to Moynier, envisioned it as a temporary committee whose task was mostly that of establishing a network of societies that would carry on its mission.[30]

In its interactions with national actors, the ICRC was concerned about unwittingly undermining trust between local governments and their respective NRCs. In 1871 France, for example, the Paris Commune identified the Paris-based NRC with international agents, accused it of spying, and confiscated its supplies. Its staff protested to no avail: "the Society has always been above political, military, or religious questions or involvement . . . the Society is a national society, and not regional, municipal, or Parisian."[31] Thus, the ICRC exercised its influence cautiously so as not to exacerbate such suspicions, and placed much of the responsibility for the creation of local organizational structures on local volunteers.[32] The reasoning was that local notables (such as state officials, philanthropists, and physicians) would be more likely to move state governments to establish an aid society than a foreign committee that may be unaware of local specificities or be perceived as interfering in state affairs.[33]

However, maintaining decentralization was easier said than done, as the ICRC gained public visibility that attracted unwelcome attention from enthusiastic actors believing it to possess powers it did not have. A report of ICRC activities during the Franco-Prussian War complained:

> There have been some grave misconceptions about our responsibilities. We have seen, for example, people of all countries pouring into our offices, coming to join the *International,* as they say, thinking that there was only one society operating on both sides, and that we have the capacity to enlist them or to direct sanitary societies, and the ability to confer upon them absolute

inviolability by giving them an international armband. The need to disabuse these applicants and to refer them to the proper authorities has been, for some weeks, fairly demanding work.[34]

While the ICRC maintained that the NRC volunteers must be granted neutrality by the local military authorities, this misunderstanding pervaded into some of the Red Cross societies themselves. Vice president of the French NRC, Vicomte de Melun, wrote in an 1871 report:

> The Convention opened the battlefield to the French [Red Cross] Society, as well as to societies of other countries that were placed under its legal power; it has promised the Society freedom of movement, even across enemy lines, the inviolability of its delegates and their auxiliaries, respect for the places where they shelter the wounded, and the possibility of extending these immunities to all those with whom the society affiliates.[35]

Regardless of their legal accuracy or of ICRC approval, statements representing the Geneva Convention as a document empowering humanitarians and elevating them beyond mundane political considerations of battlefields and international relations became common in late-nineteenth-century publications.

The powers of patriotism

ICRC leaders—alongside their critique of the brutalities of war—espoused a positive view of the potential of patriotism to motivate humane conduct. ICRC leaders spoke of NRCs as "primarily *national*, and not *international*, as they are often believed to be," since each one of them was "born under the joint inspiration of charity and patriotism":[36]

> What is essentially international in the Red Cross Societies is the spirit that animates them, that spirit of charity that moves them to wherever blood flows on the battlefield, experiencing as much solicitude for foreigners as for their compatriots when they are injured . . . [but] most of the work of each society will concern the army of its country; they are thus eminently national institutions . . . they cannot repudiate this character. By proclaiming it, they affirm their autonomy, which is a condition for their vitality . . . this is a guaranty for their success both with relation to their nation and with relation to their government.[37]

Movement advocates thus described nationalism and humane conduct as fully compatible with each other, often citing America and the various humanitarian initiatives it saw during the Civil War as a model:

America . . . with the energy, spontaneity, and unwavering commitment that distinguish its children, and also—we should add—with a deep sense of patriotism and a tender and compassionate love that is one of the most precious fruits of Christianity, responded without hesitation [to the Civil War].[38]

Such endorsements of patriotism made it easier for NRCs to present the Red Cross project to local contributors and statesmen as directly aligning with their national interest and well-being. For example, the statute declaration of the Magdeburg provincial society explained:

The international character taken by the [Red Cross] not only responds to the voice of philanthropy, but also satisfies national patriotism. We find in it a guaranty that the wounded and the sick of the Prussian army will be treated fraternally, even if they are in an enemy country, and our own assistance could not reach them.[39]

Reports of successful cooperation between NRCs of different states or between themselves and foreign military authorities reinforced these understandings. When Strasbourg was occupied by the victorious Germans in 1871, the local auxiliary Red Cross committee, which was part of the French Red Cross, had to negotiate for supplies and freedom of movement with the foreign powers. The committee reported to Paris: "Our work, which had been primarily *national*, became *international*, and could continue unhindered thanks to the cooperation, fairness and good sense of Mr. Schenck."[40] The latter, who was the Baron of Schweinsberg and helped the local Red Cross committee resume its activities, "was awarded by the Strasbourg Committee . . . honorary membership in testimony of its gratitude."[41] Elsewhere, the Spanish Red Cross reported about its cooperation with the Society of the Holy Cross and of May Second, which was "eminently patriotic, and this origin makes its adherence to universal principles of charity [i.e., the Geneva Convention] all the more moving."[42]

The interweaving of national and transnational orientations also appeared in the letters and memoirs of the relief workers themselves. ANRC founder Clara Barton, for instance, saw the future of transnational humanitarianism as dependent on "the union of beneficent action between people and Government, [which] when once comprehended and effected . . . shall constitute a bulwark against the mighty woes sure to come sooner or later to all peoples and all nations."[43] Commenting on the Red Cross intervention in the Armenian massacre of 1896, Barton exclaimed that "never has America cause to be more justly proud and grateful than when its sons and daughters in foreign lands perform deeds of worth like that."[44] Similar sentiments came from England, where philanthropists described the successes of their charitable work overseas as being "most consistent with the character of our nation."[45] Moynier himself confessed a "feeling of patriotic satisfaction" at the Swiss origins of many humanitarian initiatives. This, to him, was a "guarantee and a pledge of their Helvetic neutrality, to which all of Switzerland attaches great value."[46] Volunteers at work expressed similar national sentiments. A British nurse, reporting on her work in a makeshift hospital, wrote, "One feels one can be of use, then one is proud of one's Queen and Country."[47] Iowan women who taught Russians to cook with corn took pride in "teaching hungry peasants how to prepare and cook palatable and nutritious dishes made from American grain."[48] Foreign visitors to Japan similarly noted the fervent patriotism that accompanied the Red Cross volunteers' meticulous care for Russian soldiers.[49] In other words, not only was nationalism not considered a barrier in the way of universal, impartial care, but it was often considered to be a *reason* for extending help toward people of all nations.

The Red Cross linkage between nationalism and charity latched on to already-existing types of charitable volunteer work that had become popular among aristocratic women in previous decades and was often tied to the royal houses.[50] With the mass conscription of men and with the multiple wars that erupted in the second half of the nineteenth century, this system of quasi-national service provided women and noncombatant men with prestige and recognition that greatly resembled military honors. In Prussia and postunification Germany, Empress Augusta awarded humanitarian volunteers (both in the service of the Red Cross and in other societies) badges of honor, and the Japanese empress followed suit in the 1890s.[51] By creating NRCs (or relabeling an existing society as such) and providing it with national recognition, state leaders helped bestow prestige on humanitarian work and, at the same time, singled out the Red Cross as an exemplary humanitarian organization.

Varieties of national humanitarian projects

The growing legitimacy of Red Cross societies helped state leaders present themselves as morally superior to their neighbors once their NRC was well established. They did so, however, in different tenors. The Franco-Prussian War saw both belligerents exchanging accusations of mistreatment of enemy wounded soldiers, with Prussia, in particular, brandishing its compliance with the Geneva Convention, its superior Red Cross society, and the generosity and compassion of its broader humanitarian community in the face of its enemy.[52] Such legalistic claims for national superiority were a common way in which nations competed in the late nineteenth century.[53] But NRCs made other types of claims for superiority as well. The Dutch NRC, for example, congratulated its nation for being the "only country in which an aid society was established by the initiative of the King himself . . . for the good of the nation and of humanity."[54] Franz von Arneth, writing for the Austrian society, reported a "curious fact: that the Red Cross has cared for infidels; in Dalmatia, several soldiers from the Ottoman armed forces benefitted from the care of the [Austrian] patriotic Society," while the latter offered no equivalent care.[55] The Austrian society also reported proudly its support of both sides of the Franco-Prussian War: "We sent to the Berlin Committee seventeen packages containing 1,015 pounds of lint, 420 pounds compresses, and 2,115 bandages, and to Paris eighteen packages containing 1,023 pounds of lint, 380 pounds compresses, and 2,200 bandages."[56] American commentators—both professionals and journalists—often cited the U.S. Sanitary Commission, which worked during the American Civil War, which was in their eyes the American precedent to the Red Cross:

> The operations of the United States Sanitary Commission during our late war taught a valuable lesson to the nations of Europe, for they have since adopted our Christian-like system of nursing the sick and wounded during their numerous campaigns. With a happy foresight the Geneva Cross Convention made that system universal throughout Europe.[57]

The additional meanings local activists ascribed to the idea of Red Cross humanitarian relief can be illustrated by comparing the early Japanese and United States societies. Figure 3.2 presents a Japanese woodblock print depicting the Red Cross volunteers at work in the Russo-Japanese War. It depicts well-organized and compassionate Japanese aid workers recovering wounded Russian soldiers from the battlefield, and meticulously caring for them in a field hospital under a proud Japanese flag (a similar scene is presented in figure 3.4). In contradistinction, a smaller frame at the top of the print shows Russian soldiers kicking Japanese women and children. European visitors to Japanese Red Cross hospitals reported an unusually large, orderly, and hierarchical society, with staff members professing their

Figure 3.2. "Russo-Japanese War: Great Japan Red Cross Battlefield Hospital Treating Injured." Utagawa Kokunimasa (Ryûa), 1904. Jean S. and Frederic A. Sharf Collection, The Museum of Fine Arts in Boston.

devotion to their work as an expression of their devotion to the Empress (who headed the society) and to Japan itself,[58] in particular during war. The society worked closely with the military and thus often presented itself as an auxiliary to the armed forces.[59] However, its humaneness and efficiency in dealing with foreign nationals received international praise—especially when it came to treating Russian soldiers during war. The Japanese Red Cross presented itself (and was presented by others) as an extension of Japanese moral superiority in relation to its enemies.[60]

By contrast, the aid society that Reverend Henry Whitney Bellows founded in New York in 1866 failed to gain much government or public support and disbanded in the mid-1870s. In the early postbellum era, the U.S. government was more invested in Reconstruction than in preparation for future wars.[61] Not having heard from Bellows in a long while, the impression of the ICRC was that "the remoteness of the New York Committee from all European centers removed it from the influence of the global movement" and that "a sort of weariness descended upon the friends of our mission after the colossal activity that was carried out by the Sanitary Commission during the civil war."[62] Moreover, while appreciative of the initiative, the U.S. government itself (like many potential donors) was confident of existing medical facilities and, with the Civil War concluded, had little interest in making new arrangements for wartime relief. The relief society itself remained small and failed to represent itself as bearing a national mission. In Geneva, ICRC leaders Gustave Ador and Gustave Moynier concluded several years later that the committee had truly disbanded.[63]

When Clara Barton reconstituted the American National Red Cross in 1881, the U.S. was still enjoying relative peacefulness and there was little interest in battlefield relief.[64] However, the 1880s saw a series of natural disasters ravage the Midwest and South—forest fires in Michigan in 1881, tornados in upstate New York in 1883, and flooding so severe that an 1884 relief mission to Cincinnati "found the city afloat."[65] The need for natural disaster relief work was a far better platform from which Clara Barton could draw attention to the Red Cross project. Thus, the ANRC grew to fame by helping (both domestically and internationally) victims of floods, famines, and fires, with wartime relief being only one of its many functions. Although the ANRC developed close ties to the government, it had little contact with the armed forces in its first decades compared to its Japanese counterpart.[66] As a result, the ANRC grew decentralized with many of its interventions obtaining a distinct grassroots character.[67] By the end of the century, the ANRC presented itself as an international carrier of American charity and voluntarism, supplying gifts provided "by the people of America for the innocent, unfortunate sufferers" in other countries, as opposed to the military-focused Japanese Red Cross.[68]

Although the Red Cross movement provided activists and state officials with the means to portray their nations as morally superior to others, it also provided activists with ways to criticize their state leadership for failing to adopt humanitarian customs. The emerging NRCs also used the logics of the nascent humanitarian field to criticize their own national leadership. Bellows, surprised at the American government's reluctance to endorse the Red Cross project or to ratify the Geneva Convention, wrote to Dunant that he and his colleagues are "not a little mortified that America should be among the last powers to come into a convention so creditable to the civilization of the nineteenth century."[69] The 1860s Austrian committee was similarly exasperated with the reluctance of its government to support the Red Cross and appealed to the ICRC to intervene on its behalf.[70]

Red Cross in national imagery

National systems of representation framed Red Cross activism as the movement spread into new countries, visually rendering helping foreign nationals as an expression of national morality.[71] Well into the twentieth century, Red Cross missions proudly carried the Red Cross flag and their own

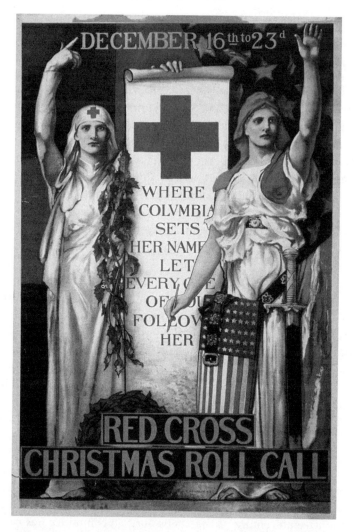

Figure 3.3. Mythical national figures were often recruited to represent national Red Cross societies (Edwin H. Blashfield, 1918).

national flag conjoined. Mythical national figures were similarly recruited for the propagation of the movement's mission. The American Red Cross adopted the figure of Columbia, the feminine personification of the United States, who appeared on various visual representations of the society in the late nineteenth and early twentieth centuries. In an early-twentieth-century poster (figure 3.3), a Red Cross nurse, decked with a Christmas wreath, stood side by side with Columbia. The latter carried a sheathed sword on her belt under her outstretched left hand. In her right hand, she held a pen, pointing to the inscribed banner the nurse holds up. "Where Columbia sets her name let every one of you follow her," read the banner.

The French NRC adopted Joan of Arc as its patron saint, and one of its posters displayed a haloed image of her tending to a wounded soldier against the background of horsemen in the battle. The German NRC's publications featured a Red Cross nurse in knight armor, slaying the dragon of tuberculosis. This trend peaked during World War I. The names the NRCs initially used were also indicative as to the patriotic terms in which they conceived of their missions and the nature of the fields in which they stood (the Austrian society, for example, was officially named the Patriotic Aid Society for Wounded Soldiers).

Modeling new nationhood through humanitarian activism

The Red Cross also helped model ideas of what the nation ought to look like for emerging nation-states. The newly unified German Red Cross proudly reported the cooperation of the preunification German humanitarian community during the Franco-Prussian War across existing borders:

> We saw the Order of St. John and the Knights of Malta, the Sisters of Charity, the deacons, the brothers of mercy, and the country deacons (especially from Duisburg, Berlin, and Erlangen), . . . [and] hospital trains from all parts of Germany, led by the best doctors and students and devoted men, heading for the battlefield . . . to make themselves useful or to bring back to their homeland those who need to be brought back.[72]

This wide cooperation across German religious, medical, and charitable sectors signified to the committee and to its admirers the successful unification of their nation. The German NRC quoted proudly a letter Emperor Wilhelm I sent to Empress Augusta in 1871:

> My heart was profoundly and joyfully moved by the loving care devoted to the army by the entire German homeland under your direction. . . . German unity has already been achieved in the field of humanitarianism by the Central Committee of the German Aid Societies for Wounded Soldiers.[73]

For the new nation-states that fought for independence in the 1870s and 1880s, establishing an NRC was a declaration of self-determination and of belonging to the family of nations. Montenegro, Serbia, and Romania featured NRCs months and even years before the international community recognized them as independent states. The national revival of Hungary within Austro-Hungary saw the establishment of a Magyar society in Budapest in 1881, which mobilized its own Hungarian imagery, language, and personnel in contradistinction to the German-speaking society that had represented the entire empire. The society's founders negotiated with the imperial court specific rules to distinguish themselves from the preexisting Vienna-based society, and insisted that the "organization should be autonomous [from the Austrian NRC] and purely Hungarian."[74]

In the non-European world, some states supported a strong humanitarian field led by an NRC for similar reasons. The Ottoman Empire, Siam, and Japan established their own societies, as part of a general wave of reforms aimed at presenting themselves as equals to Western nations. These states faced considerable threats of Western coercion and domination, and thus struggled to assert their independence and equal worthiness in the "civilized" family of nations.[75] ICRC members were initially incredulous, and initially thought that "it would be foolish to demand of the savages or the barbarians . . . to follow suit" and adopt the humanitarian principles of the Red Cross.[76] They were surprised to find that the Japanese emissaries to Geneva "could not be more charitable, even at the era of enlightened men, who observed the committee's efforts sympathetically."[77] Reports of the devoted care extended to wounded enemy soldiers, including approximately 70,000 Russian prisoners of war, in the 1905 Russo-Japanese War overcame the initial skepticism toward the Japanese Red Cross.[78] Siam modeled its own NRC after the Japanese chapter, as officials were taken by what they saw on a visit to Japan.[79]

Expansion into the Ottoman Empire was not without its difficulties. The Society for Assistance to the Wounded and Disabled in Action was established in Constantinople in 1868, in response to the original call from Geneva to establish aid societies in each capital. However, the Ottoman government initially rejected the initiative of Ottoman physicians to recognize the society as a national aid society. Moynier personally urged the Imperial Medical Society in Constantinople to advocate for the society in 1876, as the Red Cross movement would not transfer donations to unrecognized aid societies. In 1877, the Ottoman government announced that its national aid society would use a red crescent as its neutrality-conferring emblem (while recognizing the red cross emblem as a sign of neutrality for other aid societies.) The ICRC agreed to this arrangement for the duration of the Russo-Turkish War (1876–1878), but de facto accepted the use of the crescent indefinitely (although it continued to raise concerns about a lack of uniformity across various aid societies in this regard).[80]

Sensational internationalism

In numerous countries, NRCs fostered close relations with local news outlets, which were enthralled with the melodramatic accounts of humanitarian hardships and triumphs the new movement provided and of the cosmopolitan ethic nations espoused. News commentators marveled at how the "Russians nurse the Turks" and "how loyally and how disinterestedly the Red Cross of Japan worked in the Chinese war [of 1894–1895], caring for the brutalized Chinese with the same tenderness with which they nursed their own heroic sons" (see figure 3.4).[81]

The Belgian Baroness de Crombrugghe reported from the Franco-Prussian battlefront; her reports were printed in numerous magazines: "What I can say . . . is that at Saarbrücken, Metz, Rémilly, in a word, wherever I met French prisoners and wounded, I could find that their opponents treated them with all the consideration that their position demanded."[82]

The Red Cross's involvement in brokering large-scale international aid projects similarly propelled its recognition. During the 1885 Serbo-Bulgarian War, news of the Bulgarian need for medical supplies spread over Europe. NRCs existed in both countries, and the ICRC appealed to neutral countries to ask that help be sent to the Austrian Red Cross, which would transfer it to Bulgaria. Since the only route to Sofia went through Serbian territory, the ability of the Austrian NRC to arrange their safe passage in coordination with the Serbian chapter won considerable international praise.[83]

Rising Prestige Breeds Local Competition

The interweaving of Red Cross activism with notions of national morality, as well as the specific type of relationship the ICRC fostered with the national committees, caused structural changes within domestic humanitarian communities. These transformations solidified a leadership position for the Red Cross in different countries and drew new parties to model their own organization after the Red Cross template.

One crucial aspect of ICRC policy was crucial for its downstream effect on domestic humanitarian communities. Despite its efforts to efface its central role in the movement, the ICRC kept control of an important resource: recognition of the official NRC in each state.[84] The ICRC adopted a policy of

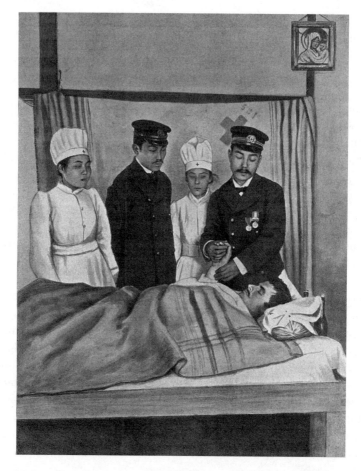

Figure 3.4. Japanese Red Cross nurses, depicted in 1904 in *The Sphere* assisting army surgeons caring for a Russian soldier. Note the Russian Orthodox icon in the top right.

communicating with only one central NRC in each state,[85] which would, in turn, communicate with the provincial societies within its jurisdiction. ICRC recognition as an NRC had clear advantages. First, it provided societies with access to an alternate source of funding that, once emergency struck, could circumvent the state's financial influence on the organization. Second, it gave societies access to a channel of information and a network through which to exercise moral agency (either by sending donations or by traveling to disaster-ridden areas). Like other decentralized movements, the Red Cross's growing network facilitated learning across different types of humanitarian actors. This structure allowed the movement to draw from experience in multiple locations and incorporate it into its policy.[86] Third, ICRC recognition conferred prestige upon an NRC, marking it as part of an internationally acclaimed group of elite institutions and—no less important—marking it as being an exemplary carrier of impartial humanitarianism.[87] This helped movement chapters position themselves in relation to other actors engaged in relief work in their own countries. Fourth, without needing to micromanage each branch from the top, the ICRC could take advantage of the flexibility of the movement as a whole and rely on local knowledge, initiatives, funding, and energy as the network of humanitarian organizations extended through its expanding national chapters.[88] These benefits—taken together—provided NRCs with considerable leverage in their home countries and attracted the attention of royal houses and volunteers alike (with Japan, Prussia, and Saxony being prime examples).

However, these rewards led to various local squabbles between societies presenting themselves as belonging to the movement, as being impartial, and as representing the international Red Cross in their country.[89] In Belgium, the NRC warned Geneva about a competing society named the Société nationale belge de la Croix-Rouge, which "did not possess as recommendable a character as its name suggests."[90] In France and Britain, copycat Red Cross societies appeared—often taking similar organizational forms as the official NRC—and vied for funds and prestige. An English letter to the ICRC warned that a competing society was a "political and combatant aid society,"[91] and another confessed that "the National Red Cross Society has many enemies in England and among the worst are those who try to take its place in order to obtain the credit for its work."[92] Volunteers on the battlefield were also complaining about "individuals who have usurped the right to wear the armbands of the Red Cross, thereby compromising . . . the work of the Society."[93] Reports about a Hungarian copycat society in the 1880s prompted the ICRC to ask the NRCs to seek legal protection for their exclusive use of the Red Cross insignia and name in their countries.

The nature and extent of the competition in each national-level humanitarian field greatly depended on the level of state contribution and support. In some states, enthusiastic state involvement produced highly hierarchical and structured NRCs that were quasi-state organizations and produced little competition between actors over symbolic capital. In other cases (e.g., the Ottoman Empire), NRCs remained weak and, with little interest from the state level, gave rise to little competition or public attention. But in most cases, NRC work interacted with varying levels of state involvement to consolidate nationally bounded fields of humanitarianism, in which providing impartial help (and, no less importantly, being recognized for this) was an object of some competition.[94] Whether in competition or cooperation, the emergence of new NRCs had the effect of orienting existing charitable societies, which had already been a staple of midcentury aristocratic social life, toward the template of the Red Cross. NRCs often formed close relations with preexisting charitable religious societies with similar aims.[95]

As new Red Cross societies emerged over the 1870s and 1880s, and as many of those societies attracted local attention and competition, the symbolic value of saving lives impartially increased. The stakes for these competitions were dual: on the one hand, different parties competed over which of them best emulated the values of their nation, and on the other hand, those parties competed over which best expressed the impartiality and neutrality the ICRC articulated.

"Humanitarian Colonialism": The Red Cross and the Scramble for Africa

The growing prestige of the Red Cross was also usurped for colonialist ends during the Scramble for Africa, as the European expansion into Africa was occasionally presented as humanitarian rather than exploitative. Belgian King Leopold II's Congo Free State was the most prominent example.

Even though King Leopold did not manage to convince the Belgian government that establishing a colony in Africa was necessary, he established the International African Association in 1876 in order to promote the establishment of a new colony in the Congo Basin under his own rule. The association was short-lived, but it achieved its goal of convincing international powers that Leopold's colony would serve as a humanitarian project that would alleviate public health threats and at the same time provide European education to the Africans. The king invited Gustave Moynier to the association's 1877 conference in Brussels. Hearing the proposal, Moynier was initially concerned about the legal status of indigenous people under this colonial plan, as well as the potential for conflict between nations over territory. However, he became gradually convinced that a colony in the Congo would spread Christianity and European education in Africa and would help stop slavery and the slave trade.[96]

The 1877 conference focused on the administrative details of the proposed colony. The Congo Red Cross recounted that, during discussion of the appropriate flag for the Congo Free State, one of the delegates suggested "protecting the humanitarian work that was going to be undertaken [in the Congo Free State] under the folds of the white flag with the red cross—the one adopted by the Geneva Convention for the no less humanitarian work of the assistance of wounded soldiers." Moynier did not waste a second. "He understood that his duty was to oppose . . . [and] had no difficulty in making his opinion prevail." According to the Congo Red Cross, "this incident did not even leave any trace in the printed protocol of the meeting, having undoubtedly been judged by the secretary to be too insignificant to appear there beside the serious subjects under discussion."[97]

The Institut de droit international gradually became supportive of the Congo Free State, as its members believed that the ultimate aim of the colony was the abolition of slavery and slave trade in the Congo Basin.[98] Their opinion added credibility to King Leopold's project. As the Congo Free State began to materialize, Moynier spoke in favor of the project but insisted that one of the key intents of the colony would be abolishing slavery and ending the slave trade.[99]

The Congo Free State was formally established in 1885. In 1888, it ratified the Geneva Convention,[100] and in 1889 it asked the ICRC to recognize as its NRC the Société congolaise et africaine de la Croix-Rouge (the Congolese and African Society—referred to commonly as the Congo Red Cross), which was formed the previous December in Brussels.[101] The society's newsletter proclaimed proudly: "The Red Cross . . . has spread successively into all parts of Europe. The Sovereign of the Congo Free State has just given it Africa."[102] The Congo Red Cross became a full member of the Red Cross movement and sent delegates to its international conferences. It worked to build hospitals and sanitariums in the colony, notably in Léopoldville (today Kinshasa) and Boma. At the same time, much of its administration and fundraising efforts remained in Belgium, primarily in Brussels and Antwerp. Although the society was established to provide assistance both to Europeans and to indigenous people, the reports from Congo focused on the care given to all European travelers (even congratulating the society for caring for Europeans beyond the boundaries of the state) and said relatively little about what the society concretely achieved in terms of caring for Africans. Some reports stated that Africans received care only as out patients,[103] but others described hospitals being set up with stretchers for European patients and hammocks for African ones.[104]

The Congo Red Cross framed its project as part of a broader civilizing mission for Africans. Commenting on the future of its work in 1903, the society wrote:

In Japan, where the Red Cross has made contact with the yellow race, it has triumphed marvelously . . . ; it is the natives themselves who lead there, so progress has definitely won in that part of the Far East. In Congo, the Red

Cross proceeded differently, in the face of the excessive and inveterate savagery of the Negroes. The Red Cross is directed there at this time only by Europeans because the blacks are not yet able to cooperate, except as subordinate agents. But with patience, this will change: the example and the education that the Belgians provide to their African pupils will certainly influence the blacks, and will gradually civilize them. . . . The progress already made is promising and the friends of the Red Cross can rejoice.[105]

But at the same time that the Congo Red Cross was voicing such aspirations, the brutalities of King Leopold's regime were coming to light internationally. The state, having initially failed to profit from rubber extraction, had handed swaths of land over to private companies in the 1890s. These companies were allowed to exploit the local population in any way they saw fit, leading to mass enslavement and inhuman work conditions. The state enlisted Africans to enforce obedience and ensure profit maximization; they—alongside Europeans—exercised brutal violence against forced laborers. To add to the misery, Europeans and Arab slave traders communicated diseases like sleeping sickness and smallpox, which ravaged the locals.[106] British and Swedish missionaries working in the Congo were among the first to raise the alarm in Europe about the atrocities, and a movement to free Congo from Leopold's rule emerged in the United States and the United Kingdom. Although Leopold waged a propaganda war against the allegations against him, increasing international pressure and public outrage pushed the Belgian government to annex the Congo Free State in 1908 and to convert it into its own colony, the Belgian Congo.[107]

The Congo Red Cross made few public comments about the controversy and confined its reports to discussion of disease treatment and hospital building. When the Congo Free State was dismantled, the main concerns the society voiced were about continuing operations in its hospitals during the transition to Belgian sovereignty. In the meeting of the general assembly of the society, Louis, the prince of Ligne, serving as the society's president, moved to disband it now that Congo was no longer a state and could not possess a "national" Red Cross society of its own.[108] The assembly voted unanimously to dissolve and sent its final report to Geneva in January 1909.[109]

The Congo Red Cross received relatively little public attention throughout the propaganda war, and the international Red Cross leadership's naïve acceptance of the humanitarian proclamations of the Congo Free State was not held against it. The ire of those international critics working against the Congo Free State was directed at King Leopold himself and at the formal state structures; the Congo Red Cross was not perceived as truly annexed to the state but as independent. Overall, this episode did not tarnish the reputation of the Red Cross movement, and certainly did not raise questions about the strong public association of universally oriented humanitarian projects with national pride.

National Sentiments as Mediators of Global Action

The nineteenth-century Red Cross movement was not unusual for its time in its intermingling of nationalism and universality. Two similar examples are the Olympic movement and the Scouting movement. The Olympic movement was founded in 1894 in Paris (moving in 1915 to Lausanne) with the global aim to encourage sports matches, to spread agreed-upon ethics in sports, and to propagate a spirit of fair play and friendly competition that would contribute to world peace.[110] The Scouting movement, which espoused universalist ideas about the proper physical and mental development of boys, was officially established in 1908 and within two years had chapters in more than twenty countries.[111] Much like the Red Cross, the rising popularity of both movements across borders relied heavily on their ability to elicit and emulate a sense of national commitment and pride in each state. These movements shared the emulation and dissemination of international and supposedly universal values through multiple national iterations.

As the Red Cross movement expanded, it carried with it a key principle across national borders: that good humanitarian aid is provided impartially, preferably by volunteers. In many cases, state actors were actually the key sponsors for relief organizations, and numerous states eventually dominated some (or all) of their local Red Cross organizations.[112] However, at the same time that humanitarian societies expressed patriotic pride, they increasingly worked to assert that they operated independently from state interests, according to a universal ethic that consecrates saving lives regardless of national origins. The depoliticized approach with which the emerging humanitarian sector addressed suffering stood in direct opposition to their pacifist and socialist contemporaries by offering assistance without criticizing the conditions that cause social suffering in the first place.

Throughout its expansion, the Red Cross movement set in place the infrastructure for the transnational humanitarian field by introducing clear criteria to evaluate good humanitarian work, and by establishing itself as the internationally recognizable model for such criteria.[113] By the 1880s, humanitarian activists across borders recognized the Red Cross insignia and mission as representing an elite form of relief work, and even though some of the humanitarian associations of the late nineteenth century were quite critical of one another, few of them could disagree that the ICRC possessed unique prestige and influence over international organizations.[114] Despite national and religious differences, actors across three continents now sought to emulate the Red Cross norms as codified in the Geneva Convention and began to struggle—domestically and internationally—over which of them best represented those values. It provided criteria on what forms a "good" humanitarian, thereby allowing different parties to struggle over which best emulated the mission and values of the Red Cross, and to compete for funding, recognition, and influence over local and international politics.[115]

Studies of transnational field formation have tended to treat national-level dynamics and culture as the context from which a transnational field gains autonomy or a context into which transnational fields are interjected,[116] but have credited national dynamics or nationalist sentiments with little influence on the process. However, humanitarian work became a transnational field not by freeing itself from national constraints or by displacing preexisting humanitarian arrangements on the local level, but rather by actively engaging with national culture as humanitarian activists made impartial relief under the Red Cross flag into an expression of national pride. While the patriotic zeal some of these early humanitarians harbored occasionally inhibited cross-national cooperation, their nationalist sentiments have also had a generative effect on spreading internationally what are known today as humanitarian norms.[117]

Contemporary humanitarian INGOs tend to highlight their global aspirations and to downplay their national affiliation, and many commentators see national sentiments as hindering humanitarian efforts.[118] Providing relief "without borders" has become the ideal for good humanitarian work in the last four decades, and the efforts NGOs have taken to reach beneficiaries without regard for national sovereignty have been internationally celebrated. However, the idea that providing impartial relief to all those who suffer stands in opposition to national sovereignty or sentiments is a new phenomenon. The nationalistic underpinnings of nineteenth-century humanitarianism occasionally inhibited cross-national humanitarian action, but at the same time, nation-level dynamics and nationalist sentiments have made an undeniable contribution to the emergence of the transnational humanitarian field.

The interrelationship between the transnational humanitarian field and its various national counterparts helps make sense of the continuing salience of national boundaries in the contemporary humanitarian sector. Despite the cosmopolitan attitudes many actors in the contemporary transnational humanitarian field espouse, humanitarian INGOs continue to be swayed by national dynamics in their states of origin as well as by beliefs about the relationship between their nationality and their global work. Studies of humanitarian work have shown that activists still tend to link the form of universal aid they provide with their national values and character,[119] and more general studies of NGO work have shown that national and regional associations greatly influence their work.[120] The Red Cross movement itself has historically seen disputes between its national chapters over which of them is best suited to undertake impartial humanitarian tasks on behalf of humanity as a whole, and what qualifies as impartiality in the first place. (This topic will be covered in chapter 5.) Similar patterns exist in other domains, such as the environmental field, where actors in different locations engage with the global task of counteracting climate change by construing links between that ideal and their national character and values, drawing motivation from a sense of unique responsibility and dedication that makes them feel best suited for such a task.[121]

Even though little research has considered what specific meanings actors attach to nationalism, and how those meanings may affect international structures,[122] scholars have highlighted the role of nationalism in providing the cultural frameworks that render action toward global causes imaginable and feasible.[123] While national exceptionalism *may* take the stance that one's nation is uniquely blessed and is charged with exporting its ideological system throughout the world, it may also take the stance that a specific set of national founding ideals are of potentially universal significance.[124] In this, national culture may endorse global initiatives such as transnational humanitarianism as a reflection of national responsibility toward the world.

FOUR

The Spread of Humanitarian Logics into New Domains

For its first decades, the International Committee of the Red Cross spent much energy on separating what it saw as "true" humanitarian work from other types of benevolence. In a wide array of publications, ICRC officials asserted that their aid societies were unique in that they were permanent, rather than ad hoc; neutral, rather than on a side in a conflict; and, first and foremost, that they were impartial and worked according to their own code of humane values rather than partisan interests. But just as the emerging humanitarian world was defining its boundaries, *other* emerging professions began employing its discourse and practices to resolve problems and to advance causes in their own domains. Nurses began championing their involvement in the Red Cross and drawing on its symbolic imagery to highlight the humanitarian needs on the battlefield. Journalists, who had been increasingly critical of the conditions on the battlefield, used Red Cross figures and operations to represent humanity in warfare. International lawyers employed the Geneva Convention as a measure for humane conduct in their own countries and used their association with the Red Cross to disseminate it. The symbolic language the Red Cross disseminated worked in such emerging occupational worlds and, in this, disseminated the logics of humanitarian work across professions.

Existing research on humanitarian work has highlighted how interest-driven parties (most often politicians) have often usurped humanitarian language and organizations. For example, scholars such as Didier Fassin and Alex de Waal have demonstrated how politicians use the notion of "humanitarian emergency" to disguise aggressive military endeavors as being aimed solely at saving lives. The examples provided in chapter 3 have similarly shown that the air of disinterestedness the Red Cross afforded served state leaderships in bestowing moral superiority on their respective nations. However, as groups outside of the humanitarian sector gradually adopted the Red Cross moral economy, they also reinforced the notion that humanitarian work is truly impartial, neutral, and independent. Once journalists began employing the Geneva Convention as a standard of humane conduct, nurses found social legitimacy and respect by volunteering to the Red Cross, and international lawyers began using international humanitarian law to influence goings-on in their own countries, the Red Cross confirmed its status as an elite organization that demonstrates the way "good" humanitarian work ought to be conducted.

Studies on the emergence of new fields tend to focus on how they attain autonomy from preexisting social structures. However, there is little research on why and how actors outside of a field endorse that field's autonomy. While some fields are enclosed by impermeable borders, others have porous boundaries that allow for the cross-travel of symbolic goods among fields.[1] In the case of the humanitarian field, the independence of humanitarians to act according to their own ethical code relied on the extent to which actors in other fields accepted their project as being on a different register. In particular, the Red Cross needed other actors in the battlefield to agree that humanitarian volunteers should be considered inviolable in order to credibly present themselves as neutral agents. This chapter argues that the autonomy of the humanitarian field could only be ratified once professional parties emulated the Red Cross's language and logic, and then employed this new cultural framework to resolve tensions they had experienced in their own worlds. To this end, the chapter traces the circulation of the moral economy the Red Cross propagated across four adjacent fields, starting with the religious field.

The Religious Field

As the Red Cross movement grew in later decades of the nineteenth century, ICRC leaders made conscious efforts to downplay the religiosity of their organization,[2] to reaffirm their open invitation for people of all faiths to participate.[3] This became more pressing as its identification with Christianity brought the movement some unwelcome attention outside of Europe. Reports from the Serbian battlefield complained about Ottoman troops mistaking the cross emblem for enemy insignia, "the flag of the Red Cross particularly exacerbating their fury."[4] (The Ottoman replacement of the cross with a crescent partially alleviated this concern.) Downplaying the religious affiliation of the movement helped establish links and new societies in states such as Persia, Siam, and Japan, thereby expanding the reach of the transnational humanitarian field beyond the Christian world.[5]

While the Red Cross presented itself, in its later years, as *accepting* all religions, much of its staff, affiliates, and supporters continued to see it as a religious endeavor. While ICRC leaders claimed that their movement espoused "no confessional character," they insisted that the project was "born of Christian sentiments."[6] Understating the Calvinist character of the society helped secure the help of Catholic and non-Christian states, but such growing cross-denominational support only served as proof, in the founders' minds, of the universal validity of their faith.

In keeping with the Red Cross founders' pragmatically nonconfrontational character, explicit critiques of their secular counterparts were kept to a minimum, but such undertones surfaced at times in their writings. In the introduction to one of his publications, Moynier mentioned his contemporaries and confessed his wish, through the Red Cross's work, "to rattle their secular chains or at the very least to loosen them!"[7] Letters, diaries, and even official reports in late nineteenth-century displayed many of the same convictions, confirming that the leaders (as well as many followers) of the movement saw it as a religiously oriented project well past its early years. The belief that the Red Cross is specifically Christian also helped European actors make sense of the fact that the Japanese society rapidly grew to be the largest NRC in the world in the 1890s. As a member of the French Academy said in an annual meeting of the French society,

> If the French society is less powerful than the Japanese society . . . it is animated by a purer and livelier spirit. Japanese charity is based primarily on patriotism; Christian charity, which is driven by spirit and by religious ideals, is based on the words of Christ: "love one another." Under this inspiration, it is not likely that the former would fall under the fluctuations of patriotism. It will remain rooted in the eternal base of eternal charity.[8]

Thus, while Moynier and his associates were conscious of the adverse effects of the Red Cross's conspicuous Christianity, the movement retained its religiosity in many ways. Relations between the Red Cross and the religious field remained close, even if strictly informal, well into the twentieth century.

The cross-denominational appeal of the Red Cross project facilitated its mass dissemination in the 1860s and 1870s. The Red Cross developed informal ties with churches, religious orders, and prominent clergy members who, in turn, saw in the movement the furtherance of their own religious aspirations for the realization of Christian projects in Europe and the United States. Ties with faith-based relief associations and movements were particularly common in Prussia, where the Red Cross worked alongside a host of religious relief organizations that were now afforded neutral status thanks to the Geneva Convention. The cooperation between the early Prussian Red Cross and the myriad religious aid societies impressed ICRC officials, who cited specifically the Lutheran deaconesses of Berlin, Kaiserswerth, and Wurttemberg, the Deacon House of Duisburg, the Rauhe Haus Field Deacons, and the Catholic Alexian Brothers of Aachen.[9] This association promoted the Red Cross and motivated volunteers to join. Numerous church leaders and religious activists described it as a clear sign of Christianity's regained eminence in late-nineteenth-century societies. One of the movement's strongest American allies, New York Unitarian pastor Rev. Henry W. Bellows, described the expansion of the Red Cross into the United States as testifying "of the oneness of America and Europe in all that touches the permanent interests and triumphs of Christian charity and universal brotherhood."[10] Papal approval of the Red Cross provided the movement with additional leverage. Upon presenting Dunant with a portrait of Pope Leo XIII, seated and appearing to be signing a document, the bishop of the Roman Catholic Diocese of Saint Gallen wrote, "the dictum—fiat pax in virtute tua Deus [peace be your God]—and the signature of his hand will prove to you that he appreciates the Geneva Convention and the merits of its authors."[11]

The affiliation with Red Cross societies became even more important for preachers on the battlefield. The inclusion of clergy in the Geneva Convention as one of the parties that all sides should consider neutral was particularly important. French pastors during the Franco-Prussian War used Red Cross flags to allow them to proselytize.[12] Protestant pastors appreciated the newfound safety, given the rampant anti-Protestantism in some parts of mid-nineteenth-century France.

Churches in support of the Red Cross

Churches were important sources of support for the Red Cross. Bellows's own church, as well as other New York religious institutions, was central recruiting sites for volunteers in subsequent decades. Local churches occasionally proclaimed "Red Cross Sundays" to raise funds and awareness, and to solicit spiritual support for the Red Cross. The *Hartford Courant* reported in 1898 that on one such Sunday, collections were taken up for the aid of the work of the Red Cross . . . [and] the women of the churches were also urged to assist in the making of the 1,000 pajamas which have been assigned to the local branch of the society in Hartford. Special, patriotic services were held in some of the churches and the presence of the flag draped about the pulpits was noticeable.

The piece named numerous Congregationalist, Episcopalian, Methodist, and Baptist churches in the city in which special sermons were read, alongside an 1897 appeal to the American public from President McKinley, to help raise funds and donations for the American National Red Cross's work in Cuba.[13] Bellows reported that thousands of New York women had also followed his call to volunteer during the Franco-Prussian War.[14] Similarly, before one of the movement's meetings in Berlin, prayers were said to have been said in all churches in the city, in support of the Red Cross.[15]

Popular Christian interpretations of the Red Cross

The movement (and its effects on the growing transnational humanitarian field) was similarly received as a religious project by the press and "lay" supporters. American newspapers reported that "Europe is to have a Christian Commission" after the signing of the Geneva Convention, which is "owing to the efforts of a Swiss Christian who witnessed the unalleviated horrors of Solferino."[16] An American historian wrote to Dunant, suggesting in excited words that the Cross of St. George may have inspired the Red Cross insignia. If this was true, she claimed, "that would make the modern [Red Cross] society the last link in a chain whose first link was the Christian spirit of passive resistance to the persecutions of Diocletian, and another of those links is the Crusader's spirit of active resistance to the advances of the Turks."[17] Letters to the committee congratulated it for its "godly work" and for working toward the realization of "the civilization of God."[18] In Christian communities, the religious affiliation of the Red Cross helped not only to expand the movement, but also to expand the activism that characterized it and thereby spread its ideas about how humanitarian activism should be undertaken.

The persisting affinity to religious field sentiments and imagery was an important channel through which the ideals of the transnational humanitarian field were disseminated. The existing infrastructure of churches and faith-based movements provided the movement with much transnational leverage in raising funds, recruiting volunteers, and inspiring similarly minded societies to form.[19]

Professional Nursing

Although the founders of the ICRC and the participants in the founding conferences of the Red Cross were uniformly men, women were as deeply involved in the movement from its inception. As Clara Barton—founder of the American National Red Cross—reported,

> In most countries the co-operation of women has been eagerly sought. It is needless to say it has been as eagerly given. In some countries the central [Red Cross] committees are mixed, both sexes working together; in others, sub-committees are formed by women, and in others, such as the Grand Duchy of Baden, woman leads.[20]

While many women advocated and collected donations for the movement, women predominantly served the movement as nurses in its hospitals and on the battlefield.

Nursing: an emerging profession

Although women had served in nursing roles (often as part of their domestic tasks) far before the nineteenth century,[21] the nineteenth century saw the rapid dissociation of nursing from domestic caregiving and its professionalization as a disinterested occupation. Early-nineteenth-century European newspapers already brought forth news and depictions of Sisters of Mercy from various parts of Europe, and tied the assiduous care they reportedly provided to their gender. The Basque women during the First Carlist War (1833–1839) were said to "make excellent nurses in a military hospital" with

> no false notions of delicacy [that] interfere with their indispensable services . . . they seldom faint, and the wounded are attended all the better for their *hardiesse*. . . . Man was indeed doing his utmost to bring a hell upon earth; but there were yet lingering on it spirits of a finer, purer, and nobler order, whose example and influence still preserved a portion of the blessings designed for it by heaven.[22]

As noted in chapter 1, British, French, Irish, and Russian faith-based Sisters of Mercy orders also appeared in news reports and literary depictions of the war throughout the 1850s and 1860s. The midcentury saw the rapid professionalization of what was until then the domain of faith-based women's associations.[23]

The rise of nursing as a profession and nurses' involvement in transnational humanitarianism should be understood in the context of the unprecedented numbers of women in the Victorian era who were moved by a sense of vocation to leave their homes and engage in charitable or religious work. One result of this tendency was the revival in the 1830s of the orders of Lutheran deaconesses, which were devoted to pastoral care for women in the community (their roles often extended to liturgical functions as well). Deaconesses also traveled to parishes other than their own and often served as powerful role models for younger women, helping them find their own calling in the process. In doing so, they contributed to an already-existing movement of higher-echelon bourgeois young women toward the newly established profession of nursing. Agnes Jones, the first nursing superintendent at the Liverpool Workhouse Infirmary, wrote about her meeting with deaconesses in her early life reaffirming her preexisting religious devotion and kindling her desire to serve those in need,[24] and Florence Nightingale similarly recounted deeply shaping experiences at a Lutheran deaconess motherhouse in Kaiserswerth.[25]

Much like journalism, the nursing profession was fast becoming a distinct field in the mid-nineteenth century, with its own set of positions, hierarchies, norms, and stakes.[26] With the establishment of nursing schools in midcentury, the profession became an acceptable alternative social trajectory for upper-class women to express Victorian sensibilities. As commentators saw it, the

> trained nurse . . . was simply the ideal "lady," transplanted from home to hospital and absolved of reproductive responsibilities . . . she exhibited the deep religious conviction and piety necessary to serve God through man.[27]

Florence Nightingale's *Notes on Nursing: What It Is and What It Is Not*, published in 1860, was an extremely influential book containing specific advice on numerous nursing tasks and had great influence on the establishment of nursing as a field.[28] She established her own School of Nursing and Midwifery a year later in London, alongside the Bellevue Hospital School of Nursing in New York (established 1873), and American nurse Linda Richards established several other schools in the United States, Europe, and

Japan. Many of these women earned international renown, both for their professional opinions and for their exemplary devotion.

Where nuns have traditionally performed most battlefield tasks identified today with nursing, the Crimean War was the first major battlefield in which an independent group of women, led by Florence Nightingale, received government authorization to travel to the Crimea and to care for the wounded soldiers in various stages of recovery. Newspapers gave the work of this pioneering group of battlefield nurses considerable attention, and Nightingale rose to celebrity status, becoming an authority in her profession in Great Britain and beyond. While the presence of nurses on the battlefield was initially under the sponsorship of the military, women were also appearing unsolicited on various frontlines in the hope to offer help. The introduction of organized aid societies, and then the Red Cross, was a key way for nurses to reach the battlefield en masse.[29]

Women's aid societies and the Red Cross

Women's aid societies were becoming a staple of European and American civil societies in midcentury. In Europe, these societies were often established by (or under the patronage of) aristocratic women, who were an important group in facilitating the Red Cross's influence in diplomatic and governmental circles. The aid societies provided a central outlet for mid-nineteenth-century women to participate in civil life with unprecedented vitality. As the century progressed, women's involvement in humanitarian causes became acceptable and later even expected in aristocratic circles.

One front in which women figured prominently was the diplomatic one, as aristocrats across the continent were some of the Red Cross movement's strongest allies and advocates. Their activism also opened the way to the battlefield for nurses. While the ICRC famously excluded women from committee membership until the early twentieth century, aristocratic women were the driving force behind many of the local committees, both in convincing their governments to establish them and in operating them. This was especially true for the royal families of Europe. Empress Augusta of Prussia was an avid supporter of the movement and donated substantial funds and often appeared in public wearing the Red Cross armband. During the 1864 Second Schleswig War, when visiting wounded soldiers in the hospital, she reportedly explained, "In the present crisis, I neither speak nor feel as a queen, I simply express my sympathy as a female for suffering humanity."[30] In England, Queen Victoria and Princess Louise personally donated many items from their households to the British society, as did Russian Empress

Maria Feodorovna to the Russian society. Empress Eugénie of France was a strong supporter of the Geneva Convention and advocated the expansion of its guidelines to maritime battles.[31] Unusual in her devotion was Empress Shōken of Japan, who not only helped develop in Japan what grew to be the largest and reportedly most efficient NRC and served as honorary president with numerous members of the imperial family members at her side, but also personally visited hospital beds in wartime and tended to the wounded—Japanese and foreign alike. Empress Augusta, Empress Maria Feodorovna, and Empress Shōken endowed funds that remain active within the ICRC today.[32]

The Germanic Confederation was particularly rife with various charitable "patriotic societies" when the Red Cross movement was established. These societies actively invited women to take up nursing and—once war broke out—to partake in a national effort to care for the wounded. English-born German royalty were instrumental in developing nursing as a profession in the German states and bringing it into the aid societies. Prussian Empress Victoria was involved for much of her tenure as princess royal and her short imperial reign in importing the English model of nursing to Germany. She established numerous nursing schools and aid societies according to this model.[33] Alice of Hesse, one of the more energetic aristocrats in this area, employed trained nurses in the society under her patronage, and through her urging, the British National Red Cross established a hospital at Darmstadt, which English physicians and local nurses staffed together.[34]

In recapitulating the charitable activities during the Franco-Prussian War, the president of the German committee pointed to the plethora of women's societies in each German state, and their organization under local royalty:

> Germany is rich with associations of women who marched together with the male societies during the war to rescue the wounded. . . . The most important are . . . the Patriotic Women's Society in Berlin. . . . placed under the patronage of the Empress of Germany; the Association of Bavarian Women . . . under the patronage of the Queen Dowager Marie; the "Albert Society" in Dresden, under the protection of the Royal Princess Carola; the League of Württemberg Women, under the protection and direction of Queen Olga; the Society of Baden Women, embracing all parts of the Grand Duchy under the direction of the Great Duchess Louise; the "Alice Society" of Darmstadt, under the direction of Princess Ludwig of Hesse, born a princess of Great Britain; finally, . . . the Women's Society of Saxe-Weimar, under the patronage of the great Duchess Sophie.

Once the various societies were unified as the German Red Cross under the direction of Empress Augusta, the tasks women volunteers were to perform in peacetime and war were also formalized:

> According to the project they would pursue the following common goals: In peacetime, they would devote themselves to caring and alleviating the pressing miseries in their respective constituencies, and engage in development work to care of the sick. In war, the societies would care for the wounded and sick in the battlefield, and support the institutions created for this objective. . . . In extraordinary circumstances caused by natural causes such as epidemics or major disasters, they help each other promptly in cash or supplies, and, if appropriate, by a nursing staff. . . . The union badges are the red cross on a white background.[35]

With the growing need to mobilize masses for war, the new feminized public role of nurses took the extension of care as its own link to the state. Existing women's societies provided the clear majority of Red Cross volunteers in the German states, and their already-existing infrastructure was crucial in facilitating the extraordinary success of the movement in preunification Germany.[36] The Red Cross societies allowed women to receive some of the glory previously reserved for men. The various relief organizations "intertwined the soldier and the civilian volunteer in an elaborate system of honors and rewards, feasts and festivals that bound them to the state," as historian Jean Quataert observed.[37]

Nurses in the service of the Red Cross

Thus, nurses soon became the lifeblood of the NRCs. The general assumption was that women are much better suited for this occupation than men. Barton wrote:

> There are numbers of men and women who have the will and devotion necessary to lead them into hospitals or to battlefields, but very few of them are capable of performing well the duties of nurses. . . . The relief societies soon found that women were by nature much better fitted for this duty than men can be.[38]

The growing number of women turning to nursing education meant a growing number of trained Red Cross volunteers who could now offer help where needed. Red Cross nurses were, in many cases, those who introduced new knowledge about the importance of sterilization into the battlefields, rather than state medical personnel.[39] The increased attention to hygiene was key in decreasing field hospital gangrene and amputation rates.

Nurses also turned to organizations such as the Samaritan Society, which was educating volunteers in first aid. The society, founded by the German surgeon Friedrich von Esmarch in Kiel in 1882, established various "Samaritan schools" throughout Germany.[40] This was, in part, an inspiration from the British St. John Ambulance, and soon inspired similar initiatives in various countries, as far as Argentina.[41] The movement similarly had ties to the Red Cross, and some local Red Cross societies implemented its training.

The mass involvement of nurses in the Red Cross movement came as the movement gradually assumed a more socioemotional type of work. Humanitarian organizations also worked in areas that many late-nineteenth-century states left open, and thus addressed many of the war-related anxieties of the home front. While much of the ICRC leadership had traditionally insisted that the movement ought to help only the wounded soldiers (and had, in fact, officially named itself as being an aid society for wounded soldiers), the movement soon entered the domain of prisoners of war (as early as the Franco-Prussian War). The task of searching for missing persons and prisoners of war was previously conducted sporadically, as part of individual initiatives (e.g., during the American Civil War).[42] Over the first decades of its existence, the ICRC and many of the national committees were in a much better position than governments to collect information about the conditions of prisoners and to communicate it to their families. The German society took upon itself the task "to send news to the parents of wounded and sick soldiers, by correspondence and by establishing an information bureau."[43] As late as World War I, various NRCs served as "the eyes and ears of the families at home," as organized state facilities for the communication of news about the welfare of soldiers at the front were often inefficient. In some instances, much of the consolation and moral support clergy and social workers typically performed fell upon the shoulders of Red Cross volunteers.[44] Peacetime activities—taking care of the recovering wounded or institutionalized children (figure 4.1), for example—were also highlighted in Red Cross propaganda.

New systems of reward

Queen Victoria established the Royal Red Cross award in 1883. This award— conferred only upon women—honored nurses (both military and nonmilitary) for extraordinary efforts in caring for sick and wounded servicemen.[45]

PEACE HATH HER DUTIES NO LESS THAN WAR—A Rer Cross nurse, off duty, passing her vacation at New York's seaside home for children.

Figure 4.1. Red Cross nurses became active care givers beyond the battlefield. *The Sunday News Tribune*, 1898.

The queen regularly honored Red Cross nurses with a medal, and the women were, in turn, honored in newspapers ("Each nurse wore her distinctive nursing uniform, and no Court dress of plume and train could have been more dignified than their simple robes of gray and brown").[46] German empress Augusta Victoria followed suit in 1899 and created a similar decoration, awarded to "persons belonging to the Red Cross Association who distinguish themselves particularly by their zeal."[47] Such decorations were often described as true equivalents to those awards conferred upon men:

> Instances of excellence in knighthood, and of faith, true-heartedness and purity in womankind, have been recorded with love and reverence by old chroniclers, but her Majesty is first on the roll of English sovereigns to acknowledge and reward the qualities of patience and loving-kindness exhibited with rare disinterestedness and self-devotion by women in time of war.[48]

Emma Pearson and Louisa MacLaughlin

The intertwined life stories of two English women demonstrate how the Red Cross empowered nurses in the public sphere. Emma Maria Pearson (1828–1893) was born in East Anglia. Her father was a naval officer. Louisa Elisabeth MacLaughlin (1836–1921) was the daughter of an Anglican priest. She was raised in Nice where her father served as minister and was trained by pioneer nurse Sister Dora. Pearson and MacLaughlin worked together at the National Health Society, a public health association, but soon joined the National Society for Aid to the Sick and Wounded in War, which was the British NCR. They were sent to the front to help the wounded in the Battle of Gravelotte, and then joined a field hospital, the Anglo-American Ambulance.

The Anglo-American Ambulance began its work with one half of its employees nursing the wounded Prussian and Bavarian soldiers at Balan, in the Ardennes, and the other half working with French prisoners at Sedan. Once the latter group completed its work in Sedan, it attempted to reach the besieged city of Paris but failed, and remained in Orléans with few resources. In November 1870, Pearson and MacLaughlin traveled to London and requested funds from the National Health Society, but were denied. Emma Pearson published an appeal in the *Times*, signing her letter as the "Superintendent of Nurses of the Anglo-American Ambulance," leaving their cause "with all confidence to the kindly sympathy of [their] countrymen and countrywomen who . . . will always appreciate real, hard, practical work."[49] Toward the conclusion of the war, in February 1871, Pearson appealed again from Orleans. The Prussian military had ravaged through the city and the surrounding villages, and Pearson wrote to the *Times* about the condition of the local population. Pearson wrote, "We have rare opportunities of seeing what can be done for little cost, and with English energy, for we see it done ourselves. If some English friends would only collect and send us some money, they would do infinite good."[50]

They each received the Militär-Sanitäts-Kreuz decoration from the Grand Duke of Hesse Darmstadt in 1872, "for the recognition of services rendered to the wounded in the Franco-Prussian War."[51] Several years later, the two were on their way to Serbia to continue their work in the Serbo-Bulgarian War, when their luggage was searched at a Cologne train station and they were treated rudely. A Hessian officer happened to pass by and, recognizing their decorations, intervened on their behalf.

The Red Cross thus supplied women with a clear channel to mobilize, to leave the traditional social trajectory assigned to them, and to receive honors equivalent to those of men. While at times treated humorously (see figure 4.2), the involvement of women in general and of nurses in particular was widely praised and contributed greatly to the establishment of humanitarian work as a field.

Journalism

Like nursing, the journalistic field was gradually consolidating in the mid-nineteenth century. Like the field of nursing, the journalistic field established a strong interrelationship with the humanitarian field, primarily through the Red Cross movement. In 1898, Clara Barton published a book summarizing the endeavors of her organization to date. Like many of her counterparts at the ICRC and in other NRCs, Barton took care to mention the special relationship between the media and the Red Cross:

> To the American newspaper press, and perhaps to the New York *Herald* more than any other . . . , the Red Cross is indebted for timely aid and noble furtherance of its objects and aims. . . . Not less than three hundred periodicals and papers have, within the last two years, laid upon our desk their graceful tribute of encouraging and fitly spoken words.[52]

The press was a key avenue through which the Red Cross movement could build its reputation. It allowed activists to demonstrate abstract Red Cross

IN HARD LUCK.

Terrible situation of Henpeck, who enlisted to get away from his wife and found her at the front as a Red Cross nurse.—N. Y. Evening Journal.

Figure 4.2. The increased independence the Red Cross afforded many women was also portrayed humorously. *Jackson Daily Citizen*, 1898.

principles in action. Barton herself fostered special relations with various news outlets, who were enthralled with the stories of hardship and triumph she readily provided. Herself a skilled writer, she contributed pieces that were published nationwide and grew dramatically in fame (figure 4.3).[53] Similar partnerships existed in Belgium, France, and Switzerland, among other states. The reasons for this partnership, though, were rooted in processes under way within the journalistic profession, as reporters sought ways to criticize the conditions on the battlefields.

War journalism in transition

Journalists had been present on battlefields for several decades by the mid-nineteenth century, but they were usually commissioned by military leaders

Figure 4.3. Clara Barton reported regularly about Red Cross activities. *The San Francisco Call*, 1899.

to glorify their own accomplishments.[54] But by the 1860s, reporters were rapidly gaining independence from the military. Journalistic production costs had become affordable enough to independently include foreign news, opinions, and a variety of other features. Furthermore, journalists and publishers were fending off (with varying levels of success) censorship attempts, and—especially British journalists—published scathing critique of their governments.[55] Thus, reports from the Irish Potato Famine as well as the various wars that erupted across the continent became a common sight in mid-nineteenth-century West European newspapers.[56] With the increasing mobility of news through railroads and the telegraph,[57] European and American readers were receiving daily news of war carnage, and such reports often elicited public outrage.[58]

A critical turning point was the Crimean War (1853–1856), in which the detailed reports of inefficiency at the battlefield communicated by the "first war correspondent" William Howard Russell voiced unprecedentedly staunch criticism of state failures.[59] His reports of the rampant disease in the soldiers' camps and of the incompetency of the medical staff, and his appeal in favor of nursing aid, contributed to the commissioning of Florence Nightingale and her team of nurses.[60] As the war progressed, Russell reported approvingly of Nightingale's endeavors in the Crimea:

> The noble devotion of Miss Florence Nightingale, and her band of English sisters, who some time in November started on their mission of mercy, to nurse the sick and wounded soldiers in the hospitals near Constantinople, ought to be held in grateful remembrance by all whose sympathies are excited by human suffering, and who can appreciate the self-sacrificing goodness which encounters every risk and welcomes every labor or trial that may relieve it.[61]

Thus, even before encountering the Red Cross, the press was doing much more than simply informing the public about conditions in the battlefield— it was framing them as catastrophes. The notion of *humanitarian emergency* or *crisis* was becoming increasingly familiar to newsreaders, as news reports became increasingly more immediate thanks to the introduction of the telegraph. This included not only reports of the conditions of the listeners' own national forces but also of their enemies. Reporting from the Crimean War in 1856, Russell wrote:

> Nearly all [the Russian] dead were killed by shot and shell. Some of them were so mangled as barely to be recognizable for human remains. It is awful to stand on one of the heights and look over the field. The ground is hidden

by the corpses. Round the little battery which was taken and retaken so often, are 2500 dead Russians. For about fifty yards around the outside of the battery, the corpses literally lie two and three deep.[62]

The British press was quick to denounce the British government's support of Constantinople and spurred public protest.[63] News reports caused a stir in the House of Commons, who exerted considerable pressure on the prime minister; the reports reached Queen Victoria, who denounced in her diary the Ottoman soldiers as "horribly cruel mutilators."[64] In the United States, newspapers were publishing lists of casualties (since official protocol of notifying family members was rudimentary if it even existed at all) and, in cases where the casualty could not be identified, deathbed photos of the deceased.[65] This only contributed to the closeness with which relatives of soldiers followed the news from the front.

The Red Cross and journalists on the front

The nascent humanitarian field and the mid-nineteenth-century journalistic community developed ties on multiple levels over the next several decades. The Red Cross and war correspondents crossed paths frequently from the earliest relief missions the movement organized. Since both war correspondents and relief workers are auxiliaries to the armed forces, they are often placed together during war. Pearson and MacLaughlin noted that they met numerous English war correspondents in Belgrade when they arrived to enlist for the Serbian Red Cross during the Serbo-Turkish War in 1876,[66] and British war correspondents and illustrators reported in journals such as *The Graphic* their experiences accompanying the Red Cross to the Balkan fronts.[67]

The press also became crucial for the Red Cross to receive news of distant suffering and to prioritize their actions.[68] Clara Barton wrote of the Russian famine,

> The foreign journals began to tell us of the apprehension caused by an unusual failure of the crops in Central Russia. . . . Eighteen hundred and ninety-one found the old-time granaries empty, and a total failure of the crops, and a population of thirty-five millions of people, paralyzed with the dread of approaching famine.[69]

Aid societies often reciprocated, as the American Red Cross volunteers, for instance, alerted the media to the conditions in certain disaster-ridden areas, as was the case in the devastating rise of the Ohio River in 1884. "Telegraphing from there to our agents of the Associated Press, we proceeded to Cincinnati, to find the city afloat. . . . These conditions were [also] telegraphed."[70]

Thus, the Red Cross was becoming a familiar feature in war correspondents' accounts of the battlefield. Journalists such as Archibald Forbes and Januarius MacGahan offered frequent praises to the movement in their reports.[71] While the latter reporters worked for "serious" news outlets, illustrated magazines were another form of increasingly popular media that contributed to the Red Cross. French newspapers such as *Le Petit Journal* and *Le Petit Parisien* and British magazines such as *Illustrated London News* and *The Sphere* offered illustrated accounts of the Red Cross in action. These newspapers offered sensationalized news rather than the more reserved format of their senior counterparts and the propaganda-infused party-affiliated outlets. The heroism of relief workers on the front—especially women— quickly caught the attention of these newspapers. Accounts of "exotic" lands and peoples engaging in humanitarian work were also prized. In an account of the Japanese Red Cross, *The Sphere* reported that Japan was waging the war "after the fashion of the civilised nations. . . . In few respects is this more noticeable than in the admirable hospital arrangements that the Japanese have made for the campaign. This is even more remarkable since the Japanese soldier is probably less afraid of death than any fighter in the world."[72]

While skeptics were often critical of Red Cross efficiency during the Spanish-American War, Clara Barton garnered much praise for her personal efforts. An American colonel serving on the warfront recalled:

> When I saw Miss Barton, with another lady, arrive on an army wagon, over one of the worst roads in the world, and, without any rest, go to work and prepare soup over a camp fire, I realized that a society inspired by such a leader could not help being fruitful of good results. Therefore I obeyed a very natural impulse when, at Santiago, the day before her departure, I called on Miss Barton and, in the name of the Medical Department, expressed to her my grateful acknowledgments for all her society had done for us in our times of need.[73]

The journalistic field adopts humanitarian language

But the Red Cross supplied the press not only with sensational stories, but also with the language to criticize human rights violations. The Balkan conflicts of the mid-1870s were particularly marked by reports of humanitarian crises, especially with reports of Turks "massacring" Christian communities in Serbia and Bulgaria. In 1876, for example, news reporters from various newspapers were sent to report on the Balkan crisis (including renowned American journalist Januarius MacGahan), once rumors of a violent Ottoman repression of the Bulgarian uprising began to spread.[74] Newspapers such as *The Times* and *Daily News* adopted the term *massacre* to describe what they saw, sights that were conveyed and denounced in harsh terms. MacGahan reported from a Bulgarian village:

> Neither age nor sex was spared. The town was pillaged, then fired; about one fourth of the houses were burnt, people were cut down in the streets, on their own doorsteps, on their own hearthstones. Old men and women begging for mercy, and children and infants screaming in terror, perished alike beneath the swift and certain sabre.[75]

Such accounts invoked the Geneva Convention as a measure of humanity on the battlefield, denouncing its violations as "an outrage upon Europe."[76] The extent to which the Ottomans adhered to the Geneva Convention became a matter of public interest in Britain and France, and links were made between doing so and protecting European civilization. Newspapers reported about the urgings of state officials such as Austro-Hungarian foreign minister Count Gyula Andrássy and philanthropists such as Count Houdetot, the president of the Society for the Amelioration of the Condition of Prisoners of War, as they attempted to persuade the Ottoman government to implement the convention. Some correspondents took a more active role in calling for reprimands of breaches of the convention. *The Times* correspondent to the Russian army in 1877 reported a Russian attack on incapacitated Ottoman soldiers to the Ministry of Foreign Affairs, resulting in a formal complaint.[77]

The press was also a key channel by which the Red Cross sought to inform the public about the Geneva Convention and other humanitarian guidelines. This was especially pertinent in the 1860s and 1870s because many armies—notably the French and the U.S.—failed to educate their soldiers in the tenets of the convention, which their governments had ratified, resulting in the convention often being applied one-sidedly.[78] During the Franco-Prussian War, at Henry Dunant's pleading, the French minister of war agreed to publish a notice in the *Journal Officiel* reminding "the public of the provisions of Article 5" of the convention, which establishes neutrality for humanitarian agents in the battlefield.[79]

Newspapers also took it upon themselves to interpret the Red Cross proposals and to encourage their governments to comply:

The sufferings of mutilated and disabled foes have no military value whatever, and it can never be the object of a commander to prolong or aggravate
them, or to place obstacles in the way of medical succor and religious consolation. . . . From the moment that an enemy is physically incapacitated from
fighting, he ceases to be an enemy in any real military sense. . . . All civilized
Governments will, we trust, hasten to give in their adhesion to a humane compact which in no way limits the effective rights and powers of belligerents, and
which no nation, therefore, can have any possible interest in repudiating.[80]

The coverage of the Red Cross and other humanitarian organizations was
far from uniform. Some journals criticized the "prejudiced and sensational
articles which have appeared in the daily press from correspondents and
from certain hysteric members of the Red Cross, seeking to aggrandize their
own services by belittling the work and results of the Medical Department
of the Army."[81] Nevertheless, the close relations between humanitarian organizations and the press expanded the scope in which the logics of the
Red Cross circulated. The widening exposure conferred specific distinction
on the Red Cross as an exemplary movement that demonstrates universal
human values.

International Law

The humanitarian field and the field of international law underwent similar
processes of professionalization in a similar time frame, and the connections between them emerged from the very beginnings of the Red Cross.
Gustave Moynier, before serving as president of the ICRC from 1867 to 1910,
was a Sorbonne-trained jurist and had a lifelong interest in international
law. Red Cross officials were involved in the drafting, promotion, and implementation of humanitarian law since the inception of the movement.

The ICRC is the sole INGO the Geneva Conventions of 1949 mentions
specifically. The conventions specify, for example, that parties to an international armed conflict "shall accept without delay an offer which may be
made by the International Committee of the Red Cross or by any other organization which offers all guarantees of impartiality and efficacy" to serve as
a protecting power for civilians affected by the conflict.[82] The parties are also
required to "grant to the International Committee of the Red Cross all facilities within their power so as to enable it to carry out the humanitarian functions assigned to it."[83] Belligerents are obligated to allow the ICRC access to
prisoners of war and may not restrict shipments delivered through the ICRC

to detainees.[84] The ICRC is also identified as the authority on matters related to the emblems the Geneva Convention recognizes as conferring neutrality.[85] The conventions further specify that, in any case, their provisions "constitute no obstacle to the humanitarian activities which the International Committee of the Red Cross or any other impartial humanitarian organization may, subject to the consent of the Parties to the conflict concerned, undertake for the protection of wounded and sick, medical personnel and chaplains, and for their relief."[86] Additional resolutions passed at the 1949 conference in Geneva recognized "the necessity of providing regular financial support for the International Committee of the Red Cross."[87] Perhaps most indicative of the importance of the Red Cross is the stipulation in the conventions that "the special position of the International Committee of the Red Cross in this field shall be recognized and respected at all times."[88]

The ICRC cultivated a stronger relationship with the field of international law than other relief groups or disarmament movements. The Prussian Order of St. John of Jerusalem, for example, rarely engaged in legalistic work and concentrated on medical and religious work. The League of French Women, a disarmament advocacy movement, was hardly mentioned by legal scholars at the time and had few jurists speak in their conferences. By contrast, the Red Cross project and the Geneva Convention spoke directly to issues that preoccupied the legal scholars of their time. International law specialists were particularly the audience for these new developments. Members of this relatively new profession were the ones to translate international law into concrete military codes of conduct, and to advise states about how to implement the law with relation to their militaries. While international lawyers were hardly uniform in their support of transnational humanitarianism, they played an important role in converting the Geneva Convention and its offshoots into concrete military practices.[89]

The emergence of the field of international law

The nineteenth century saw remarkable professionalization in the field of international law.[90] International lawyers, having become considerably more relevant after the 1806 dissolution of the Holy Roman Empire, were striving to formalize their profession and—inspired by the positivist philosophical currents of their time—sought to portray their field as quasi-scientific. This drive was also intertwined in the movement away from *natural law* toward *positive law*—that is, from the view that international law is predetermined by nature and therefore precedes human agency to the view that international law is constituted only upon the aggregate of the agreements formed between states themselves. Thus, international law became *state* centered (rather than universalistic) and fragmentary.

Crucially, jurists dealing with positive law espoused a technocratic outlook and thus depoliticized the profession of international law. The preceding decades have seen natural-law jurists denounce in the roundest possible terms acts that they saw as contradicting universal principles; conversely, the positivist international lawyers of the mid-nineteenth century insisted on a sharp division between questions of *politics* and questions of *legality*, lending themselves an air of impartiality. The field thus became increasingly self-regulating by the middle of the century. Two central bodies established in 1873, the International Law Association in Brussels and the Institut de Droit International in Ghent, supported the autonomous stance of this field. It became a separate area of study in numerous European and American universities in the same time frame.[91] Crucially, positivist international law crystalized the notion that war, beyond its political and military aspects, is not exempt from objective legal evaluation.[92]

The ICRC as a legal agent

Even though the ICRC had advocated that states be held accountable to an international body of law, it was extremely resistant to attempts to pull it into disputes between nations and refused to lay blame on one party or another during armed conflicts. This tendency was at odds with its accumulating power in the global political sphere, as demonstrated in the previous chapter. At the same time, the ICRC was concerned about the application of the Geneva Convention within the signatory states and its implementation within their militaries. One of the key implications of the prominent role of *national* settings in the emergence of the transnational humanitarian field is that the responsibility for properly applying international humanitarian law and the attendant provisions on the battlefield fell directly on local governments rather than the international community.

In order to promote adherence to the Geneva Convention on the individual state level, the ICRC communicated regularly with the NCRs, both to receive information about their legal status in the various states and to encourage local activists to advocate for the adoption of the Geneva Convention articles into military penal codes. In many states, they succeeded. Switzerland had preexisting regulations about treating the wounded on the battlefield, enacted in 1861, and it adopted into its military rules the recognition of the Red Cross flag and armband in 1866. Baden, Bavaria, the Netherlands, Russia, and Württemberg made significant moves to adopt the Geneva Convention articles into their own military instructions and penal law, and Prussia added the entire convention into its military instructions.[93] The Hessian minister of war invited the local NCR to actively advise the military authorities on incorporating the Geneva Convention into their regulations.[94]

In addition, in some cases Red Cross societies acted as interpreters of the law in relation to their own specific circumstances. One example is the endeavors of the Spanish NRC during the Third Carlist War (1872–1876). The Geneva Convention applied specifically to international conflicts, and yet Red Cross volunteers were on the ground attempting to care for the wounded under the same umbrella of neutrality that covered them in international conflicts. The Spanish committee did its best to highlight the relevance of civil wars for the Red Cross project:

> Some argue that since our association derives its origin from an international act recognized by a diplomatic convention, its objectives must be confined to the relief of the suffering caused by major international conflicts. . . . We should remember that the first and greatest manifestation of the spirit of our work . . . appeared in a civil war—that of the United States.[95]

The Geneva Convention supplied local jurists with a language to critique the conduct of states during war and to further their own professional goals. After the Franco-Prussian War, for example, the Geneva Convention provided Prussian lawyers with means to accuse the French with barbarian conduct during the war, and the same was true for the Danes after the Second Schleswig War.

International lawyers and the Geneva Convention

In addition to the various state-level implementations of the Geneva Convention, international law scholars also took an interest. American legal scholar Francis Lieber wrote to Charles S. P. Bowles, the U.S. Sanitary Commission representative to the 1864 Geneva Convention:

> I . . . take the deepest interest [in the Geneva Congress] because . . . it assembles for the promotion of humanity in the midst of war, and for the purpose of settling some more points in the law of nations in peace and war, which will be one of the greatest, perhaps, taken all in all, the greatest achievement of modern civilization.

Lieber conceived of the Geneva "Congress" as a step toward fulfilling his aspirations for the field of international law:

> Ever since I have made the Law of Nations a particular subject of my studies, I have thought that the greatest good could be done by unofficial congresses of jurists, plainly acknowledged to be among the foremost in their respective countries, which should settle some great international points, yet allowed to float in an undetermined state. If works of single jurists acquire authority, how much more would the results of such united deliberations between German, French, Italian, English, and American jurists aid the great cause of our family of nations?[96]

Thus, Lieber not only envisioned international lawyers as those who can resolve international affairs, but also endorsed the Geneva Convention as the type of forum in which they could work.

A key figure in establishing the status of the Geneva Convention was Swiss legal scholar Johann Caspar Bluntschli (1808–1881).[97] Although Bluntschli was not a pioneer in the area of international humanitarian law, he was inspired by Francis Lieber's codification of the laws of war, and based much of his own work in the area on these instructions, as well as on a long correspondence with Lieber himself.[98] Bluntschli included the neutrality of ambulances and aid workers as an integral aspect of the laws governing warfare in his 1868 comprehensive codification of international law. He attributed this article of the law to Dunant and Moynier and recounted favorably their endeavors to develop and promote the Geneva Convention.[99] Bluntschli's codification became an authoritative source for legal scholars internationally, and—despite not having been translated to English—was cited by U.S. courts.[100]

The unenforceability of the Geneva Convention

The ICRC began its work with the working assumption that a code of honor would ensure states' adherence to the Geneva Convention. But the Franco-Prussian War demonstrated to the committee how unreliable the convention was without any means of enforcing it.[101] Moynier became convinced that an international arbitration tribunal would be necessary in order to manage infringements of the convention. Although this tribunal would not under any circumstance be affiliated with the Red Cross, Moynier believed such an arrangement would promote respect for the convention and, by extension, ensure that humanitarian volunteers be protected on the battle-field. He wrote a detailed blueprint for such a legal body.[102]

Moynier had met the Belgian jurist Gustave Rolin-Jaequemyns at an 1862 international charity conference in London, and was taken by the latter's enthusiasm and expertise in international law. Rolin-Jaequemyns established the journal *Revue de Droit International et de Législation Comparée* with two colleagues. Writing about the ways in which to prevent abuses in the battle-field, he appeared to share Moynier's concerns:

> Apart from the sense of honor, which will always be the first guarantee in this matter (but cannot be ensured by any legislation), it will necessarily seek to prevent [such] abuse by each state taking a positive duty to properly instruct its soldiers, and alternatively of stipulating legal measures [in their own jurisdiction].[103]

In 1872, Moynier visited Rolin-Jaequemyns in Ghent to try to convince him to establish such a tribunal. Some of Moynier's contemporaries—Francis Lieber in particular—did not welcome his proposal. Lieber thought a tribunal would be too restrictive to be acceptable for state leaders.[104] However, the idea of establishing a group of international lawyers that would observe and debate unresolved tensions within world issues appealed to Rolin-Jaequemyns, as Lieber had already written to him with similar sentiments. Moynier's idea, according to Rolin-Jaequemyns, aligned precisely with Lieber's wishes: that "a congress or perhaps a conference of international jurists for the purpose of conferring collective academic authority upon and accordingly recommending to the general public and to governments certain proposals of international law that specifically meet present needs."[105]

The group of jurists Rolin-Jaequemyns invited to the institute figured prominently in discussions of new treaties. On the initiative of Czar Alexander II of Russia, delegates of fifteen European states met in Brussels on July 27, 1874, to examine the draft of an international agreement concerning the laws and customs of war that the Russian government submitted to them. Moynier was dissatisfied with the treatment of the Geneva Convention as simply a part of this new international agreement, as in his mind this would dilute the power of the treaty. He asked the various NRCs to attempt to convince their respective governments to postpone discussions in order to reexamine the issue.[106] Ultimately, the conference accepted the draft with minor alterations, but it was never ratified since the governments were unwilling to accept the Brussels Declaration as a binding convention.

The project nevertheless was an important step in the movement for the codification of the laws of war. In the year in which it was approved, the Institute of International Law, at its session in Geneva, appointed a committee to study the Brussels Declaration and to submit to the institute its opinion and supplementary proposals on the subject. The efforts of the institute led to the adoption of the Manual of the Laws and Customs of War at Oxford in 1880. Since there was considerable confusion among governments about which instructions they should be giving their soldiers, Moynier thought the manual would change existing customs in ways conducive to humanitarian work and that the institute should help promote it internationally. However, he continued to regret the absence of an international judiciary that would enforce the convention.[107]

The Geneva Convention as a symbol of neutrality

One general effect of the legalization of Red Cross norms was the wide dissemination of quasi-legalistic knowledge among civilians about the protections that the Geneva Convention and the Red Cross emblem provided them. When Dunant had worked in Castiglione in 1859, he noted that panic erupted when the locals thought that the Austrian army was making its way back to the village, and that all French flags that had been hung in celebration were immediately taken down and replaced by Austrian ones. By contrast, over the 1860s, the Red Cross flag became widely known as the standard for protection. In Nancy, on the eve of the arrival of the Prussian army in 1870, a volunteer saw "many families open their houses and received each a few [French] wounded. They hastened to make our [Red Cross] flag and hang it from their windows, thinking, doubtless, that when the Prussians arrive, which now, indeed, was not far distant, it would protect them."[108] A Red Cross doctor accompanying the French army in 1870 learned from Prussian prisoners that the Red Cross insignia "were well known to them, and that [the volunteers] should not be fired upon by their troops."[109]

As an effect of the strengthening relations between humanitarians and international lawyers through the Geneva Convention, the state itself became an object to scrutinize and—at times—manipulate. It also became a central moral agent, one that a community of impartial spectators standing in the name of humanity could reproach. However, despite Moynier's advocacy for the establishment of an international judiciary institution, no attempt to create a formal international tribunal that would actively enforce the Geneva Convention on its signatory states bore fruit until the 1899 establishment of the Permanent Court of Arbitration in The Hague, which itself was not strictly an enforcing body but an arbiter in disputes between states.

Balancing Interconnectedness and Autonomy

In the nascent humanitarian field, the outward flow of symbolic goods and their valuation by actors in other fields was crucial for gaining prestige. The growing recognition of the Red Cross across borders and professions provided figures ranging from jurists like Gustave Moynier to nurses like Emma Pearson leverage in their own professional fields. The humanitarian authority of the Red Cross served as capital within the nascent humanitarian field of the nineteenth century, but was also exportable to other domains.[110] Through the work of these early figures, the humanitarian principles of the Red Cross came to be valued across a wide array of professions.

The religious, legal, nursing, and journalistic fields were the closest neighbors of the humanitarian field and remain connected to it to present day. The close relationships these fields fostered were crucial for humanitarian societies to gain a permanent stance in late-nineteenth-century societies. Actors in each of these fields evoked Red Cross language, norms, rules, figures, and values differently, for many different reasons. But across this diversity, the Red Cross resonated with the different actors who were invested in it, and was institutionalized as an elite in the humanitarian field through the links those actors made between their work and the humanitarian relief work this movement modeled. While local competitions over resources and public attention occurred sporadically,[111] on the whole the relationships were cooperative. The influence of the Red Cross emerged when their measures of worth resonated with cultural processes under way in adjacent fields. The influence of the Red Cross not only within the humanitarian field but also in other fields provided the humanitarian field with prestige, exposure, and leverage in multiple contexts.

FIVE

Sans-Frontiérisme and the Rise of "New Humanitarianism"

Although the International Committee of the Red Cross (ICRC) has remained a leader in the global humanitarian sector over the last century and a half, the 1970s saw the rise of a very different type of humanitarian work that departed from traditional Red Cross norms. "New humanitarianism"[1] intertwines the provision of medical aid in emergency situations with outspoken criticism of the conditions that create such emergencies in the first place.[2] Where Red Cross organizations have traditionally refrained from publicly criticizing belligerents and have opted for discreet behind-the-scenes diplomacy, new humanitarian movements have taken to the public sphere in their condemnation of battlefield practices. Furthermore, where national Red Cross societies (NCRs) provide aid through collaboration with national governments, new humanitarians often work without securing the approval of local sovereigns, at the cost of putting themselves at risk of deportation or retribution.

New humanitarianism emerged through the work of Médecins sans Frontières (Doctors without Borders, or MSF), an organization established when several volunteer physicians broke off from the French NCR in 1971. Their highly independent approach to humanitarian aid came to be known as *sans-frontiérisme*.[3] Because MSF activists have been some of the strongest critics of Red Cross policies and ethics, many authors have described the birth of this movement as a radical break with the past.[4] Such work tends to attribute the emergence of MSF to late-twentieth-century sociopolitical developments—for example, the 1949 Universal Declaration of Human Rights, the increasing global awareness new media afford, a post–World War II "never again" commitment, French intellectual currents—rather than to the preexisting field logics of the Red Cross.

However, while MSF certainly carved out a new position for itself in

the humanitarian field and provided the space for other outspoken organizations to follow suit, its break from the past was far from radical. As
this chapter demonstrates, MSF's attempt to reinvent humanitarianism—
despite its self-portrayal as entirely novel—stayed within the confines of
the already-existing cultural framework of its field. Although MSF disagrees
with the Red Cross about what impartiality might concretely mean when
emergency strikes, it accepts the parameters of humanitarian work modeled by the Red Cross since the mid-nineteenth century—especially with
regards for the ethical value of impartiality.[5] Where the ICRC contended that
the impartiality Dunant and Moynier advocated can be achieved through
discreet, nonjudgmental diplomatic work, MSF countered that impartiality
means bearing witness to atrocities and speaking out to help stop them.[6] As
existing work on social fields shows, while fields are characterized by some
level of contention and cross-arguments among different actors seeking to
dominate, the fundamental stakes these actors assign to their work remain
constant across such struggles.[7]

The emergence of new humanitarianism in the 1970s is rooted in the
history of the ICRC over the twentieth century, in which its unchallenged
authority over humanitarian affairs began to crack. New actors joined the
humanitarian field, with competing ideas of how humanitarian work ought
to be conducted and who should lead it, setting the stage for the emergence
of MSF. This chapter will first trace the increasing challenges to the authority
of the ICRC over the twentieth century and highlight the tensions that have
built up within the humanitarian community since the middle of the century. It will then examine the emergence of MSF and its early endeavors, demonstrating the continuity between the late-nineteenth-century ideals of the
Red Cross founders and the late-twentieth-century new humanitarianism.

A Turbulent Century for the ICRC

The Second Boer War (1899–1902) was a high point in the history of the Red
Cross movement. Despite the geographic distance, as well as some resistance
from the British army, Red Cross organizations were heavily represented on
South African battlefields. The United Kingdom, the South African Republic,
and the Orange Free State each had an NRC, but Belgian, Dutch, French,
German, and Russian NRCs, among others, also sent significant reinforce-
ment and, in many ways, saved the Boer medical facilities from complete
collapse.[8] In many ways, the efforts of the ICRC over the preceding thirty-five
years appeared to have borne fruit.

The now-experienced NRCs coordinated local relief work efficiently and won considerable praise in their home countries.[9] Most NRCs underwent rapid professionalization due to the accumulation of NGO management expertise as well as generational turnover. In the U.S., for example, Washington, D.C. socialite Mabel Boardman replaced Clara Barton as president of the American National Red Cross (ANRC) in 1904. While certainly a visionary, Barton was also an inefficient executive who delegated little authority to others and failed to raise sufficient funds for the proper functioning of her organization. Almost forty years her junior, Boardman was an experienced philanthropist and a levelheaded manager. During her tenure, the ANRC established itself as an effective leader of the U.S. humanitarian community and grew in international influence as well.[10]

In Geneva, Gustave Moynier manned the helm at the ICRC until his death in 1910. His forty-six-year tenure as the president of the committee remains by far the longest. His successor was his own nephew, long-time committee member Gustave Ador (1845–1928), who served as ICRC president until his own death. Ador was deeply connected to Swiss politics, being a member of the Swiss National Council from 1889 to 1917 and serving as the president of the Swiss Confederation for a one-year term in 1919. Internationally, he was a supporter of the establishment of the League of Nations, and did much to secure international recognition of the neutral status of Switzerland. Under his watch, the ICRC coordinated World War I humanitarian activities, and in particular expanded in the area of maintaining contact with prisoners of war. The International Prisoners-of-War Agency, which the ICRC established in Geneva in 1914, registered close to two and a half million prisoners and informed family members of their location. Red Cross representatives visited many of those prisoners and arranged for them to receive parcels from home.[11] For this work, in 1917 the ICRC received the only Nobel Peace Prize awarded during the war years.[12]

But alongside the institutionalization of the Red Cross as a leader in all things humanitarian, the ICRC continued to face challenges to its authority from outside critics and also from within the movement. On the one hand, the Red Cross movement faced severe criticism from its contemporaries in their first several decades—particularly from parties that had other models of relief work in mind. In keeping with the spirit of the founders of the movement, NRCs have tended to work closely with their national militaries, and—while occasionally offering advice about implementations of the Geneva Convention—have refrained from criticizing warfare as such or taking steps to prevent future wars. Peace activists, dismayed by what historian John Hutchinson called the "militarization of charity,"[13] continued to criticize the Red Cross movement as helping militaries wage wars through their charitable work. As late as 1914, British journalist Edith Durham remarked that "no Red Cross aid ought to be sent out in war" because "to heal men's wounds and send them back to the front as soon as possible is to prolong war indefinitely."[14]

On the other hand, even within the Red Cross movement itself, a disagreement brewed over the extent to which NRCs ought to involve themselves in disaster relief work and in promoting public health. Although the ICRC restricted the Red Cross mission scope primarily to wartime intervention, many of the NRCs were de facto occupied in disaster relief and development work during peacetime. In 1919, Henry Pomeroy Davison—chairman of the war council of the ANRC during World War I—spearheaded the creation of a new international coordinating body, the League of Red Cross Societies (today known as the International Federation of the Red Cross—the IFRC). The NRCs of France, Italy, Japan, the U.K., and the U.S. formed this new body jointly in order to coordinate Red Cross peacetime activities. Davison, who became the first president of the league, voiced exasperation over the restriction of membership in the ICRC itself to Swiss persons alone, and envisioned the league as opening the way for all NRCs to help steer the movement. The ICRC, concerned about the loss of cohesion and direction within the movement, had numerous reservations about this move, which caused concern among some of the national societies as well.[15] A series of conferences over the course of the 1920s spelled out new guidelines for cooperation among the organs of the movement and helped alleviate some of the tensions, leaving the ICRC fully in charge of coordinating all wartime activities. However, the ICRC no longer possessed the same unchallenged leadership position that it had held for the first fifty-five years of the movement.[16]

The ICRC in the Second World War

Shortly after the internal dispute between the ICRC and the League of Red Cross Societies was resolved, a far greater challenge emerged. In August 1933, initial reports of political detainees being held in appalling conditions in German concentration camps reached the ICRC. Three months later, Germany nationalized the German Red Cross and stripped it of its independence. The German Red Cross transformed overnight into an active participant in the Nazi project, and its staff took part in running the *Lebensborn* houses, in populating military medical facilities, and in promoting Arianizing eugenics across Germany. Gustave Ador's successor, ICRC president Max Huber (1874–1960), felt unable to intervene or to expect the

German Red Cross to deliver accurate information about the conditions in Germany.[17] Although ICRC visits to Dachau were arranged in 1935 and 1938, the visitors found the conditions harsh but not inhumane.[18] However, increasingly alarming reports of deportations of Jews and of additional concentration camps continued to reach Geneva. The ICRC asked the German Red Cross to arrange a visit to Poland to inquire about the conditions in the camps in 1939, and was denied.

By late 1942, the ICRC had clear information about a genocide in progress.[19] The committee drafted a general appeal on violations of international humanitarian law in Germany, but finally decided not to publish it, in an effort not to compromise the meager cooperation it had with Germany, thus remaining silent about the extent of the genocide. In addition, the ICRC exercised strict caution in its dealings with Germany—for example, not derecognizing the German Red Cross as a member of the movement despite its Nazi nationalization—and did not develop any systematic policy with regards to the concentration camps.

In 1944, Red Cross representatives visited the Theresienstadt concentration camp, which had been prepared as a model camp for outside observers. King Christian X of Denmark had insisted over the preceding months that the Danish Red Cross should be allowed to visit Danish deportees and to evaluate their conditions. Wishing to maintain some level of positive standing in Denmark, German authorities agreed to allow a Red Cross visit to Theresienstadt, hoping to whitewash their war practices.[20] ICRC investigator Dr. Maurice Rossel headed the Red Cross delegation to Theresienstadt. Rossel reported back to Geneva about a clean, orderly camp that included reasonable accommodations as well as medical, cultural, and religious facilities. Later in the same year Rossel managed to reach Auschwitz and was received for a short meeting with a commander, but was not permitted to inspect the camp itself.[21]

Although the ICRC failed to intervene in the matter of the camps, it had some significant achievements throughout the war. Red Cross representatives worked to provide humanitarian relief to prisoners of war on both sides and to contact their relatives with information. The ICRC was able to negotiate the delivery of aid parcels to detainees whose whereabouts were known, and sent more than 120,000 such parcels. Friedrich Born, the ICRC delegate to Budapest, made considerable efforts to protect Hungarian Jews and, while most of his efforts came to nothing once deportations began in 1945, he did succeed in stopping the deportation of 7,500 Jews to Auschwitz.[22] ICRC delegates managed to establish a presence in some of the camps toward the end of the war, to distribute aid parcels, and to offer preliminary assistance where possible.[23] As German forces retreated, NRCs also entered the camps and began administering aid to survivors.[24]

The war had a mixed effect on the ICRC. It regained leadership in the humanitarian community as soon as the war ended, and was key in coordinating relief efforts for refugees—both Axis and Allied—and in reconnecting those who have been separated during the war. In 1949, a major expansion and consolidation of the Geneva Conventions, including the adoption of a Convention Relative to the Protection of Civilian Persons in Time of War, helped bolster the position of the ICRC as an authority on international humanitarian law. The committee also received considerable state donations that helped cover its wartime deficit.[25] Nevertheless, the shortcomings of the ICRC in addressing the genocide now marred its reputation. In the aftermath of the war, considerable criticism was directed at the ICRC for favoring diplomacy and legalism over basic concern for human lives.[26]

The question of World War II impartiality revisited

The ICRC kept its World War II files confidential for more than forty years, until releasing them to the U.S. Holocaust Memorial Museum in 1996. The files confirmed that the organization knew of the Nazi concentration camps, and that its leaders felt unable to speak out publicly on the matter.[27] Several years later, ICRC president Jakob Kellenberger explained that the failure to intervene stemmed from the commitment of the ICRC to remain in the vicinity of the victims of armed conflict and to provide relief, with "all other consideration—with the exception of security— . . . strictly subordinated to this goal."[28] Precisely because the ICRC does *not* make regular public appeals, and when it does it avoids "one-sided or at least too explicit condemnations of individual parties to conflict,"[29] it possesses considerable sway in gaining access to victims. Kellenberger maintained that speaking out against Germany had to be weighed against the costs of losing access to almost two million Allied prisoners of war, who were under the ICRC's care. "Being consistent in public comment and in public silence is a fundamental prerequisite for the ICRC's credibility," Kellenberger concluded.[30]

The ethical dilemma about whether or not to speak out became more complicated once it became apparent that the Swiss Federal Council (the president of which also served on the ICRC assembly) pressured the ICRC in real time not to make the information it received about the Holocaust public, so as not to upset relations between Bern and Berlin.[31] The deep interlinking between Swiss and ICRC policy highlighted the extent to which the ICRC was open to Swiss governmental influence, as a result of the strong ties cemented during Ador's tenure with the National Council. While the ICRC instituted restrictions on cross-membership in its assembly and in Swiss government agencies, and by the 1960s forbade them altogether, the suspicion of interests foreign to humanitarian considerations tainting its decision processes continued to lurk both within and outside the organization.[32]

While the ICRC regained much of its credibility through notable interventions in the 1950s and 1960s in Algeria, Greece, Hungary, and Yemen, the memory of its conduct during the war continued to trouble the organization and to occasionally resurface, especially in Holocaust studies circles, but also by philanthropists and activists.[33] This continuing tension intensified in the 1960s and 1970s, as the organization proved itself unable to engage with an emergent and newly politicized generation of young doctors and volunteers.

The French Doctors in Biafra: New Humanitarianism Emerges

Sociologist Alberto Melucci claimed that "new social movements," often associated with the student movements of the 1960s, focus on employing unconventional means in their endeavors, and often present themselves as "changing the rules of the game" due to the inadequacy of existing channels.[34] As sociologist Claus Offe claims, "The space of action of the new movements is a space of noninstitutional politics which is not provided for in the doctrines and practices of liberal democracy and the welfare state."[35] Such movements are often engrossed with identity, autonomy, self-realization, and the politicization of everyday life.[36] New humanitarianism evolved precisely as a new social movement, as emerging humanitarian movements placed a renewed and enhanced emphasis on the volunteers themselves, their conscience, and their ability to fulfill an idealized humanitarian mission—both in the field and in their home countries.[37]

One of the main factors in the rise of new humanitarianism was an influx of baby boom–generation French physicians into humanitarian NGOs over the second half of the 1960s. One reason for this influx was that by the middle of the decade, the French job market was saturated with doctors who found themselves working in menial positions (if any), many of whom were seeking alternate (and possibly more exciting) employment opportunities.[38] This stagnation was at odds with the exciting activist atmosphere on French campuses in the late 1960s, which gave rise to a cohort of new physicians who had been active in radical left-wing movements with a globalist bent (e.g., MSF leader Rony Brauman was associated with a French Maoist movement, and Bernard Kouchner was a communist activist).[39] With the lack of available means in France to fulfill professional and ideological aspirations, many such doctors turned to relief work in the Third World.[40] The type of work offered in armed conflict there, according to one activist, "put into practice this idealism that lies dormant deep inside every physician, and without which a physician risks being nothing but a merchant."[41]

The Nigerian Civil War (1967–1970) was the first destination for many such doctors. When the southeast provinces of Nigeria attempted to secede and form the new Republic of Biafra, armed conflict erupted between the Nigerian federal military forces who attempted to reclaim the region and the scantly armed but fiercely determined Biafran armed forces. The conflict had high international stakes in part because France and the UK were heavily invested in Nigerian oil extraction and processing and were competing for influence in West Africa.[42] Before the war concluded with the federal victory in Biafra, it claimed between one and three million civilian casualties who perished either by armed assault or by the widespread famine the blockade on the region caused.[43]

Although the ICRC was involved in humanitarian relief work from close to the start of the war, its initial means were limited. It received some support from the Swiss Red Cross and from the World Council of Churches, but did not manage to recruit many volunteers or raise sufficient funds. However, the war caught considerable media attention starting in the summer of 1968, and as a result the ICRC welcomed an influx of volunteers and partner organizations. The Salvation Army, Oxfam, the Lutheran Church–Missouri Synod, Save the Children, and other organizations sent personnel and raised funds internationally. The Nigerian Red Cross Society became heavily involved in humanitarian aid on the ground, and the Red Cross societies of Denmark, Finland, Norway, Sweden, the Netherlands, Yugoslavia, and the United States joined the mission.[44]

The French Red Cross mission to Biafra brought together future MSF founders such as physicians Marcel Delcourt, Xavier Emmanuelli, Bernard Kouchner, Vladan Radoman, and Max Recamier. The Red Cross maintained a presence in Biafra even during the most violent points of the conflict, but with the atmosphere being as explosive as it was (and with humanitarian volunteers often being targeted alongside civilians), it was careful to retain its neutral standing. As per Red Cross policy, volunteers were instructed to refrain from interviewing or speaking out about the events and conditions they witnessed in the field. Nevertheless, Kouchner, Recamier, and numerous other physicians volunteering for the French Red Cross, appalled by the conditions in Biafra and by the Red Cross's compliance with Nigerian demands in the field, broke with this policy upon returning to France and published articles about their experience in *Le Monde*.[45] Forming an association named GIMCU (Groupe d'intervention médico-chirurgicale d'urgence—Group for Medical and Surgical Emergency Intervention) in 1970, they undertook the critical mission of bringing attention to the atrocities they witnessed in Biafra. A second association, SMF (Secours médical français—French Medical Relief), was formed in the same year by physicians and journalists seeking to direct attention to the conflict in East Pakistan (later Bangladesh), which was already escalating to the level of genocide.[46]

The two organizations merged to form Médecins sans Frontières. MSF, according to its founding declaration, "brings care to people in precarious situations and works towards helping them regain control over their future." Its actions primarily consist of "providing curative and preventive care to people in danger, wherever they may be . . . in crisis periods when a system is suddenly destabilised and the very survival of the population is threatened." Bernard Kouchner saw this new movement as claiming "the right to interfere," which later activists reformulated as "the duty to interfere" wherever human rights and welfare were compromised. Ideally, this would involve an immediate and direct response to human catastrophe, wherever it takes place and without regard for national borders.[47] Movement founders also saw the principle of *témoignage* as central to the identity of the movement. *Témoignage*, according to their founding declaration, means bearing witness to human rights abuses and being willing to speak publicly on behalf of the recipients of aid, leaving open "the possibility to openly criticise or denounce breaches of international conventions."[48] According to the MSF declaration, *témoignage* is "done with the intention of improving the situation for populations in danger," which requires the physical presence of volunteers on the ground as caregivers *and* witnesses.[49]

The ICRC initially welcomed the French doctors' call for volunteer physicians for the Biafra cause and even reprinted excerpts from the *Le Monde* articles in the *International Review of the Red Cross*.[50] However, it soon found itself facing a solid competitor for funds and public attention, and—no less important—over authority within the humanitarian field.[51] MSF rapidly grew into a multinational federated INGO over the last decades of the twentieth century. It founded operational centers in Amsterdam, Barcelona, Brussels, Geneva, and Paris, its total income grew to €938 million in 2012,[52] and it currently employs almost 32,000 staff members (most of whom are volunteers). MSF centers have exercised caution in dealing with national governments out of fear of cooptation, and where ICRC funding comes mostly from government contributions (approximately 80 percent),

89 percent of MSF's overall funding in 2012 came from private donors. The movement has prided itself on providing care to casualties of conflict and disaster—especially civilians—with or without the consent of their governments (e.g., MSF has set up two hospitals in opposition-held regions of Syria despite not receiving authorization from the Syrian government).[53] Despite their differences, the ICRC remained for the most part cordial with MSF and established a working relationship with the new competitor where possible.

Polluting the Red Cross: the memory of Auschwitz returns

The 1971 "rebellion" against the Red Cross figured strongly in the ways MSF founders framed the orientation of the movement over the course of its expansion. MSF activists have suggested that Red Cross–type aid does not live up to the transnational ideals of humanitarianism it speaks of, in particular in the battlefield realities of the 1970s. Rony Brauman, former president of MSF-France, explained:

> Until the beginning of the 1960s, the Geneva-based ICRC carried out its duties without sending medical units to battle sites . . . the ICRC was not encouraged to send out medical units because most conflicts in the past century involved either industrialized nations opposing each other or industrialized nations opposing their colonies. In both types of conflict medical care was provided by the military of the countries involved. In the first type of conflict most victims were soldiers. The armies facing each other were medically well equipped: each had its own medical unit to treat its own wounded. Military doctors were assisted by nurses and stretcher bearers from the Red Cross sections of only their own countries. In the second type of conflict, the colonial powers used the principle of noninterference to outlaw any foreign medical assistance to nationalist guerrillas. Here, too, war medicine was limited to military medicine.[54]

The ICRC's relative silence on the matter of the Holocaust appeared in these accounts as an example of the failures of the Red Cross to provide aid in real time and it pointed to its preference of confidential diplomacy over speaking out in the face of genocide. Although the scholarly debate over the extent to which the ICRC's silence enabled the genocide was still ongoing in the 1970s, numerous leading French humanitarian aid figures and journalists adopted this belief, drawing on the potent metaphor of the Holocaust to describe Biafra as a breaking point. As Bernard Kouchner put it,

We [the French doctors in Biafra] knew that after an October 14, 1942, decision of the executive committee [of the ICRC], during World War II [the organization's leaders] in Geneva had chosen not to reveal the existence of the extermination camps and to consider the Jews—intended victims of the final solution—as prisoners no different from the others. We rejected that complicity. We refused to participate in the selection of the sick or to collude with the executioners. Much later, during a host of other crises, we saw that speaking out provided protection against murder and that the media were our allies.[55]

MSF activist Claude Malhuret voiced similar sentiments when he advocated for a strong interventionist stance toward Khmer Rouge Cambodia: "People are dying of hunger in Cambodia, and we can't intervene. If you had known about Auschwitz, would you have buried your head in the sand?"[56]

For new humanitarian activists, "modern humanitarian aid was born in the summer of 1968 [and] in the Biafran War." As Médecins du Monde activists proclaimed, "Faced with this horrific situation, [French Red Cross doctors] decided to break the vow of silence they had taken when the ICRC hired them, rejecting the guilty neutrality of the doctors and representatives who visited Auschwitz during the Nazi genocide."[57]

Glorifying Sans-Frontiérisme

With these grand proclamations framing their activities in the early 1970s, MSF founders—and in particular the outspoken Bernard Kouchner—were celebrated by the media, and enthralled readers with depictions of their courageous missions in places where other NGOs feared going.[58] MSF volunteers have furnished the humanitarian world and many "lay" readers with harrowing tales of the danger and peril in which they have worked. Their esteem within the organization was often measured not by their "real" training but by the sites in which they have served: the greater the danger, the greater the prestige, the greater the public interest.[59]

Furthermore, like their Victorian-era predecessors in the early Red Cross, MSF volunteers often recounted their "adventures" in excited tones: "It's more fun than sitting in an office. After running a hospital and doing surgery, you could never be a nurse in Europe and wear your funny little hat again." One volunteer's worst nightmare is "to be married with two children and a mortgage." Another volunteer says that she loves Africa because "Here, everything is real, not phony, it's life and death."[60] They also tend to emphasize the transformative effects of volunteering in conflict zones:

"Physicians returning from such missions," stated one of MSF's founding members, "will no longer be entirely the same,"[61] having fulfilled the true calling of their profession. Ethnographers studying the movement have offered similarly romanticized descriptions: "Becoming an MSFer is . . . a kind of *dis*alienation. Membership liberates them as human beings, allows them to explore fully their potential as they seize the opportunity to act. With that liberation comes a profound conviction of the purity of what they do, of the moral superiority of their agency and themselves—a belief so powerful, a satisfaction so intense, that it sustains them through whatever they must do."[62]

MSF appealed to the rising suspicion of state sovereignty and the cosmopolitanism that characterized many intellectual communities at the end of the twentieth century.[63] A French sociologist, commenting on the shift from the "old" humanitarianism to *sans-frontiérisme*, wrote that as "calls for help can be heard from oppressed people and minority groups . . . Western countries have neither the financial and military clout, nor, above all, the political will to impose a new world order based on respect for human rights. The international community's response will only be prompted by . . . media visibility and the sustained pressure of public opinion."[64] French sociologist Guy Hermet commented: "Geneva-style [ICRC] humanitarianism . . . applied only to foreign or civil wars—in short, to the effects of belligerency in a spirit of reciprocity on the part of the warring parties. It has *not* affected the cornerstone of the sovereignty of every state. . . . Governments and even blood-soaked tyrants have continued to enjoy a free hand on their own territory." However, Hermet asserts that in the post–World War II era, and thanks to the continuing action of new humanitarian movements, matters have been irreversibly altered. Rather than continue to accept state sovereignty as a given, recent resolutions in the UN have granted the international community the right to impinge upon states that are found to violate their citizens' rights.[65]

Troubled Institutionalization

While ideas about recovering the true impartial ethic of their field have excited the imagination of the founders of MSF, the movement also learned some hard lessons about the fate of well-intentioned humanitarian interventions in conflict-ridden areas over the 1970s and 1980s. These revolved around the operational implications of their initial disregard for state sovereignty, with the repercussions of speaking out against belligerents, and with the unpredictable conduct of some of the MSF actors who expected the organization to fully live up to its promise of criticizing all violations of human rights without regard to possible retribution by state authorities.

In line with its ethos of rejecting outside interference with humanitarian work, the nascent MSF refused to invest in a fundraising infrastructure or to cooperate with existing government programs. Instead, MSF activists valued an informal, nonhierarchical organizational structure and scoffed at notions of bureaucracy.[66] As a result, MSF could only send its own volunteer teams while relying on other aid organizations to provide the infrastructure for aid delivery. While operations in Vietnam in 1975 and in Lebanon in 1976 helped establish MSF as a serious organization, its lack of organizational resources hindered its efforts to be first on the scene when emergency strikes.

Operationally, the insistence on not directly cooperating with host states soon began to take its toll. In Pakistan, in Honduras, in Thailand, and in Zaire, MSF set up infirmaries and shelters, and claimed neutrality for its operations, but ultimately discovered that guerilla factions used the cover of neutrality to recuperate and to recruit new members.[67] The international aid community faced additional dilemmas in its dealings with authoritarian regimes such as North Korea, where food supplies were reportedly not reaching the population, and yet aid organizations continued to supply the nation with food, thus strengthening its governmental distribution system.[68] Elsewhere, MSF relief programs were becoming a tool at the hands of local powers who used the promise of medical care and food supplies to move populations according to government needs.[69] Such recurring botches have led to counterarguments against humanitarian actors, pointing to the fact that humanitarian efforts have unintentionally led to the escalation of warfare.[70] A related concern during wartime was that by their mere presence in the field, humanitarian NGOs may be contributing to the war economy. Through taxes, housing, security payments, employment of local staff, and local transportation, humanitarian agents have both directly and indirectly brought cash into local belligerents' treasuries.[71]

Témoignage reconsidered

An additional challenge MSF met was belligerents' response to international censure brought on by humanitarian organizations working within their territories. In 1985, for example, food distribution centers in Ethiopia were discovered to be used as means by the government to relocate populations. MSF activists, wishing to exercise *témoignage*, spoke to the media and called for international censure of the Ethiopian government. MSF was consequently expelled from the country.[72] ICRC workers, in contrast, are not allowed to testify in court or to speak to the media without prior approval so as not to sour relations between the organization and belligerent parties.[73]

As a result of the challenges of confronting national sovereigns, the activist, outspoken character that MSF initially heralded soon caused disagreements about the respective roles of *témoignage* and providing assistance within the movement. In 1977, Claude Malhuret was elected as president of MSF. Malhuret, a French doctor and lawyer, had worked as an epidemiologist in India for the World Health Organization. He had already worked for MSF in Asia, and notably condemned the Khmer Rouge violence in an interview on French television upon returning from Cambodian refugee camps in 1977. As president, he represented a very different type of leader than Kouchner and other first-generation MSF members and aimed to introduce some measure of professionalism to the NGO, along with a coherent fundraising scheme. For Kouchner, these moves posed the danger of "bureaucratization" and dilution of MSF's original intentions.

MSF, after its first few years in the field, has become much more cautious and aware of possible implications of speaking out. In 1977, MSF revised its charter to specify that members should avoid "any interference in States' internal affairs" and abstain from "passing judgment or publicly expressing an opinion—either positive or negative—regarding events, forces, or leaders who accepted their assistance." MSF-France leadership announced in 1978 that the organization's bureau would make all decisions about reporting human rights violations moving forward. Under Malhuret's leadership, the status of *témoignage* grew more symbolic and less practical in MSF's policies, and emphasis was placed instead on organizational sustainability and longer-term programming. Thus, the difficulties of aligning its critical mission with the realities in the field brought MSF closer to traditional Red Cross policies.

Despite these restrictions, MSF continued to work in a very public manner. In 1980, as news of famine in Cambodia became widespread, MSF representatives Rony Brauman and Claude Malhuret joined the organizations Action Internationale Contre la Faim (AICF) and the International Rescue Committee (IRC) and approached the Cambodian border with about a hundred protesters and a food convoy. Although the initiative failed and the envoy was turned away, the media coverage was widespread. MSF helped raise the attention of numerous aid organizations, celebrities, and state officials regarding the state of Cambodia at the time.

At the same time, an unapproved mission to Vietnam, headed by Bernard Kouchner himself and staffed by reporters and medical professionals, was considered too much of a publicity stunt by the president and council, leading to the 1979 departure of Kouchner and several others to establish the new NGO, Médecins du Monde (MDM). Kouchner's view was that *témoignage* was the most ethical and effective way to address human suffering, especially when the populations that suffer do not have the means to represent themselves in international media. MDM views MSF critically as having backed out of its own commitments to rejuvenate humanitarian work, and continues to present itself as expressing "true" humanitarian ethics. Like MSF, Médecins du Monde found itself subject to retaliation when local sovereigns accused it of interfering with state affairs. Notably, when the International Criminal Court in The Hague indicted South Sudan president Omar al-Bashir for war crimes in 2009, South Sudan expelled Médecins du Monde from Darfur for supposedly aiding rebel groups and spying on the movements of the national armed forces.[74]

Despite the talk of novelty and reinvention around the birth of new humanitarianism, the parallels between the rise of the Red Cross in the 1860s and the rise of MSF in the 1970s go beyond the similar language used in describing humanitarian action. MSF's mission to raise public awareness draws directly from the transnational humanitarian field's preexisting "emergency imaginary," the position according to which the world is incessantly in peril and parties in various locations require immediate help.[75] The Red Cross used the same type of discourse in the 1860s to justify the permanent existence of humanitarian associations, as chapter 1 has shown. While the Red Cross has tended to work outside of the public eye, it has nonetheless provided publics and decision makers with powerful appeals on behalf of their beneficiaries. In addition, the notion that humanitarian actors occupy a special position from which they can observe impartially how belligerents conduct themselves is identical to the position the Red Cross had taken a century earlier. The Red Cross's self-positioning was constituted on presenting itself as expressing a universal human ethic that affords it the capacity to remain impartial in its survey of world politics and conflicts. While MSF activists labeled new humanitarianism as the true manifestation of universal humanitarian ethics, this movement relies on the logics the Red Cross brought into the field of humanitarianism a century earlier.

Ongoing Tensions in the Humanitarian Field

In a 2012 article in the ICRC journal *International Review of the Red Cross*, former MSF-France president Rony Brauman highlighted what he saw as the crucial difference between the ICRC and MSF responses to the Syrian crisis. After praising the fruitful cooperation that has characterized ICRC and MSF relations over the years and downplaying the severity of the split between the French doctors in Biafra and the ICRC, Brauman gets to the heart of the matter. The ICRC, according to him, chose to engage in dialogue with Damascus and to dispense aid with the Assad regime's approval. While the ICRC first turned to the regime in the hope of reaching all those in need within Syrian territory, this move de facto aligned it with the regime and hindered its efforts to deliver aid across lines. Furthermore, the ICRC dispensed some of the aid through the Syrian Arab Red Crescent (SARC). SARC, being largely identified as a national organization and thus affiliated with the regime, suffered attacks from opposition groups and was thus unable to act in many of the conflict zones where its help was most needed. By contrast, MSF set up field hospitals without seeking approval from Damascus. In Brauman's view, "for MSF, as soon as it becomes thinkable, and hence possible, to set up medical services in an area controlled by an opposition force, it is *necessary* to do so."[76] The *International Review* editor, however, added a note to point out that there are many instances of the ICRC working across Syrian conflict lines, including cities like Homs and Harasta that witnessed some of the most violent battles.[77] Despite the enduring cooperation between the Red Cross and MSF, the critique of the ICRC—whether justified or not—continues to be a salient feature of MSF organizational culture to the present day.

Both the ICRC and MSF occupy the *autonomous* pole of the humanitarian field—that is, the side of the field predominated by field-specific capital and most resistant to influences from other fields. But as Krause showed, the ICRC and MSF differ in the way they are autonomous. The ICRC places an emphasis on absolute neutrality, but since it accepts the legitimacy of nation-state sovereignty, it is susceptible to state interest "pollution." MSF, by contrast, has adopted a confrontational attitude toward governments, but this has often inadvertently aligned it with rebel nonstate actors.[78] However, despite these differences, MSF and the ICRC share an underlying belief in the virtues of independence, neutrality, and impartiality—as each defines it. As this chapter has shown, even when opposing the Red Cross, MSF has continued to employ the same fundamental assumptions about humanitarian work. The Red Cross's influence in shaping the field of transnational humanitarian activism thus extends from the mid-nineteenth century directly to the early twenty-first century.

CONCLUSION

Reconsidering the Culture of
the Humanitarian Field

This book argued that the institutional dynamics of the humanitarian field over the past 150 years are rooted in the values that animated the early founders of the Red Cross. Specifically, it showed that the ethical principles humanitarian NGOs tout today—impartiality, neutrality, universality, independence—emerged from the organizational logics the Red Cross drew from its Calvinist heritage. These principles have served as a common denominator for cooperation among humanitarian relief projects at times, but have also been subject to controversy and conflict at various points in history. They have allowed relief organizations to reach beneficiaries across political boundaries, but have also generated the impossible dilemmas humanitarian NGOs face: is speaking out against human rights abuses the right way to be truly impartial, or must one remain nonjudgmental at all costs? Should NGOs collaborate with local sovereigns in order to reach the maximum number of beneficiaries, or does such cooperation compromise neutrality during conflict? Should humanitarian NGOs engage in peace building, or would such an act compromise their apolitical position? None of these questions has easy answers and, if anything, the unruly and rapidly growing corpus of reflections and theorizing on these topics by scholars and practitioners alike suggests that these quandaries will remain unresolved for the foreseeable future.[1]

Across the chapters of this book, I have argued that culture—in the forms of beliefs, codes, and symbols—played a central role in the genesis and mass expansion of the humanitarian field. While religious beliefs were central to its formation and shaping, nationalist sentiments and imagery played an equally important role in transmitting it across borders and rendering it meaningful in new contexts. An interest in beneficence across different professions provided humanitarianism with leverage across professional worlds. Although there is no denying that political interests and structural organizational dynamics played parts in the story, the common thread was the cultural resonance of the project the Red Cross was advocating: an independent, impartial, and neutral sector of humanitarian NGOs. The fact that culture plays such a key role in field emergence extends far beyond the humanitarian field, and should inform studies of other fields—adjacent ones like the field of human rights or development, but also more distant ones like scientific or technological fields. Understanding field emergence as culturally dependent helps explain why field actors value certain institutional arrangements more than others and what alternate paths those fields could have taken.

In these last several pages, I outline two implications this book bears for contemporary conversations about humanitarian practices and ethics. The first relates to the role religion plays, and ought to play, in contemporary humanitarian work, and the second expands the conversation on humanitarian ethics beyond the scope outlined in this book.

Religion and Humanitarian Work Reconsidered

Despite the pervasive involvement of religious actors in the humanitarian sector, there is a growing stance among some members of the humanitarian community that humanitarian work stems from a secular tradition and that religion, if anything, is one of the causes of the suffering humanitarians address. Public discourse on peace building, scholarly research on humanitarian NGOs, and NGOs' own policies reflect this stance.

Numerous public intellectuals have attacked the role of religion as a peace-building framework in recent years. In particular, the "new atheists"— figures like Richard Dawkins, Daniel Dennett, Sam Harris, and Christopher Hitchens—have spent much ink attempting to attribute human violence to religious beliefs (notably, Hitchens's book is titled *God Is Not Great: How Religion Poisons Everything*).[2] Psychologist Steven Pinker, for example, dismissed religion as a foundation for moral reasoning, instead calling the Bible "a manual for rape, genocide, and the destruction of families" and attributing to religion "stonings, witch burnings, crusades, Inquisitions, jihads, fatwas, suicide bombers . . . and mothers who drown their children in the river."[3] His own book, *The Better Angels of our Nature*, argues that violence has greatly declined over human history with the historical turn to reason, and claims that the "theory that religion is a force for peace . . . does not fit the facts of history."[4]

Many scholars commenting on humanitarian organizations, and especially new humanitarians, similarly see irreligion as a precondition to true impartiality and religion as either irrelevant or a barrier to humanitarian work. Referring to the Red Cross as "MSF's most directly contrastive corollary and ancestor," anthropologist Peter Redfield describes MSF as assuming "a secular humanitarian worldview as its moral norm, whereby facts of widespread human suffering—rather than sin, salvation, or liberation—define the essential gravity of moral discourse."[5] Elsewhere, British anthropologist Jonathan Benthall notes that "historically, the creation of MSF resulted mainly from an alliance of medicine, journalism and the political left—all entirely secular institutions."[6]

This broad aversion to religion is not only confined to the bookshelf but has practical implications for the work of humanitarian organizations in the field as well. Nonreligious humanitarian NGOs often present themselves as neutral with regards to religion and claim that this neutrality is what helps them work across boundaries. After acknowledging that in some cases religious faith may be helpful for humanitarian efforts, Polly Markandya, director of communications for MSF UK and Ireland, articulates this position well:

> We witness first hand the strife and hatred that religious divisions can foster. People fight over religion and politics—so for us to help those caught in the midst of these conflicts, where our help is needed the most, we simply cannot take sides or carry any of those labels. Separating our organisation not just from religious but also political, racial and philosophical tenets is what makes our work possible and is our passport to reaching those in greatest need—especially in warzones.[7]

As a result of this view of religion as hindering true neutrality, many nonreligious NGOs treat faith-based humanitarian organizations with suspicion, and often draw boundaries between their work and their own work. The suspicion, as policy analyses and interviews with staff members have shown, is that faith-based organizations are either partial to one side of a conflict or are using the veil of humanitarian relief to mask an underlying proselytizing mission.[8]

However, as this book has shown, such stances are historically shortsighted and simplistic. Religious faith not only motivated the founders of the humanitarian field to pursue charitable works, but actually supplied the specific characteristics their emerging field should espouse. Historically, religious actors have led the way for the humanitarian world, and while enlightenment theorists may have provided some of the initial mobilization, the ones that have acted upon them were religious actors, seeking to restore a modicum of morality into the violence that Europe (under the flag of secular nationalism) had descended into since the late eighteenth century. When humanitarian organization staff members declare their stance as impartial and autonomous from all other considerations—including religious ones—they are ironically articulating a stance derived from one specific tradition, early-nineteenth-century Swiss Calvinism.

Today, faith-based organizations remain prominent in the humanitarian aid sector. Alongside nonreligious organizations, NGOs such as Lutheran World Relief, Catholic Relief Services, and the nondenominational evangelical Samaritan's Purse have received consistently high rankings from charity watchdog organizations like Charity Navigator in terms of their financial stability, accountability, and transparency.[9] Without acknowledging the legitimacy of religion in the humanitarian field, secular humanitarian organizations risk marginalizing religious language, ideology, and experience in humanitarian work on the ground. Humanistic aspirations notwithstanding, humanitarian agencies often serve deeply religious populations, and many of their locally recruited staff members share the beneficiaries' faith, rather than determined secularism. By professing an ideological indifference to religion, humanitarian NGOs set the expectations that religious beliefs remain confined to the private lives of their workers and beneficiaries.[10]

Furthermore, improving coordination between nonreligious and faith-based humanitarian NGOs can provide the former with access to funds and volunteers, as well as to preexisting congregation-based networks to locate beneficiaries and provide assistance. In some contexts, religious actors are more successful humanitarian responders than their secular counterparts. The humanitarian response to the 2017 crisis in Puerto Rico in the wake of Hurricane Maria is one example. Although Puerto Rico received considerable media attention and several celebrities made impressive fundraising efforts after the hurricane struck, logistical shortcomings and a slow U.S. government response left many Puerto Ricans with little more than the meager aid their local government could offer. On the island, Caritas Puerto Rico, the local branch of Catholic Charities International, was initially slow but gained traction once distribution logistics were resolved. Crucially, across denominations, church organizations mobilized networks between Puerto Rican churches and their mainland U.S. counterparts to intercede much faster than government agencies. Both Catholic and Protestant congregations were able to send funds, supplies, and volunteers through church networks, and no less importantly, to distribute them through local religious organizations.[11] Other examples—both historical and contemporary—exist, and the humanitarian sector as a whole would benefit from bolstering co-operation with such religious networks.[12]

This book joins a growing literature demonstrating that belief structures matter greatly in motivating large-scale human rights, humanitarian, and development projects.[13] Attuning emergency relief schemes to the centrality of faith in the global field of humanitarianism will facilitate more efficient aid projects.

Rethinking the Mission of Humanitarianism

By tracing the logics of the humanitarian field to one specific Calvinist tradition, this book has highlighted the historical variability of the ethics that guide humanitarian work. Although many contemporary NGOs assume that humanitarian aid should be provided by impartial and neutral agents who are independent from the state, other ethical frameworks for thinking about relief work exist and should be taken into consideration in contemporary policy discussions. Indeed, religious and nonreligious movements that were contemporaneous with the early Red Cross envisioned much more global solutions to social suffering.[14] The Society of Friends (the Quakers), for example, has continued to support projects that intertwine relief work with active attempts to prevent war and to encourage pacifism. The work of the American Friends Service Committee, with its active advocacy against the Cold War, its relief efforts in numerous wars, and its work toward social justice, has earned it considerable public praise (along with the continuing scrutiny of the Federal Bureau of Investigation).[15]

The predominant ethical framework for humanitarian NGOs outlined in this book was conceived from a much more pessimistic view about the ability to truly overcome war and to work toward perpetual peace. Gustave Moynier and Henry Dunant, both in their public roles as founders of the movement and in their personal writings, imported a key dialectic from the religious to the humanitarian field: on the one hand, a profound sense that Christianity will serve to promote peace, but on the other hand, a belief that wars will *not* diminish in the foreseeable future due to the inherent sinfulness of humankind. The relatively limited project the Red Cross took upon itself, then, was confined to saving lives and eschewed any grander involvement in concrete peacemaking or any other political project. Although Red Cross societies—both historically and presently—have certainly been supportive of peace-building efforts,[16] their determination to remain disinterested has precluded them for helping beneficiaries seek long-term political solutions to their needs. While new humanitarian organizations like Médecins sans

Frontières have aspired to address the causes of social suffering by defying national boundaries and by speaking out publicly about human rights infringements, this commitment has become hard to juggle with their determination to remain completely impartial. With impartiality, neutrality, and complete independence being *the* markers of authority in the humanitarian field, few organizations would want to compromise their position by interceding directly in political questions.

At the same time, there has been a growing criticism of independent humanitarian NGO work and calls for reform. In particular, although NGOs are certainly accountable to their sponsors, they are not usually accountable toward their beneficiaries—in keeping with their independence—and are rarely required to make themselves available to public scrutiny.[17] While some INGOs (international NGOs) have made impressive efforts to include beneficiaries in their decision-making processes and to employ locals among their staff, they remain a minority in the humanitarian aid landscape, and NGO decision makers often misunderstand realities on the ground as a result.[18]

Over the long term, such lack of direct accountability can become a serious problem when NGOs maintain a prolonged presence in the field without working to rebuild local self-governance capacities.[19] Sadly, in some instances the relationships between humanitarian organizations and recipient populations take on a patronizing and colonialist hue,[20] and may encourage phenomena like volunteer tourism ("voluntourism") that further exploit local distress.[21]

Proponents of *rights-based humanitarianism* seek to address some of these limitations by expanding humanitarian work beyond the traditional confines of impartiality and neutrality and into developmental and human rights agendas. Rights-based humanitarian actors seek not only to address the emergency at hand but also to identify its causes and to address them at their root, with an emphasis on restoring and securing human rights through humanitarian and development work.[22] As part of this approach, humanitarian NGOs would work to strengthen the ability of local state organizations to provide for the population and would help prevent exploitative parties from taking advantage of the local humanitarian needs. Oxfam, for example, has been central in an ongoing struggle in El Salvador's fight against predatory mining and exploitation of its natural resources. Oxfam helped its El Salvador partners win a 2016 case in the International Court for the Settlement of Investment Disputes at the World Bank, where the court upheld the country's right to regulate mining in its territory.[23]

While rights-based approaches have made considerable headway in the development sector since the mid-1990s, they have gained less traction in humanitarian aid organizations. Most humanitarian organizations prioritize providing relatively short-term assistance over longer-term transformations and capacity building that are largely the domain of development agencies like the International Monetary Fund or the World Health Organization. Humanitarian organizations tend to steer clear of the public advocacy and calls for judicial remedial action that characterizes human rights organizations like Amnesty International and Human Rights Watch. Furthermore, rights-based humanitarianism comes with its own set of critics, who have questioned the extent to which promoting human rights is within the capacity of humanitarian organizations and whether it might not lead to adverse results like instilling false expectations among local populations.[24] Others have noted that in complex humanitarian emergencies, where local governments are either incompetent or uncooperative, a rights-based approach is unrealistic to begin with.[25]

Despite these difficulties, solutions like these push beyond the traditional scope of relief work, and—if anything—help shed a comparative light on existing humanitarian policies. Continuing this conversation by considering alternatives to the Red Cross paradigm will certainly help develop policies that both protect the rights of beneficiaries and respond to their emergency needs.

Conversations over humanitarian policy have diversified over the past decades, with difficult questions arising from sites like Haiti, Srebrenica, and Libya. Nevertheless, the humanitarian community continues to valorize the parameters the founders of the Red Cross introduced more than a century and a half ago, and NGO intervention is often perceived as better than other possible channels of aid. In this, those organizations that can present themselves as completely disinterested by keeping all political questions at an arm's distance still exert extraordinary influence over international humanitarian affairs and will continue to do so in the foreseeable future. The understanding that their ethical stance is historically contingent should be in integral part of any discussion of the future of humanitarian aid.

ACKNOWLEDGMENTS

I am indebted to Jeffrey C. Alexander, Philip S. Gorski, and Philip Smith for guiding me through this project from its earliest iterations to the final product. I am similarly thankful to Eva Illouz for introducing me to cultural sociology and for many conversations about this research over the years.

At Yale, I greatly benefitted from conversations with Julia Adams, Scott Boorman, Emily Erikson, Ron Eyerman, Sigrun Kahl, and Peter Stamatov. At Harvard, Yael Berda, Barış Büyükokutan, Michèle Lamont, and Jocelyn Viterna provided valuable feedback and advice. Over the years, numerous colleagues and friends have volunteered their time to read chapter drafts and to provide comments, and I am deeply grateful for their help: Laura Adler, Matt Andersson, Annika Arnold, Elena Ayala-Hurtado, Roger Baumann, Aina Begim, Noli Brazil, Adrienne Cohen, Philip Jun Fang, Maleah Fekete, Limor Gabay-Egozi, James Hurlbert, Kristian B. Karlson, Gabrielle Kelly, Kwan Woo Kim, Matthew Lawrence, Peggy Levitt, Thomas Lyttleton, Timothy Malacarne, Syeda Masood, Sakhile Matlhare, Bo Yun Park, Candas Pinar, Laura Rienecker, Derek Robey, Hosna Sheikholeslami, Samuel Stabler, Amy Tsang, and Hernan del Valle.

I presented parts of the research at the Yale Center for Cultural Sociology Workshop, the Yale Comparative Research Workshop, the Yale Macmillan Center Initiative on Religion, Politics, and Society, the Harvard Culture and Social Analysis workshop, the Indiana University Lilly Family School of Philanthropy Workshop in Multidisciplinary Philanthropic Studies, the Social Science History Association Annual Meeting, and the American Sociological Association Annual Meeting. A 2011 presentation at the Konstanzer Meisterklasse helped me formulate the empirical questions raised in chapter 3, and I am obliged to Bernhard Giesen for inviting me to this workshop. I am similarly thankful to Julian Go and Monika Krause for inviting me to participate in the Fielding Transnationalism project, where I developed much of the theoretical framing for chapter 3, and for their feedback.

My first two years at Yale were supported by a Fulbright doctoral fellowship provided by the United States–Israel Educational Foundation. Funds for three additional years at Yale came from the Thomas A. Emerson Fund and the Joseph Hopkins Twichell Memorial Financial Aid Fund. My travels to Geneva were supported by a George M. Camp grant. A generous dissertation completion fellowship, provided by the Lake Institute on Faith & Giving at the Indiana University Lilly Family School of Philanthropy, allowed me to finish the research, and a Harvard College Fellowship provided me with the time and resources to complete the book manuscript.

I am grateful to the International Committee of the Red Cross and to the Library of Geneva for allowing me to research their archives. Their archival staff—and particularly Fabrizio Bensi at the ICRC—have been most helpful in locating material and in identifying the best strategy for my research. Volkmar Schön at the German Red Cross and Wolfgang G. Fischer at the Rauhe Haus provided additional assistance with locating primary sources.

At the University of Chicago Press, I am grateful to Douglas Mitchell and Elizabeth Branch Dyson for seeing the book project through from start to finish. Doug passed away several months after the book was accepted for publication, and I am lucky to have benefitted from his depth of knowledge, editorial eye, and friendship. I am also indebted to Michael Koplow for the careful copyediting, and to Mollie McFee, Tyler McGaughey, Lauren Salas, and Kyle Wagner for their assistance throughout the production and marketing process. In addition, the anonymous outside readers provided feedback that has greatly improved the final manuscript.

Many others have helped throughout the journey in countless ways, both professionally and personally. In particular, during the last stretch of the work, Rabbi Hirschy and Elkie Zarchi gave me a home away from home and offered both spiritual and concrete support, and Rabbi Menachem Altein took great pains to deepen my engagement with Judaism.

Finally, my family—Uri, Dalia, Yael, Danny, Maya, Itai, Idan, and Peter—has been an inexhaustible source of strength, despite being half a world away. Over the long writing process, Blake Scalet, my partner, has personally exemplified the affinity of faith and humanitarianism with which this book is concerned.

APPENDIX: SOURCES AND METHODOLOGY

My research included multiple sources of data, including documents generated by the Red Cross and its personnel, news reports and commentary, and
responses to the activities of the Red Cross in the legal, medical, and journalistic field. The bulk of the data came from the archives of the International
Committee of the Red Cross and of the Library of Geneva, where many of
the personal documents of early Red Cross activists are housed. Until the
late 1990s, much of the historiography of the ICRC has been written under
its own sponsorship, and was thus largely uncritical. In fact, for much of its
history, the ICRC has insisted on reviewing and authorizing scholarly work
based on their material and placing other restrictions on its use. It was only
in the 1990s, after mounting criticism of failure and misconduct, that the
archives were opened to the public, and new historiographies were offered.

For the current research, the ICRC archive provided mainly internal communications and memos of the ICRC and communications between the
ICRC and non–Red Cross actors such as government officials, clergy, philanthropists, and journalists, as well as personal documents and diaries of
early Red Cross activists. The private files of Gustave Moynier, the president
of the ICRC from 1864 to 1910 (which his family donated to the ICRC) shed
much light on the internal workings and dilemmas the organization and its
leaders faced in its early years. The personal files of Henry Dunant, which
are housed at the Library of Geneva, provided great insight into the religious
and philanthropic culture in Geneva in the mid-nineteenth century and its
influence on the founders of the movement, as well as on Dunant's own
beliefs and undertakings. Additional information about early Red Cross collaborators came from the archive of the Rauhe Haus Foundation. In addition to these primary sources, the periodical *Bulletin international des sociétés
de secours aux militaires blessés* (founded in 1869) served as a key resource.[1]

This quarterly, published by the ICRC, has provided each national society with space to report its activities and to voice concerns about operational and ethical issues. ICRC circulars, recommendations, and reports similarly appeared in this journal. The *Bulletin* was a key channel of communication for the Red Cross in its first decades, and as such it provides much insight into the self-presentation and self-conception of the movement. In addition, the sermons and letters of Swiss theologians François Louis Gaussen and Jean-Henri Merle d'Aubigné, along with the theological writings of several of their contemporaries, provided insight into the religious teachings that shaped the early Red Cross.

Additional material came both from existing historiographies of the journalistic field, the international law field, the religious field, and the nursing field, and from published works and documents by key actors in those fields in the mid-nineteenth century. In addition, English- and French-language newspaper repositories were consulted in order to better understand how the public sphere mediated the cross-influence between the transnational humanitarian fields and these adjacent fields. Finally, material on the processes under way in the humanitarian field in the 1970s came from published interviews and commentaries by early Médecins sans Frontières activists, as well as those of related movements, along with their existing historiographies.

NOTES

PREFACE

1. "Public Release of Initial MSF Initial Review," Médecins sans Frontières, last modi-fied November 5, 2015, http://www.msf.org/sites/msf.org/files/msf_kunduz_review _041115_for_public_release.pdf/; "Updated Death Toll—42 People Killed in the US Airstrikes on Kunduz Hospital," Médecins sans Frontières, December 12, 2015, http://www.msf.org/en/article/kunduz-updated-death-toll-%E2%80%93-42-people -killed-us-airstrikes-kunduz-hospital.

2. "Afghanistan: UN Strongly Condemns 'Tragic, Inexcusable' Kunduz Hospital Air-strike," UN News, last modified October 3, 2015, https://news.un.org/en/story/2015 /10/511652-afghanistan-un-strongly-condemns-tragic-inexcusable-kunduz-hospital -airstrike.

3. Malaka Gharib, "MSF Director Unsatisfied with Pentagon's 'Admission of Gross Neg-ligence,'" NPR, November 25, 2015, accessed November 18, 2018, https://www.npr .org/sections/goatsandsoda/2015/11/25/457393164/msf-director-unsatisfied-with -pentagons-admission-of-gross-negligence.

4. Hamid Shalizi and Peter Graff, "U.S. Strikes Killed 140 Villagers: Afghan Probe," Reuters, May 16, 2009, accessed November 18, 2018, https://www.reuters.com/article /us-afghanistan-civilians-idUSTRE54E22V20090516. See also Eric Schmitt and Thom Shanker, "U.S. Report Finds Errors in Afghan Airstrikes," New York Times, June 2, 2009, accessed November 18, 2018, https://www.nytimes.com/2009/06/03/world /asia/03military.html.

5. Rod Nordland, "NATO Acknowledges Civilian Deaths in Afghan Airstrike," New York Times, August 6, 2010, A6.

6. "Afghan Urges Obama to End Civilian Deaths," Wall Street Journal, November 6, 2008, 11.

7. Clancy Chassay, "'I Was Still Holding My Grandson's Hand—The Rest Was Gone,'" The Guardian, December 15, 2008, accessed November 29, 2018, https://www .theguardian.com/world/2008/dec/16/afghanistan-taliban-us-foreign-policy/.

INTRODUCTION

1. Alexandra J. Lee, Resilience by Design. Advanced Sciences and Technologies for Security Applications (Cham, Switzerland: Springer, 2016), 57–90.

2. USIP, *Haiti: A Republic of NGOs?* (Washington, DC: United States Institute of Peace Briefs, 2010).

3. Jocelyn Viterna and Cassandra Robertson, "New Directions for the Sociology of Development," *Annual Review of Sociology* 41 (2015): 261.

4. Kathleen Jobe, "Disaster Relief in Post-Earthquake Haiti: Unintended Consequences of Humanitarian Volunteerism," *Travel Medicine and Infectious Disease* 9 (2011): 1–5; Vijaya Ramachandran and Julie Walz, "Haiti: Where Has All the Money Gone?" *Journal of Haitian Studies* 21 (2015): 26–65; Nezih Altay and Melissa Labonte, "Challenges in Humanitarian Information Management and Exchange: Evidence from Haiti," *Disasters* 38 (2014): S50–S72. For examples of similar situations in other states, see James Pfeiffer, "International NGOs and Primary Health Care in Mozambique: The Need for a New Model of Collaboration," *Social Science and Medicine* 56 (2003): 725–738; Stephen Knack, "Aid Dependence and the Quality of Governance: Cross-Country Empirical Tests," *Southern Economic Journal* 68 (2001): 310–329.

5. Oxfam International, *Oxfam Annual Report 2015–2016* (Oxford: Oxfam International, 2016); Médecins sans Frontières, *Médecins sans Frontières 2016 Annual Report* (Geneva: MSF International, 2017); CARE, *CARE USA 2016 Annual Report* (Atlanta, GA: CARE USA, 2017). International relations scholars have further documented the myriad ways in which INGOs increasingly influence global political, economic, and social processes. Margaret E. Keck and Kathryn Sikkink, *Activists beyond Borders: Advocacy Networks in International Politics* (Ithaca, NY: Cornell Univ. Press, 1998); Ann Marie Clark, Elisabeth J. Friedman, and Kathryn Hochstetler, "The Sovereign Limits of Global Civil Society: A Comparison of NGO Participation in UN World Conferences on the Environment, Human Rights, and Women," *World Politics* 51 (1998): 1–35; Richard Price, "Reversing the Gun Sights: Transnational Civil Society Targets Land Mines," *International Organization* 52 (1998): 613–644.

6. Groupe URD, "L'espace humanitaire en danger" (Plaisians, France: Université d'Automne de l'Humanitaire, 2006), 105. See also Michele Acuto, ed., *Negotiating Relief: The Dialectic of Humanitarian Space* (London: C. Hurst, 2014).

7. Sarah Collinson and Samir Elhawary, *Humanitarian Space: A Review of Trends and Issues* (London: Overseas Development Institute, 2012), 1.

8. Several critics have claimed, for example, that humanitarian NGOs employ the notion of *humanitarian emergency* in a way that ultimately benefits their Western donors. See Mark Duffield, *Development, Security, and Unending War: Governing the World of Peoples* (Cambridge, UK: Polity, 2007). For more general discussion of the uses of emergency discourse in humanitarian action, see also Craig J. Calhoun, "The Idea of Emergency: Humanitarian Action and Global Disorder," in *Contemporary States of Emergency: The Politics of Military and Humanitarian Intervention*, ed. Didier Fassin and Mariella Pandolfi (Cambridge, MA: Zone Books, 2010), 29–58; Craig J. Calhoun, "The Imperative to Reduce Suffering: Charity, Progress, and Emergencies in the Field of Humanitarian Action," in *Humanitarianism in Question: Power, Politics, Ethics*, ed. Michael Barnett and Thomas G. Weiss (Ithaca, NY: Cornell Univ. Press, 2008), 73–97.

9. Charitable humanitarian associations with universal aspirations were, of course, not new in themselves in the mid-nineteenth century. Moniz, among others, demonstrates that transatlantic humanitarian societies have worked across borders since the eighteenth century. However, the use of notions like neutrality and impartiality in order to evaluate humanitarian work and to orient a sector dedicated to humanitarianism was new to the 1860s. Chapter 1 will demonstrate this in further detail. See

Amanda B. Moniz, *From Empire to Humanity: The American Revolution and the Origins of Humanitarianism* (New York: Oxford Univ. Press, 2016).

10. Although this committee was established in 1863, it only adopted the name International Committee of the Red Cross in 1876.

11. Geoffrey Best, *Humanity in Warfare: The Modern History of the International Law of Armed Conflicts* (London: Methuen, 1983). See also Cecelia Lynch, "Peace Movements, Civil Society, and the Development of International Law," in *The Oxford Handbook of the History of International Law*, ed. Bardo Fassbender and Anne Peters (Oxford: Oxford Univ. Press, 2012).

12. Comité international de la Croix-Rouge, *La Conférence Internationale réunie à Genève les 26, 27, 28, et 29 Octobre 1863 pour étudier les moyens de pourvoir à l'insuffisance du service sanitaire dans les armées en campagne, deuxième édition* (Geneva: Comité international de la Croix-Rouge, 1904).

13. John Boli and George M. Thomas, eds., *Constructing World Culture: International Nongovernmental Organizations since 1875* (Stanford, CA: Stanford Univ. Press, 1999).

14. E.g., Étienne Balibar, "On the Politics of Human Rights," *Constellations* 20 (2013): 18–26.

15. Michael Ignatieff, *The Lesser Evil: Political Ethics in an Age of Terror* (Edinburgh: Edinburgh Univ. Press, 2004).

16. Other scholars are similarly optimistic about NGO influence on global civil society. See Bryan S. Turner, *Vulnerability and Human Rights* (University Park: Pennsylvania State Univ. Press, 2006); Mary Kaldor, "The Idea of Global Civil Society," *International Affairs* 79 (2003): 583–593; Ann M. Florini, ed. *Third Force: The Rise of Transnational Civil Society* (Washington, DC: Carnegie Endowment for International Peace, 2000).

17. E.g., the *humanitarian governance* approach. See Michael N. Barnett, "Humanitarian Governance," *Annual Review of Political Science* 16 (2013): 379–398.

18. This line of thinking is part of a more general suspicion of international aid and the interests that underlie it. See, for example, Joseph S. Nye, "Public Diplomacy and Soft Power," *Annals of the American Academy of Political and Social Science* 616 (2008): 94–109; Joseph S. Nye, *Soft Power: The Means to Success in World Politics* (New York: Public Affairs, 2004); William F. Schulz, *In Our Own Best Interest: How Defending Human Rights Benefits Us All* (Boston: Beacon Press, 2001); William H. Thornton, "Back to Basics: Human Rights and Power Politics in the New Moral Realism," *International Journal of Politics, Culture, and Society* 14 (2000): 315–332.

19. Nicholas O. Berry, *War and the Red Cross: The Unspoken Mission* (New York: St. Martin's Press, 1997).

20. These critiques have largely remained confined to academic circles, and have made little impact on humanitarian policy. E.g., Michel Agier, "Humanity as an Identity and Its Political Effects (a Note on Camps and Humanitarian Government)," *Humanity* 1 (2010): 29–45; Mariella Pandolfi, "Contract of Mutual (In)difference: Governance and the Humanitarian Apparatus in Contemporary Albania and Kosovo," *India Journal of Global Legal Studies* 10 (2003): 369–381.

21. On points of origin, see Elisabeth S. Clemens, "Toward a Historicized Sociology: Theorizing Events, Processes, and Emergence," *Annual Review of Sociology* 33 (2007): 538; Daniel Hirschman and Isaac Ariail Reed, "Formation Stories and Causality in Sociology," *Sociological Theory* 32 (2014): 274.

22. Although humanitarian NGO work outside of Europe and North America has taken a different trajectory for some of this history, chapter 3 will show that the Geneva-based

Red Cross influenced the humanitarian sector in the Ottoman Empire, Japan, Persia, and other non-Western countries as well.

23. See also Michael Strand, "The Genesis and Structure of Moral Universalism: Social Justice in Victorian Britain, 1834–1901," *Theory and Society* 44 (2015): 537–573.

24. Alex de Waal, *Famine Crimes: Politics and the Disaster Relief Industry in Africa* (Bloomington: Indiana Univ. Press, 1997). See also John Hagan, Heather Schoenfeld, and Alberto Palloni, "The Science of Human Rights, War Crimes, and Humanitarian Emergencies," *Annual Review of Sociology* 32 (2006): 329–349.

25. Daniel P. Scarnecchia et al., "A Rights-based Approach to Information in Humanitarian Assistance," *PLOS Currents*, September 20, 2017; Celestine Nyamu-Musembi and Andrea Cornwall, *What Is the "Rights-based Approach" All About?: Perspectives from International Development Agencies* (Brighton, UK: Institute of Development Studies, 2004), https://www.ids.ac.uk/publication/what-is-the-rights-based-approach-all-about-perspectives-from-international-development-agencies/, accessed March 30, 2018.

26. Abram de Swaan, "Widening Circles of Identification: Emotional Concerns in Sociogenetic Perspective," *Theory, Culture, and Society* 12 (1995): 25–39; Thomas L. Haskell, "Capitalism and the Origins of the Humanitarian Sensibility, Part I," *American Historical Review* 90 (1985): 339–361; Thomas L. Haskell, "Capitalism and the Origins of the Humanitarian Sensibility, Part II," *American Historical Review* 90 (1985): 547–566.

27. Luc Boltanski, *Distant Suffering: Morality, Media, and Politics* (Cambridge: Cambridge Univ. Press, 1999); Eva Illouz, "From the Lisbon Disaster to Oprah Winfrey: Suffering as Identity in the Era of Globalization," in *Global America? The Cultural Consequences of Globalization*, ed. Ulrich Beck, Natan Sznaider, and Rainer Winter (Liverpool, UK: Liverpool Univ. Press, 2003), 189–205.

28. See, for example, David Brion Davis, *The Problem of Slavery in the Age of Revolution, 1770–1823.* (Ithaca, NY: Cornell Univ. Press, 1975).

29. Michael Barnett, *Empire of Humanity: A History of Humanitarianism* (Ithaca, NY: Cornell Univ. Press, 2011).

30. Steven Pinker, *The Better Angels of Our Nature: Why Violence Has Declined* (New York: Penguin Books, 2011). See also Richard Rorty, "Human Rights, Rationality, and Sentimentality," in *On Human Rights*, ed. Stephen Shute and Susan Hurley (New York: Basic Books, 1993), 111–134. However, see also critiques of this approach in Michael Mann, "Have Wars and Violence Declined?" *Theory and Society* 47 (2018): 37–60, and Larry Ray, John Lea, Hilary Rose, and Chetan Bhatt, book review symposium on Steven Pinker, *The Better Angels of Our Nature*, *Sociology* 47, no. 6 (2013): 1224–1232.

31. Miriam Ticktin, "Transnational Humanitarianism," *Annual Review of Anthropology* 43 (2014): 273–289.

32. Didier Fassin, *Humanitarian Reason: A Moral History of the Present* (Berkeley: Univ. of California Press, 2012), 4–5. For a similar approach, see Balibar, "On the Politics of Human Rights."

33. The Red Cross was certainly not the first transnational humanitarian movement, but it was the first to redefine humanitarianism as a social field. For more about preceding societies, see Thomas Davies, "Rethinking the Origins of Transnational Humanitarian Organizations: The Curious Case of the International Shipwreck Society," *Global Networks* 18 (2018): 461–478; Moniz, *From Empire to Humanity.*

34. Martha Finnemore, "Rules of War and Wars of Rules: The International Red Cross and

the Restraint of State Violence," in *Constructing World Culture: International Nongovernmental Organizations since 1875*, ed. John Boli and George M. Thomas (Stanford, CA: Stanford Univ. Press, 1999), 149–165. As Boli and Thomas show in the same volume, the late nineteenth century saw the rapid dissemination of the INGO organizational model. The authors demonstrate that there was indeed a proliferation of INGOs beginning in 1875, but say little about the reasons the INGO model was particularly appealing to humanitarian activists. John Boli and George M. Thomas, "INGOs and the Organization of World Culture," in *Constructing World Culture: International Nongovernmental Organizations since 1875*, ed. John Boli and George M. Thomas (Stanford, CA: Stanford Univ. Press, 1999), 13–49.

35. Comité central belge, "Journal d'une infirmière, par Mme la baronne de Crombrugghe," *Bulletin international des sociétés de secours aux militaires blessés* 2 (1871): 16–20.

36. Lindsay Moir, "The Historical Development of the Application of Humanitarian Law in Non-International Armed Conflict to 1949," *International and Comparative Law Quarterly* 47 (1998): 337–361.

37. Best, *Humanity in Warfare*, 3.

38. For discussion of the effects of international treaties on social organizing, see Tamara Kay, "Labor Transnationalism and Global Governance: The Impact of NAFTA on Transnational Labor Relationships in North America," *American Journal of Sociology* 111 (2005): 715–756; Tamara Kay, "Legal Transnationalism: The Relationship between Transnational Social Movement Building and International Law," *Law and Social Inquiry* 36 (2011): 419–454.

39. John F. Hutchinson, "Rethinking the Origins of the Red Cross," *Bulletin of the History of Medicine* 63, no. 4 (1989): 557–578.

40. Monika Krause, *The Good Project: Humanitarian Relief NGOs and the Fragmentation of Reason* (Chicago: Univ. of Chicago Press, 2014), provides a compelling analysis of the struggles for domination inherent to the transnational humanitarian field. For an analysis of the often-contentious relations between aid organizations, see also Sarah S. Stroup, *Borders among Activists: International NGOs in the United States, Britain, and France* (Ithaca, NY: Cornell Univ. Press, 2012).

41. Abby Stoddard suggests that some humanitarian NGOs have developed a new paradigm over the twentieth century, straying from the original Red Cross template and becoming more amenable to cooperation with states and longer-term development work. While this shift is certainly noticeable, such organizations typically continue to define their work in terms of the Red Cross principles, which are the main concern of this book. See Abby Stoddard, "Humanitarian NGOs: Challenges and Trends," *HPG Briefing* 12 (2003): 1–4.

42. Fiona Terry, *Condemned to Repeat? The Paradox of Humanitarian Action* (Ithaca, NY: Cornell Univ. Press, 2002), 18.

43. For example, Voltaire's *Poème sur le désastre de Lisbonne* and *Candide*, or Kant's *Idea for a Universal History from a Cosmopolitan Point of View*.

44. See Peter Stamatov, "Activist Religion, Empire, and the Emergence of Modern Long-Distance Advocacy Networks," *American Sociological Review* 75 (2010): 607–28; Peter Stamatov, *The Origins of Global Humanitarianism: Religion, Empires, and Advocacy* (Cambridge: Cambridge Univ. Press, 2013).

45. Michael P. Young, *Bearing Witness against Sin: The Evangelical Birth of the American Social Movement* (Chicago: Univ. of Chicago Press, 2006). For another example, see

Robert Braun, "Religious Minorities and Resistance to Genocide: The Collective Rescue of Jews in the Netherlands during the Holocaust," *American Political Science Review* 110 (2016): 127–147.

46. This is not to discount the role religious organizations have had in providing the justifications for enslavement and segregation to begin with. See Stephen R. Haynes, *Noah's Curse: The Biblical Justification of American Slavery* (Oxford: Oxford Univ. Press, 2002); Larry Morrison, "The Religious Defense of American Slavery before 1830," *Journal of Religious Thought* 37 (1980): 16–29; Mitchell Snay, *Gospel of Disunion: Religion and Separatism in the Antebellum South* (Chapel Hill: Univ. of North Carolina Press, 1997).

47. A story about Calvinism giving rise to lasting social arrangements may immediately evoke Max Weber's *The Protestant Ethic and the Spirit of Capitalism*. However, this book draws instead on Weber's notion of sphere differentiation developed in *Religious Rejections of the World and Their Directions* because it focuses on the differentiation of new fields, rather than on the emotional outcomes of religious beliefs (namely the anxiety caused by Puritans' uncertainty about their fate) and their effects on social and economic behavior (i.e., proto-capitalism), which is the chief concern of *The Protestant Ethic*.

48. See Susanne Baer, "Privatizing Religion, Legal Groupism, No-Go-Areas, and the Public-Private-Ideology in Human Rights Politics," *Constellations* 20 (2013): 68–84. This view is part of a more general tendency of social historians to minimize the role of religion in the shaping of macro-level history, and especially in the shaping of modernity. See Philip S. Gorski, "The Return of the Repressed: Religion and the Political Unconscious of Historical Sociology," in *Remaking Modernity: Politics, History, and Sociology*, ed. Julia Adams, Elisabeth S. Clemens, and Ann Shola Orloff (Durham: Duke Univ. Press, 2005), 161–189; Penny Edgell, "A Cultural Sociology of Religion: New Directions," *Annual Review of Sociology* 38 (2012): 247–265; Philip S. Gorski and Ateş Altınordu, "After Secularization?" *Annual Review of Sociology* 34 (2008): 55–85.

49. Craig J. Calhoun, "For the Social History of the Present: Bourdieu as Historical Sociologist," in *Bourdieu and Historical Analysis*, ed. Philip S. Gorski (Durham, NC: Duke Univ. Press, 2013), 36–66.

50. For elaborate discussion, see Pierre Bourdieu, *The Field of Cultural Production: Essays on Art and Literature* (New York: Columbia Univ. Press, 1993).

51. Monika Krause, "Reporting and the Transformations of the Journalistic Field: US News Media, 1890–2000," *Media, Culture, and Society* 33 (2011): 90.

52. On field-specific capital, see also Pierre Bourdieu, *Practical Reason* (Cambridge: Polity Press, 1998 [1994]), 19–34.

53. Philip S. Gorski, "Bourdieusian Theory and Historical Analysis: Maps, Mechanisms, and Methods," in *Bourdieu and Historical Analysis*, ed. Philip S. Gorski (Durham, NC: Duke Univ. Press, 2013), 329.

54. Pierre Bourdieu, *The Rules of Art: The Genesis and Structure of the Literary Field* (Cambridge: Polity Press, 1996).

55. Existing scholarship in field analysis has tended to address field emergence in two different ways. Some authors have analyzed already-existing fields and, while acknowledging their historicity, have left aside questions of what caused these fields to emerge and what alternative paths could have shaped them differently (or, for that matter, precluded their appearance) (e.g., Helmut K. Anheier, Jürgen Gerhards, and Frank P. Romo, "Forms of Capital and Social Structure in Cultural Fields: Examining Bourdieu's Social Topography," *American Journal of Sociology* 100 [1995]: 859–

903; Damon Mayrl, "Fields, Logics, and Social Movements: Prison Abolition and the Social Justice Field," *Sociological Inquiry* 83 [2013]: 286–309). Other authors—Bourdieu included—have provided descriptive accounts of field formation by demonstrating that one type of social action came to be organized under an independent logic at a certain point in time, and that a competition for prestige and domination ensued around it. However, such work has offered little in terms of explaining what caused actors to believe that an autonomous realm dedicated to one form of action was indeed necessary (e.g., Bourdieu, *The Rules of Art*; Krause, "Reporting and the Transformations of the Journalistic Field"; Stephanie Lee Mudge, "What's Left of Leftism? Neoliberal Politics in Western Party Systems, 1945–2004," *Social Science History* 35 [2011]: 337–380).

56. Although Bourdieu intended field theory to account for both the structural and cultural sides of social hierarchies, he was explicit about the precedence the objective features of the field take in the emergence of new fields. This reflects his more general view of "principles of vision and di-vision" having a causal effect on social structure only insofar as they serve specific parties' structural interests. See Pierre Bourdieu, "The Force of Law: Toward a Sociology of the Juridical Field," *Hastings Law Journal* 38 (1987): 805–1297, and Pierre Bourdieu, "Rethinking the State: Genesis and Structure of the Bureaucratic Field," in *State/Culture: State Formation after the Cultural Turn*, ed. George Steinmetz, trans. Loïc J. D. Wacquant and Samar Farage (Ithaca, NY: Cornell Univ. Press, 1999), 53–94. Bourdieu spelled out his more general view of the relation between social and symbolic space in Pierre Bourdieu, Gisele Sapiro, and Brian McHale, "First Lecture. Social Space and Symbolic Space: Introduction to a Japanese Reading of Distinction," *Poetics Today* 12 (1991): 627–638. For a critical assessment, see also Mustafa Emirbayer and Erik Schneiderhan, "Dewey and Bourdieu on Democracy," in *Bourdieu and Historical Analysis*, ed. Philip S. Gorski (Durham, NC: Duke Univ. Press, 2013), 131–157.

57. Bourdieu, *The Rules of Art*, 61. Numerous works have expanded on the role of culture in field, but have retained the view that the cultural side of a field is harnessed to its objective structure. See, for example, Barış Büyükokutan, "Toward a Theory of Cultural Appropriation: Buddhism, the Vietnam War, and the Field of U.S. Poetry," *American Sociological Review* 76 (2011): 620–639; Joanne Entwistle and Agnès Rocamora, "The Field of Fashion Materialized: A Study of London Fashion Week," *Sociology* 40 (2006): 735–751; Agnès Rocamora, "Fields of Fashion: Critical Insights into Bourdieu's Sociology of Culture," *Journal of Consumer Culture* 2 (2002): 341–362; George Steinmetz, *The Devil's Handwriting: Precoloniality and the German Colonial State in Qingdao, Samoa, and Southwest Africa* (Chicago: Univ. of Chicago Press, 2007); George Steinmetz, "The Colonial State as a Social Field: Ethnographic Capital and Native Policy in the German Overseas Empire before 1914," *American Sociological Review* 73 (2008): 589–612.

58. For full elaboration on the theoretical assumptions here, see Shai M. Dromi, "Soldiers of the Cross: Calvinism, Humanitarianism, and the Genesis of Social Fields," *Sociological Theory* 34 (2016): 196–219. My approach conjoins field analysis with the Strong Program in Cultural Sociology, which sees culture—as beliefs, codes, narratives, symbols, and values—as an active participant in shaping social, political, demographic, and economic processes. See Jeffrey C. Alexander, "The Reality of Reduction: The Failed Synthesis of Pierre Bourdieu," in *Fin-de-Siècle Social Theory: Relativism, Reduction, and the Problem of Reason* (London: Verso, 1995), 128–217; Jeffrey C. Alexander and Philip Smith. "The Strong Program in Cultural Sociology: Elements

of a Structural Hermeneutics," in *The Meanings of Social Life: A Cultural Sociology*, by Jeffrey C. Alexander (Oxford: Oxford Univ. Press, 2003), 11–26.

CHAPTER 1

1. The ICRC also acknowledges the motto *Per humanitatem ad pacem* (With humanity, toward peace), which—since 1961—has been used more widely by the International Federation of the Red Cross (IFRC). See International Committee of the Red Cross, "Statutes of the International Committee of the Red Cross," March 10, 2013, https://www.icrc.org/eng/resources/documents/misc/icrc-statutes-080503.htm/.

2. Reportedly, the French military prepared crates with dressings that were not used due to poor organization in the battlefield and were sent back unopened to France after the battle. François Bugnion, "Birth of an Idea: The Founding of the International Committee of the Red Cross and of the International Red Cross and Red Crescent Movement: From Solferino to the Original Geneva Convention (1859–1864)," *International Review of the Red Cross* 94 (2012): 1304.

3. Henry Dunant, *A Memory of Solferino* (Washington, DC: American National Red Cross, 1939).

4. Norman H. Davis, preface to *A Memory of Solferino*, by J. Henry Dunant (Washington, DC: American National Red Cross, 1939), 5–16.

5. Historiographies of the ICRC have tended to emphasize Dunant's role in establishing the movement, but Gustave Moynier—described by Caroline Moorehead as a level-headed counterweight to Dunant's excitable evangelicalism—steered the committee for most of its first five decades of existence. Moynier was in many ways the one who shaped the committee and its international influence. Compare Jean de Senarclens, *Gustave Moynier le bâtisseur* (Geneva: Slatkine, 2000), to Pierre Boissier, *Henry Dunant* (Geneva: Henry Dunant Institute, 1974), and Corinne Chaponnière, *Henry Dunant: La Croix d'un homme* (Paris: Perrin, 2010).

6. For full history of the movement, Henry Dunant, and the Geneva Convention from the ICRC perspective, see Pierre Boissier, *From Solferino to Tsushima: History of the International Committee of the Red Cross* (Geneva: Henry Dunant Institute, 1985).

7. See, for example, Gérard A. Jaeger, *Henry Dunant: l'homme qui inventa le droit humanitaire* (Paris: L'Archipel, 2009), and David Rieff, *A Bed for the Night: Humanitarianism in Crisis* (New York: Simon & Schuster, 2002), 68–69.

8. Sandra Singer, "The Protection of Children During Armed Conflict Situations," *International Review of the Red Cross* 26 (1986): 138; Robin M. Coupland, "The Effects of Weapons and the Solferino Cycle: Where Disciplines Meet to Prevent or Limit the Damage Caused by Weapons," *British Medical Journal* 319 (1999): 864.

9. Alan Hankinson, *Man of Wars: William Howard Russell of The Times* (London: Heineman, 1982); Ilana D. Miller, *Reports from America: William Howard Russell and the Civil War* (Stroud: Sutton, 2001); Dale L. Walker, *Januarius MacGahan: The Life and Campaigns of an American War Correspondent* (Athens: Ohio Univ. Press, 1988); Leslie Williams, "Irish Identity and the Illustrated London News, 1846–1851," in *Representing Ireland: Gender, Class, Nationality*, ed. Susan S. Sailer (Gainesville: Univ. Press of Florida, 1997), 59–93.

10. Leighton S. James, *Witnessing the Revolutionary and Napoleonic Wars in German Central Europe* (New York: Palgrave Macmillan, 2013); Peter Paret, *Understanding War: Essays on Clausewitz and the History of Military Power* (Princeton, NJ: Princeton Univ. Press, 1992).

11. See, for example, Faust's compelling study of the effects of mass communication on

the families of Civil War soldiers in America. Drew Gilpin Faust, *This Republic of Suffering: Death and the American Civil War* (New York: Alfred A. Knopf, 2008).

12. John F. Hutchinson, "Rethinking the Origins of the Red Cross," *Bulletin of the History of Medicine* 63 (1989): 557–578.

13. In other words, *nomothets*. See George Steinmetz, "Bourdieu, Historicity, and Historical Sociology," *Cultural Sociology* 5 (2011): 54.

14. Eva Illouz, *Hard-Core Romance: Fifty Shades of Grey, Best-Sellers, and Society* (Chicago: Univ. of Chicago Press, 2014), 23. More broadly, social historians have long recognized the importance of accessible "recipes" for social action in facilitating humanitarian sentiments and action. See Thomas L. Haskell, "Capitalism and the Origins of the Humanitarian Sensibility, Part 1," *American Historical Review* 90 (1985): 339–361, and Thomas L. Haskell, "Capitalism and the Origins of the Humanitarian Sensibility, Part 2," *American Historical Review* 90 (1985): 547–566. For a more general discussion of resonance between texts and social experience, see also Terence E. McDonnell, Christopher A. Bail, and Iddo Tavory, "A Theory of Resonance," *Sociological Theory* 3, no. 1 (2017): 1–14. See extended examples in Terence E. McDonnell, *Best Laid Plans: Cultural Entropy and the Unraveling of AIDS Media Campaigns* (Chicago: Univ. of Chicago Press, 2016).

15. For details on mid-nineteenth-century war practices, see David A. Bell, *The First Total War: Napoleon's Europe and the Birth of Warfare as We Know It* (Boston: Mariner Books, 2007); Geoffrey Parker, "Early Modern Europe," in *The Laws of War: Constraints on Warfare in the Western World*, ed. Michael Howard, George J. Andreopoulos, and Mark R. Shulman (New Haven, CT: Yale Univ. Press, 1994), 40–54; Meyer Kestnbaum, "Mars Revealed: The Entry of Ordinary People into War among States," in *Remaking Modernity: Politics, History, and Sociology*, ed. Julia Adams, Elisabeth S. Clemens, and Ann Shola Orloff (Durham, NC: Duke Univ. Press, 2005), 249–285; Robert J. Trout, *Memoirs of the Stuart Horse Artillery Battalion: Moorman's and Hart's Batteries* (Knoxville: Univ. of Tennessee Press, 2008); Mark Grimsley, *The Hard Hand of War: Union Policy toward Southern Civilians, 1861–1865* (New York: Cambridge Univ. Press, 1997); Michael Howard, *The Franco-Prussian War: The German Invasion of France, 1870–1871* (London: Routledge, 2001); James A. Huston, *The Sinews of War: Army Logistics, 1775–1953* (Washington, DC: Center of Military History, United States Army, 1988).

16. John Ellis, *The Social History of the Machine Gun* (Baltimore, MD: Johns Hopkins Univ. Press, 1986).

17. For details about battlefield medical conditions, see John S. Haller, *Battlefield Medicine: A History of the Military Ambulance from the Napoleonic Wars through World War I* (Carbondale: Southern Illinois Univ. Press, 2011); Richard Holmes, *Redcoat: The British Soldier in the Age of Horse and Musket* (London: Harper Collins, 2001), 89–90.

18. E.g., Charles Lueder, *La convention de Genève au point de vue historique, critique, et dogmatique* (Paris: C. Reinwald & C., 1876).

19. Caroline Moorehead, *Dunant's Dream: War, Switzerland, and the History of the Red Cross* (New York: Carroll & Graf Publishers, 1999), 25.

20. See Marty Sulek, "The Last Romantic War, the First Modern War: The Crimean War of 1854–1856 and the Genesis of Contemporary Wartime Humanitarian Relief" (unpublished manuscript).

21. King-Thom Chung, *Women Pioneers of Medical Research: Biographies of 25 Outstanding Scientists* (Jefferson, NC: McFarland, 2010).

22. Andrew N. Wilson, *The Victorians* (New York: Norton, 2003), 175–178.

23. E.g., Mary A. Livermore, *My Story of the War: A Woman's Narrative of Four Years Personal Experience as Nurse in the Union Army, and in Relief Work at Home, in Hospitals, Camps, and at the Front during the War of the Rebellion* (Hartford, CT: A. D. Worthington, 1896). For more general discussion of medicine during the American Civil War, see Frank R. Freemon, *Gangrene and Glory: Medical Care during the American Civil War* (Urbana: Univ. of Illinois Press, 2001).

24. The French Société de secours aux blessés militaires—an antecedent of the French Red Cross—noted as early as 1865 in its bulletin its close acquaintance with the Sanitary Commission, and thanked the commission for sending books on their work. Société de secours aux blessés militaires (France), "Bibliographie," *Bulletin de la Société de secours aux blessés militaires des armées de terre et de mer* 1 (1865): 4.

25. For details about faith-based relief organizations, see Arthur C. Breycha-Vauther and Michael Potulicki, "The Order of St. John in International Law: A Forerunner of the Red Cross," *American Journal of International Law* 48 (1954): 554–563; Henry J. A. Sire, *The Knights of Malta* (New Haven, CT: Yale Univ. Press, 1994).

26. E.g., Louis Paul Appia, *Les blessés dans le Schleswig pendant la guerre de 1864: rapport présenté au Comité international de Genève* (Geneva: Jules-Guillaume Fick, 1864). While the Rauhe Haus was a Protestant home for troubled youth, it also supported a "Field Deacons" service ("Felddiakonie") that provided medical assistance on the battlefields in the 1864, 1866, and 1870–1871 Prussian wars. According to the German Red Cross, the Field Deacons were among the first to wear the red cross armband. Volkmar Schön, "Hamburger Betrachtungen zum Rotkreuzzeichen," *Notizen zur Hamburger Rotkreuzgeschichte* 5 (2015): 3.

27. Union League Club, *In Memoriam, Henry Whitney Bellows, D.D.* (New York: G. P. Putnam's Sons, 1882).

28. Debbie Blake, *Daughters of Ireland: Pioneering Irish Women* (Dublin: History Press Ireland, 2015). The Sisters of Mercy were often applauded, but they were greeted at times with suspicion of being untrained and ill-suited for the battlefield.

29. British Quarterly Review, "Christian Work on the Battle-field; Being Incidents of the Labours of the United States 'Christian Commission,'" *British Quarterly Review* 52 (1870): 564.

30. Mark Mazower, *Governing the World: The History of an Idea, 1815 to the Present* (New York: Penguin Books, 2013). Over the late nineteenth century, there was a significant increase in international legal instruments; see Michael A. Elliott, "The Institutional Expansion of Human Rights, 1863–2003: A Comprehensive Dataset of International Instruments," *Journal of Peace Research* 48 (2011): 537–546.

31. Roger Durand and Jacques Meurant, *Préludes et pionniers: les précurseurs de la Croix-Rouge, 1840–1860* (Geneva: Société Henry Dunant, 1991).

32. Henri Arrault, *Notice sur le perfectionnement du matériel des ambulances volantes* (Paris: Victor Rozier, 1861).

33. Francis Trépardoux, "Henri Arrault, précurseur de la convention de Genève, promoteur des ambulances volantes et ami de George Sand," *Revue d'histoire de la pharmacie* 94 (2006): 61–89.

34. Michael J. Gunn and Hilaire McCoubrey, "Medical Ethics and the Laws of Armed Conflict," *Journal of Armed Conflict Law* 3 (1998): 133–162.

35. Palasciano gave two addresses at the Accademia Pontaniana in Naples on the subject, on April 28, 1861, and December 29, 1861. Both were titled "La neutralità dei feriti in tempo di Guerra." They were included in Gaetano Mazzoni, *La neutralità dei feriti in guerra: Studio storico* (Naples: Croce Rossa Italiana, 1895), 22–31 and 37–43.

36. Mazzoni, *La neutralità*, 29.
37. E.g., Ferdinando Palasciano, *Dritto delle genti lettera su convenzione di Ginevra per neutralità dei feriti* (Naples: Tipografia di Angelo Trani, 1871). The story of Palasciano's precedence over Dunant in advocating for neutrality on the battlefield continued to circulate over the late-nineteenth-century, including in top medical journals, e.g., The Lancet, "Relief of the wounded in war," *The Lancet*, February 29, 1896, 592–593.
38. Burrus M. Carnahan, "Lincoln, Lieber, and the Laws of War: The Origins and Limits of the Principle of Military Necessity," *American Journal of International Law* 92 (1998): 213–231.
39. For further discussion of the differences between the Geneva Convention and the Lieber Code, see John Fabian Witt, "Two Conceptions of Suffering in War," in *Knowing the Suffering of Others: Legal Perspectives on Pain and Its Meanings*, ed. Austin Sarat (Tuscaloosa: Univ. of Alabama Press, 2014), 129–157.
40. For an intellectual history of the various peace movements in nineteenth-century Europe, see Thomas Hippler and Miloš Vec, *Paradoxes of Peace in Nineteenth Century Europe* (Oxford: Oxford Univ. Press, 2015).
41. Peter Stamatov, *The Origins of Global Humanitarianism: Religion, Empires, and Advocacy* (Cambridge: Cambridge Univ. Press, 2013).
42. While Mennonites and other radical Protestant denominations also participated in such advocacy, Quakers were the key religious peace activists at this time.
43. Robert Mardsen, "First Address to the Public of the Society for the Promotion of Universal and Permanent Peace, January 9, 1817," Swarthmore College Peace Collection, box 1, no. 3.
44. For more information about the main peace societies and their views on the Red Cross, see André Durand, "Gustave Moynier and the Peace Societies," *International Review of the Red Cross* 36 (1996): 532–550.
45. Mardsen, "First Address to the Public of the Society for the Promotion of Universal and Permanent Peace, January 9, 1817."
46. For more elaborate close reading, see David Warner, "Henry Dunant's Imagined Community: Humanitarianism and the Tragic," *Alternatives: Global, Local, Political* 38 (2012): 3–28.
47. Geoffrey Best, *Humanity in Warfare: The Modern History of the International Law of Armed Conflicts* (London: Methuen, 1983), 134–138.
48. Mary Seacole, *The Wonderful Adventures of Mrs. Seacole in Many Lands* (Oxford: Oxford Univ. Press, 1988 [1857]), 73.
49. Ibid., 148.
50. E.g., Emma Maria Pearson and Louisa Elisabeth MacLaughlin, *Our Adventures during the War of 1870* (London: Richard Bentley and Son, 1871); Emma Maria Pearson and Louisa Elisabeth MacLaughlin, *Service in Servia under the Red Cross* (London: Tinsley Brothers, 1877).
51. Louisa May Alcott, *The Journals of Louisa May Alcott*, ed. Joel Myerson and Daniel Shealy (Boston, MA: Little, Brown, 1989), 105.
52. On the Victorian "art" of dying, see Drew Gilpin Faust, *This Republic of Suffering: Death and the American Civil War* (New York: Alfred A. Knopf, 2008); Thomas A. Kselman, *Death and Afterlife in Modern France* (Princeton, NJ: Princeton Univ. Press, 1993).
53. On state commemoration, see Jay Winter, *Sites of Memory, Sites of Mourning: The Great War in European Cultural History* (Cambridge: Cambridge Univ. Press, 1995); David A. Bell, *The First Total War: Napoleon's Europe and the Birth of Warfare as We Know It* (Boston: Mariner Books, 2007).

54. Regarding burial practices in nineteenth-century militaries, see Timothy W. Wolfe and Clifton D. Bryant, "'Full Military Honors': Ceremonial Interment as Sacred Compact," in *Handbook of Death and Dying*, ed. Clifton D. Bryant (Thousand Oaks, CA: Sage Publications, 2003), 159–172.

55. Sally Morgenstern, "Henri Dunant and the Red Cross," *Bulletin of the New York Academy of Medicine* 57 (1981): 311–326.

56. By contrast, Bourdieusian analysis usually starts not in the preexisting beliefs and tastes of the early members of a field but rather by examining the objective appearance of new social spaces that are relatively autonomous from extraneous influences. Bourdieu claimed that only once such relatively autonomous space has materialized will "those who mean to assert themselves as fully fledged members of the [field] . . . feel the need to manifest their independence with respect to external powers, political or economic." Pierre Bourdieu, *The Rules of Art: Genesis and Structure of the Literary Field* (Cambridge: Polity Press, 1996), 61.

57. Raimonda Ottaviani et al., "The First Nobel Peace Prize Henry Dunant (Founder of the International Red Cross) and His 'Memoires,'" *Vesalius* 9 (2003): 27.

CHAPTER 2

1. Martha Finnemore, "Rules of War and Wars of Rules: The International Red Cross and the Restraint of State Violence," in *Constructing World Culture: International Nongovernmental Organizations since 1875*, edited by John Boli and George M. Thomas (Stanford, CA: Stanford Univ. Press, 1999), 149–165; John F. Hutchinson, "Rethinking the Origins of the Red Cross," *Bulletin of the History of Medicine* 63, no. 4 (1989): 557–578; John F. Hutchinson, *Champions of Charity: War and the Rise of the Red Cross* (Boulder, CO: Westview Press, 1996).

2. E.g., Steven Shapin and Simon Schaffer, *Leviathan and the Air-Pump: Hobbes, Boyle, and the Experimental Life* (Princeton, NJ: Princeton Univ. Press, 1985); Eva Illouz, *Saving the Modern Soul: Therapy, Emotions, and the Culture of Self-Help* (Berkeley: Univ. of California Press, 2008).

3. Philip S. Gorski, *The Disciplinary Revolution: Calvinism and the Rise of the State in Early Modern Europe* (Chicago: Univ. of Chicago Press, 2003); Sigrun Kahl, "The Religious Roots of Modern Poverty Policy: Catholic, Lutheran, and Reformed Protestant Traditions Compared," *European Journal of Sociology* 46 (2005): 91–126.

4. Gustave Moynier and Louis Amédée Appia, *Help for Sick and Wounded: Being a Translation of "La Guerre et la Charité," Together with Other Writings on the Subject by Officers of Her Majesty's Service*, trans. John Furley (London: J. C. Hotten, 1870), 293.

5. Ibid.

6. See Michael Barnett, *Empire of Humanity: A History of Humanitarianism* (Ithaca, NY: Cornell Univ. Press, 2011); Craig Calhoun, "The Imperative to Reduce Suffering: Charity, Progress, and Emergencies in the Field of Humanitarian Action," in *Humanitarianism in Question: Politics, Power, Ethics*, ed. Michael Barnett and Thomas Weiss (Ithaca, NY: Cornell Univ. Press, 2008), 73–97.

7. The authors also describe national sentiments as an important motivation for humane conduct and for philanthropic undertakings at times of war. Such assertions are quite at odds with contemporary sensibilities concerning transnational humanitarianism, considering the tendency of present-day intellectuals to view nationalism as anticivil and reactionary, and will be explored in detail in chapter 3. See Jeffrey C. Alexander, "Modern, Anti, Post, and Neo: How Intellectuals Explain 'Our Time,'"

in *The Meanings of Social Life: A Cultural Sociology*, by Jeffrey C. Alexander (Oxford: Oxford Univ. Press, 2003), 193–228.

8. Brian R. Mitchell, *International Historical Statistics: Europe, 1750–1993*, 4th ed. (New York: Stockton Press, 1998), 74–76.

9. In 1850, Zurich had 41,585 inhabitants and Bern had 29,670 inhabitants. "Dictionnaire historique de la Suisse," January 25, 2018, http://www.hls-dhs-dss.ch/f/home.

10. The city had 21,327 inhabitants within city walls in 1798, compared to 12,000 in Bern, 10,500 in Zurich, and 14,700 in Basel; see Olivier Perroux and Michel Oris, "Religion Affiliations in Early Nineteenth Century Geneva: The Emergence of Catholics in the 'Calvinist Rome'" (paper presented at the annual meeting of the Social Science History Association, Baltimore, Maryland, November 13–16, 2003).

11. Scott M. Manetsch, *Calvin's Company of Pastors: Pastoral Care and the Emerging Reformed Church, 1536–1609* (Oxford: Oxford Univ. Press, 2013).

12. Robert M. Kingdon, "Calvin and the Establishment of Consistory Discipline in Geneva: The Institution and the Men Who Directed It," *Dutch Review of Church History* 70 (1990): 158–172.

13. Patrick Collinson, "England and International Calvinism 1558–1640," in *International Calvinism, 1541–1715*, ed. Menna Prestwich (New York: Clarendon Press of Oxford Univ. Press, 1985), 197–223.

14. Perroux and Oris, "Religion Affiliations in Early Nineteenth Century Geneva," 4–5.

15. The Montauban Academy remained secondary to Geneva, as also evidenced by its own self-stylization as "Geneva of the Midi." For further discussion of Geneva under Napoleon, see Kenneth J. Stewart, *Restoring the Reformation: British Evangelicalism and the Francophone "Réveil" 1816–1849* (Milton Keynes, UK: Paternoster, 2006), 48–50.

16. For more on the specific features of Geneva and their contribution to the emergence of the ICRC, see François Bugnion, "Geneva and the Red Cross," *International Committee of the Red Cross* (2005), accessed March 24, 2018, https://www.icrc.org/eng/assets/files/other/geneve_et_croix_rouge_anglais.pdf/.

17. This cross-confessional cooperation was intensified by the mood of millennial optimism that pervaded many Protestant quarters during the nineteenth century. See Timothy L. Hall, *Religion in America* (New York: Facts on File, 2007).

18. Timothy C. F. Stunt, *From Awakening to Secession: Radical Evangelicals in Switzerland and Britain, 1815–35* (Edinburgh: T&T Clark, 2000), 25–26.

19. Ami Bost, *Mémoires pouvant servir à l'histoire du réveil religieux des Églises protestantes de la Suisse et de la France: et à l'intelligence des principales questions théologiques et ecclésiastiques du jour* (Paris: C. Meyrueis, 1854–1855), 36.

20. Réveil theologians at the time were fervently anti-Catholic and saw themselves in direct conflict with Rome. Gaussen wrote, "Never did the Church of Christ more need all the armour which God has provided for it against the apostasy of Rome, than it does at this time. There is a great revival of the mystery of iniquity. This might justly have been anticipated. Its fall is to be with violence, suddenness, and at once. We may expect that as Jezebel of old, just before her destruction, *painted her face, and tired her head, and looked out of her window*, hoping to win her enemies by her deceitful charms, so her true antitype, Popery, will now put on all its show and attraction." Louis Gaussen, *Geneva and Rome: Rome Papal as Portrayed by Prophecy and History* (London: W. H. Dalton, 1844), 3 (italics in original). About the changing social relations in Geneva at the time, see also Jeannine E. Olson, "Social Welfare and the Transformation of Polity in Geneva," in *The Identity of Geneva: The Christian*

Commonwealth, 1564–1864, ed. John B. Roney and Martin I. Klauber (Westport, CT: Greenwood Press, 1998), 155–168.

21. Jean-Jacques-Caton Chenevière, *Première lettre à un ami sur l'état actuel de l'église de Genève, et sur quelques-unes des accusations intentées contre ses pasteurs* (Geneva: J.-J. Paschoud, 1817), 9.

22. Blanche Biéler, *Un fils du refuge, Jean-Henri Merle d'Aubigné: ses origines, sa vie, son œuvre* (Geneva, Éditions Labor, 1934).

23. Stunt, *From Awakening to Secession*, 94–102.

24. Stewart, *Restoring the Reformation*, 96.

25. Jean-Henri Merle d'Aubigné, *La pierre sur laquelle l'académie de Genève fut posée en Juin 1559* (Geneva: E. Beroud, 1859), 17.

26. Jean-Henri Merle d'Aubigné, *Discours sur l'étude de l'histoire du christianisme et son utilité pour l'époque actuelle* (Paris: J. J. Risler; Geneva: A. Cherbuliez, 1832), 12–13.

27. E.g., Jean-Henri Merle d'Aubigné, *Jean Calvin, un des fondateurs des libertés modernes: Discours prononcé a Genève pour l'inauguration de la Salle de la Réformation, le 26 septembre 1867* (Paris: Grassart, 1868).

28. Michael Walzer, *The Revolution of the Saints: A Study in the Origins of Radical Politics* (Cambridge, MA: Harvard Univ. Press, 1965), 167.

29. Although Abraham Kuyper, founder of Neo-Calvinism, was a generation younger, he was a follower of the movement and his writings are statements of the overall Réveil theology. See Dirk Jellema, "Abraham Kuyper's Attack on Liberalism," *Review of Politics* 19 (1957): 472–485; Bob Goudzwaard, "Christian Social Thought in the Dutch Neo-Calvinist Tradition," in *Religion, Economics, and Social Thought: Proceedings of an International Conference* (Vancouver, BC: Fraser Institute, 1986), 251–279.

30. Abraham Kuyper, "Calvinism, a Life-System," in *Lectures on Calvinism* (New York: Cosimo Inc., 2007), 23. Kuyper represents a strand of Dutch Calvinism deeply affected by the Réveil.

31. Gorski, *The Disciplinary Revolution*, 55–59.

32. Bruce Gordon, *The Swiss Reformation* (Manchester: Manchester Univ. Press, 2002), 317–318.

33. By contrast, in the nineteenth-century Lutheranism and Catholicism were still very much devoted to the "confessional state" vision.

34. Abraham Kuyper, "Calvinism and Politics," in *Lectures on Calvinism* (New York: Cosimo Inc., 2007), 80–81.

35. Abraham Kuyper, *The Problem of Poverty* (Washington, DC: Center for Public Justice; Grand Rapids, MI: Baker Book House, 1991).

36. John B. Roney, *The Inside of History: Jean-Henri Merle d'Aubigné and Romantic Historiography* (Westport, CT: Greenwood Press, 1996), 99–100.

37. Daniel Warner, "Henry Dunant's Imagined Community: Humanitarianism and the Tragic," *Alternatives: Global, Local, Political* 38 (2013): 3–28.

38. Monica E. Baly, *Nursing and Social Change* (London: Heinemann Medical, 1973); Lynn McDonald, ed. *Florence Nightingale: An Introduction to Her Life and Family*, vol. 1 (Waterloo: Wilfrid Laurier Univ. Press, 2001).

39. Pierre Boissier, *From Solferino to Tsushima: History of the International Committee of the Red Cross* (Geneva: Henry Dunant Institute, 1985), 193–194. Like many other young Protestant social activists at the time, Dunant recounted a deep spiritual experience from his youth, which instilled in him a sense of calling to help others and a renewed commitment to Christianity. Corinne Chaponnière, *Henry Dunant: La croix d'un homme* (Paris: Perrin, 2010), 30.

40. Pierre Boissier, "Les premières années de la Croix-Rouge," *Revue Internationale de la Croix-Rouge* 45 (1963): 114–132.

41. International conferences are a vital site for INGOs such as the ICRC to establish themselves, providing a networking hub to strengthen social ties, an opportunity to formulate and communicate explicit ideas and theories, and a space in which to perform shared understandings of the identity of the organization. See Margaret E. Keck and Kathryn Sikkink, "Transnational Advocacy Networks in International and Regional Politics," *International Social Science Journal* 51 (1999): 93.

42. François Bugnion, "Birth of an Idea: The Founding of the International Committee of the Red Cross and of the International Red Cross and Red Crescent Movement: From Solferino to the Original Geneva Convention (1859–1864)," *International Review of the Red Cross* 94 (2012): 1299–1338.

43. Société genevoise d'utilité publique. *Compte-rendu de la Conférence internationale réunie a Genève les 26, 27, 28, 29 Oct. 1863 pour étudier les moyens de pourvoir a l'insuffisance du Service sanitaire dans les Armées en campagne* (Geneva: Imprimerie de Jules-Guillaume Fick, 1863), 7.

44. Mark Mazower, *Governing the World: The History of an Idea, 1815 to the Present* (New York: Penguin Press, 2013).

45. Letter from Henry Dunant to Herrn Dr. med Kolb, December 26, 1896, Bibliothèque de Genève, ms fr 5102 96 (109).

46. Comité international [de la Croix-Rouge], "Avant-propos," *Bulletin International des Sociétés de Secours aux Militaires Blessés* 1 (1869): 2.

47. Letter from Dr. W. Schlesinger to ICRC, November 14, 1869, Vienna, ICRC Archive, Anciens fonds 1,3/30(T).

48. The American National Red Cross was reconstituted in 1881, under the leadership of Clara Barton.

49. Société genevoise d'utilité publique, *Compte-rendu de la Conférence*, 11.

50. Ibid., 9.

51. Gustave Moynier, *La Croix-Rouge: son passé et son avenir* (Paris: Sandoz & Thuillier, 1882), 225.

52. Ibid., 259–260.

53. André Durand, "Gustave Moynier and the Peace Societies," *International Review of the Red Cross* 36 (1996): 548–550. Toward the end of his life, Henry Dunant adopted an active war abolition mission, but this was also part of his personal movement away from Calvinism. For Dunant's changing beliefs on peace, see André Durand, "The Development of the Idea of Peace in the Thinking of Henry Dunant," *International Review of the Red Cross* 26 (1986): 26–47.

54. Local committees almost immediately expanded their fields of practice into areas such as public hygiene and orphan care, but retained wartime care as their principal task. Details were mentioned in communications such as Société hessoise, "Programme de la Société hessoise en temps de paix," *Bulletin international des sociétés de secours aux militaires blessés* 1 (1870): 91–93; Société suédoise, "Assemblée générale de la Société suédoise," *Bulletin international des sociétés de secours aux militaires blessés* 1 (1870): 99–100. Discussion continued in subsequent conferences, e.g., in the Berlin Conference of Aid Societies of 1869, which met to further discuss the goals and scope of the new movement. Rudolf von Sydow, *Compte rendu des travaux de la conférence internationale tenue à Berlin du 22 au 27 Avril 1869 par les délégués des gouvernements signataires de la Convention de Genève et des sociétés et associations de secours aux militaires blessés et malades* (Berlin: J. F. Stracke, 1869).

55. Comité de Madrid, "La charité dans les guerres civiles," *Bulletin international des sociétés de secours aux militaires blessés* 1 (1870): 175.

56. The Prussian society was reported to have more than one hundred auxiliary aid societies cooperating under its broad umbrella in the late 1860s (Henry Dunant personal files, n.d., Bibliothèque de Genève MS Fr 2115N 5–1).

57. Comité central allemande, "Assemblée de Nuremberg," *Bulletin international des sociétés de secours aux militaires blessés* 3, no. 10 (1872): 57.

58. Comité international de la Croix-Rouge, *Assistance aux militaires en temps de paix*, ICRC archive, unpublished manuscript dated 1912.

59. Letter from Edward Lugard, War Office, to ICRC, February 4, 1864, London, ICRC Archive Anciens fonds.

60. J. C. Chenu, "La guerre et l'humanité au XIXme siècle, par M. L. de Cazenove," *Bulletin international des sociétés de secours aux militaires blessés* 1 (1870): 88–91.

61. Lynn McDonald, "War and Militarism," in *Florence Nightingale: An Introduction to Her Life and Family*, vol. 1, edited by Lynn McDonald (Waterloo: Wilfrid Laurier Univ. Press, 2001), 78.

62. Field-Marshal Helmuth von Moltke and General Julius von Hartmann were leading critics of organized humanitarianism. See Brian Bond, *War and Society in Europe, 1870–1970* (Montreal: McGill-Queen's Univ. Press, 1998).

63. Société genevoise d'utilité publique, *Compte-rendu de la Conférence*, 12–13.

64. Moynier and Appia, *Help for Sick and Wounded*, 220.

65. Gustave Moynier, "La convention de Genève au point de vue religieux," *Revue Chrétienne* 46 (1899): 161.

66. Despite her initial objections, Nightingale became an active supporter of the establishment of the British Society for Aiding and Ameliorating the Conditions of the Sick and Wounded in Times of War under the patronage of Queen Victoria and the presidency of the Prince of Wales.

67. Louis Paul Appia, *Les blessés dans le Schleswig pendant la guerre de 1864: rapport présenté au Comité international de Genève* (Geneva: Jules-Guillaume Fick, 1864).

68. Clara Barton, *The Red Cross: A History of this Remarkable International Movement in the Interest of Humanity* (Washington, DC: American National Red Cross, 1898), 13.

69. Comité international de la Croix-Rouge, *Résumé des travaux du Comité International de la Croix-Rouge de 1884–1890, lu à la séance du 14 Novembre 1890 par son président* (Geneva: B. Soullier, 1890), 22.

70. Letter from Henry Dunant to Empress Eugénie, August 16, 1870, Paris, Bibliothèque de Genève, ms fr 2110 (10).

71. Société genevoise d'utilité publique, *Compte-rendu de la Conférence*, 55.

72. Moynier, "La convention de Genève au point de vue religieux," 163.

73. Ibid.

74. Ibid., 164.

75. Comité central espagnol, "La guerre civile," *Bulletin international des sociétés de secours aux militaires blessés* 3 (1872): 196–203.

76. Elsewhere, however, the incorporation of civilians into the battlefield humanitarian efforts was well orchestrated. For example, ICRC officials cited approvingly the involvement of a group of sixty-eight civilian doctors from Berlin in relief efforts during the Second Schleswig War (Henry Dunant personal files, n.d., Bibliothèque de Genève MS Fr 2115N 5-1). The Baden society reported that 158 charitable societies were involved in the efforts to bring relief to the battlefield during the Franco-Prussian War, with much of their work orchestrated by Princess Louise, the Duchess

of Baden. Société de Baden, "Le secours badois pendant la dernière guerre," *Bulletin international des sociétés de secours aux militaires blessés* 3 (1872): 190–194.

77. Comité international [de la Croix-Rouge], "Travaux du Comité international pendant le dernier trimestre de l'année 1870," *Bulletin international des sociétés de secours aux militaires blessés* 2, no. 6 (1871): 81.

78. At the same time, the Geneva Convention placed few restrictions on the militaries' freedom of action. The 1906 Convention in particular, while seeking to formalize the relations between armed forces and humanitarian volunteers, effectively ensured that on no condition would the presence of civilians on the battlefield put pertinent military operations at risk. Geoffrey Best, *Humanity in Warfare: The Modern History of the International Law of Armed Conflicts* (London: Methuen, 1983), 153.

79. Leeds Mercury, "The War," *Leeds Mercury*, July 11, 1877, 5.

80. Public address by Clara Barton, delivered in 1881. Clara Barton, *The Red Cross* (Washington, DC: American Historical Press, 1906), 70.

81. Ibid., 71.

82. For example, Eva Illouz, "From the Lisbon Disaster to Oprah Winfrey: Suffering as Identity in the Era of Globalization," in *Global America? The Cultural Consequences of Globalization*, ed. Ulrich Beck, Natan Sznaider, and Rainer Winter (Liverpool, UK: Liverpool Univ. Press, 2003), 189–205.

83. Peter Stamatov, "Activist Religion, Empire, and the Emergence of Modern Long-Distance Advocacy Networks," *American Sociological Review* 75 (2010): 607–628; Peter Stamatov, *The Origins of Global Humanitarianism: Religion, Empires, and Advocacy* (Cambridge: Cambridge Univ. Press, 2013).

84. Jeffrey C. Alexander, *The Civil Sphere* (New York: Oxford Univ. Press, 2006); Richard Biernacki, "Cultural Coherence in Early Modern England: The Invention of Contract," *American Journal of Cultural Sociology* 2 (2014): 277–299.

CHAPTER 3

1. Gustave Moynier, "La convention de Genève au point de vue religieux," *Revue Chrétienne* 46, no. 8 (1899): 165. Moynier mistakenly cites Japan as Buddhist, although it had adopted Shinto as state religion under the Meiji Restoration. See James Edward Ketelaar, *Of Heretics and Martyrs in Meiji Japan: Buddhism and Its Persecution* (Princeton, NJ: Princeton Univ. Press, 1990).

2. See Rogers Brubaker, *Citizenship and Nationhood in France and Germany* (Cambridge, MA: Harvard Univ. Press, 1991), 100. The rise in xenophobia was notably felt in areas dealing with enemy civilians, who faced increased risk of forced repatriation and other forms of retribution during the late-nineteenth-century wars. See, for example, Daniela L. Caglioti, "Waging War on Civilians: The Expulsion of Aliens in the Franco-Prussian War," *Past Present* 221 (2013): 161–195.

3. David P. Forsythe, "The Red Cross as Transnational Movement: Conserving and Changing the Nation State System," *International Organization* 30 (1976): 607–630.

4. See, for example, Rachel Chrastil, "The French Red Cross, War Readiness, and Civil Society, 1866–1914," *French Historical Studies* 31 (2008): 445–476.

5. John F. Hutchinson, *Champions of Charity: War and the Rise of the Red Cross* (Boulder, CO: Westview Press, 1996).

6. Graeme Murdock, *Beyond Calvin: The Intellectual, Political, and Cultural World of Europe's Reformed Churches, c. 1540–1620* (Basingstoke, UK: Palgrave Macmillan, 2004).

7. For case studies demonstrating the importance of cultural appropriation for the international travel of texts, see Alvaro Santana-Acuña, "How a Literary Work Becomes a

Classic: The Case of *One Hundred Years of Solitude*," *American Journal of Cultural Sociology* 2 (2014): 97–149; Isabel Jijon, "The Universal King? Memory, Globalization, and Martin Luther King, Jr.," *Sociological Inquiry* 88 (2018): 79–105.

8. Jeffrey C. Alexander, "'Globalization' as Collective Representation: The New Dream of a Cosmopolitan Civil Sphere," *International Journal of Politics, Culture, and Society* 19 (2005): 81–90.

9. Brubaker, *Citizenship and Nationhood in France and Germany*, 100.

10. For elaboration on field theory and the relationship between transnational and local fields, see Shai M. Dromi, "For Good and Country: Nationalism and the Diffusion of Humanitarianism in the Late Nineteenth Century," *Sociological Review Monographs* 64 (2016): 79–97. Anthropologists and international relations scholars have highlighted the cultural dynamics involved in the travel of ideas between global and local arenas. See, e.g., Sally Engle Merry, "Transnational Human Rights and Local Activism: Mapping the Middle," *American Anthropologist* 108 (2006): 38–51. However, much of the existing literature on transnational social fields has not seen nation-level cultural processes as related to the emergence of global structures. See, e.g., Peter Dixon and Chris Tenove, "International Criminal Justice as a Transnational Field: Rules, Authority, and Victims," *International Journal of Transitional Justice* 7 (2013): 393–412; John Hagan and Ron Levi, "Crimes of War and the Force of Law," *Social Forces* 83 (2005): 1499–1534; Yves Dezalay and Bryant G. Garth, *The Internationalization of Palace Wars: Lawyers, Economists, and the Contest to Transform Latin American States* (Chicago: Univ. of Chicago Press, 2010); Stephanie Lee Mudge and Antoine Vauchez, "Building Europe on a Weak Field: Law, Economics, and Scholarly Avatars in Transnational Politics," *American Journal of Sociology* 118 (2012): 449–492.

11. Today, the ICRC coordinates NRCs in all areas concerning protection of victims of armed conflicts. It remains the sole INGO explicitly recognized by international humanitarian law. The Fourth Geneva Convention (1949) deals extensively with the activities of the ICRC and presents it as an exemplary impartial humanitarian body.

12. David Wetzel, *A Duel of Nations: Germany, France, and the Diplomacy of the War of 1870–1871* (Madison: Univ. of Wisconsin Press, 2012), 180.

13. Exact soldier death tolls vary. Compare, for example, J. David Singer, *The Wages of War, 1816–1965: A Statistical Handbook* (New York: Wiley 1972), with Gaston Bodart, *Losses of Life in Modern Wars: Austria-Hungary, France* (Oxford: Clarendon Press; New York: H. Milford, 1916).

14. François Bugnion, "The Arrival of Bourbaki's Army at Les Verrières: The Internment of the First French Army in Switzerland on 1 February 1871," *International Review of the Red Cross* 36 (1996): 181–193.

15. Comité international [de la Croix-Rouge], "Note sur le Comité de Lisbon," *Bulletin des sociétés de secours aux militaires blessés* 1 (1870): 151–153.

16. The second ANRC president, Mabel Boardman, was key to its expansion and worked particularly to define the organization as an international one, as she does in Mabel T. Boardman, *Under the Red Cross Flag at Home and Abroad* (Philadelphia: J. B. Lippincott, 1917).

17. Comité de Bade, "La Convention de Genève pendant la guerre de 1870–71," *Bulletin international de sociétés de secours aux militaires blessés* 2 (1871): 15.

18. E.g., Emma Maria Pearson and Louisa Elisabeth MacLaughlin, *Our Adventures during the War of 1870* (London: Richard Bentley and Son, 1871).

19. This journal appeared under several different names over the last century and a half,

was in later decades published in French, English, and Spanish, and today exists as the *International Review of the Red Cross.*

20. Gustave Moynier, *La Croix-Rouge: son passé et son avenir* (Paris: Sandoz & Thuillier, 1882), 280–281.

21. Clara Barton, *The Red Cross: A History of this Remarkable International Movement in the Interest of Humanity* (Washington, DC: American National Red Cross, 1898), 30.

22. Gustave Moynier, *Rappel succinct de l'activité déployée par le comité international de la Croix-Rouge à Genève pendant les quarante premières années de son existence (1863 à 1904)* (Geneva: Comité international de la Croix-Rouge, 1905), 25.

23. Ibid.

24. Comité international [de la Croix-Rouge], "De l'adoption par les diverses sociétés de secours d'une dénomination uniforme," *Bulletin international des sociétés de secours aux militaires blessés* 3 (1872): 179.

25. A rise in Spanish mentions of "Cruz Roja" can be seen in the mid-1870s—at the time of the Third Carlist War, when the popularity of the Spanish Red Cross was at its height. A jump in the English and Spanish percentages can be seen in the mid-1890s, during the Spanish-American War, which saw increased Red Cross activity on both sides (in fact, this was the first major war for the American National Red Cross).

26. Comité international de la Croix-Rouge, *La Conférence Internationale réunie à Genève les 26, 27, 28, et 29 Octobre 1863 pour étudier les moyens de pourvoir a l'insuffisance du service sanitaire dans les armées en campagne, deuxième édition* (Geneva: Publication du Comité International de la Croix-Rouge, 1904), 15; Comité international de la Croix-Rouge, *Résumé des travaux du Comité International de la Croix-Rouge de 1884–1890, lu à la séance du 14 Novembre 1890 par son président* (Geneva: B. Soullier, 1890), 5.

27. Comité central français, "France," *Bulletin international des sociétés de secours aux militaires blessés* 2 (1871): 25.

28. Comité international [de la Croix-Rouge], *La Conférence International.*

29. Since the hierarchy between the ICRC and the NRCs was informal, the ICRC even resisted the identification as a "central" committee. Ibid.

30. Moynier, *Rappel succinct,* 9–10.

31. Cte. de Beaufort, "Déclaration du conseil de la Société française de secours aux blessés des armées de terre et de mer," *Bulletin international des sociétés de secours aux militaires blessés* 2, no. 7–8 (1871): 208–212. French Red Cross leader Dr. Jean-Charles Chenu reported fully on this episode in 1874. See Jean-Charles Chenu, *Aperçu historique, statistique et clinique sur le service des ambulances et des hôpitaux de la Société française de secours aux blessés des armées de terre et de mer: pendant la guerre de 1870–1871* (Paris: Dumaine, 1874).

32. This was often complicated when local Red Cross advocates requested that the ICRC or the Swiss Federal Council intervene on their behalf with their local government.

33. Société genevoise d'utilité publique, *Compte-rendu de la Conférence internationale réunie a Genève les 26, 27, 28, 29 Oct. 1863 pour étudier les moyens de pourvoir a l'insuffisance du Service sanitaire dans les Armées en campagne* (Geneva: Imprimerie de Jules-Guillaume Fick, 1863).

34. Comité international [de la Croix-Rouge], "Comité international," *Bulletin international des sociétés de secours aux militaires blessés* 2 (1870): 8.

35. Armand de Melun, *Société française.*

36. Gustave Moynier, *Ce que c'est que la Croix-Rouge* (Geneva: Imprimerie B. Soullier, 1874), 4.

37. Comité international [de la Croix-Rouge], "Du double caractère, national et inter-national, des sociétés de secours," *Bulletin internationale des sociétés de secours aux militaires blessés* 1 (1870): 11–14.

38. Théodore Maunoir, "Note sur l'œuvre des comités de secours aux États-Unis d'Amérique," in *Secours aux blessés: Communication du Comité international faisant suite au compte rendu de la conférence internationale de Genève*, ed. Comité international (Geneva: Imprimerie de Jules-Guillaume Fick, 1864), 179–180.

39. Comité international [de la Croix-Rouge], *Secours aux blessés: Communication du Comité international faisant suite au compte rendu de la conférence internationale de Genève* (Geneva: Imprimerie de Jules-Guillaume Fick, 1864), 208.

40. However, the French Red Cross also endorsed a more belligerent form of French nationalism after the war. Over the 1880s, the French Red Cross Society led a national effort to prepare the country for a seemingly inevitable war with Britain or Germany. This campaign helped it both gain public prominence and leverage in government circles. Chrastil, "The French Red Cross," 445–476.

41. Comité auxiliaire de Strasbourg, "Compte rendu des travaux du Comité auxiliaire de Strasbourg, du 26 juillet 1870 au 31 octobre 1871," *Bulletin international des sociétés de secours aux militaires blessés* 3 (1872): 154.

42. Comité international [de la Croix-Rouge], "Progrès de l'œuvre de la Croix Rouge," *Bulletin international des sociétés de secours aux militaires blessés* 1 (1870): 173.

43. Clara Barton, *The Red Cross in Peace and War* (Washington, DC: American Historical Press, 1904), 198–199.

44. Ibid., 106.

45. Letter from Rutherford (English National Society for Aid to the Sick and Wounded in War) to the Central Committee, March 1863, London, ICRC Archive, Anciens fonds.

46. Gustave Moynier, "Ma contribution au progrès du droit international," undated manuscript, ICRC Archive, GM, p. 33.

47. Quoted in Caroline Moorehead, *Dunant's Dream: War, Switzerland, and the History of the Red Cross* (New York: Carroll & Graf Publishers, 1999), 76.

48. Ibid., 98.

49. Comité de l'Asie française, "Japon," *Bulletin du comité de l'Asie française* 69 (1906): 504–506.

50. Melinda Lawson, *Patriot Fires: Forging a New American Nationalism in the Civil War North* (Lawrence: Univ. Press of Kansas, 2002); Jean H. Quataert, *Staging Philanthropy: Patriotic Women and the National Imagination in Dynastic Germany, 1813–1916* (Ann Arbor: Univ. of Michigan Press, 2001).

51. Teresa Richardson, *In Japanese Hospitals during War-Time: Fifteen Months with the Red Cross Society of Japan* (Edinburgh: W. Blackwood and Sons, 1905). The U.S. Navy took an active interest in the activities of the Russian Red Cross at the same time, and especially in its potential military usefulness. See U.S. Navy Dept. Bureau of Medicine and Surgery, *Report on the Russian Medical and Sanitary Features of the Russo-Japanese War to the Surgeon-General* (Washington, DC: Government Printing Office, 1906).

52. Comité international [de la Croix-Rouge], "Les prisonniers de guerre," *Bulletin international des sociétés de secours aux militaires blessés* 2 (1871): 92–96. In particular, a report published by the Berlin NRC accused France of complete disregard for the convention. Comité de Berlin, *Les violations de la Convention de Genève par les Français en 1870–71: Dépêches, protocoles, rapports, etc.* (Berlin: C. Heymons, 1871).

53. Mark Mazower, *Governing the World: The History of an Idea, 1815 to the Present* (New York: Penguin Books, 2013).

54. Comité international [de la Croix-Rouge], "Assemblée générale de la société néerlandaise," *Bulletin international des sociétés de secours* 1 (1869): 31–35.

55. Dr. F.-H. d'Arneth, "Événements de Dalmatie," *Bulletin international des Sociétés de Secours aux Militaires Blessés* 1, no. 3 (1870): 124.

56. Société autrichienne, "Autriche," *Bulletin international des sociétés de secours aux militaires blessés* 2, no. 5 (1870): 27–28.

57. New York Herald, "The Red Cross," *New York Herald*, October 29, 1877, 4. For additional examples, see George Halstead Boyland, *Six Months under the Red Cross, with the French Army* (Cincinnati, OH: Robert Clarke & Co., 1873).

58. E.g., Richardson, *In Japanese Hospitals during War-Time.*

59. European commentators noted the national zeal of the volunteers. See, e.g., Nagao Ariga, *La Croix-Rouge en Extrême-Orient: Exposé de l'organisation et du fonctionnement* (Paris: A. Pedone, 1900).

60. See also Olive Checkland, *Humanitarianism and the Emperor's Japan, 1877–1977* (New York: St. Martin's, 1994).

61. Similarly, the United States did not ratify the Geneva Convention until 1882, after a long advocacy struggle by Clara Barton. See her remarks in Clara Barton, *The Red Cross of the Geneva Convention: What It Is* (Washington, DC: Rufus H. Darby, 1878).

62. Comité international [de la Croix-Rouge], "Association américaine," *Bulletin international des sociétés de secours aux militaires blessés* 1 (1869): 24–25.

63. Gustave Ador and Gustave Moynier, "Fondation d'une société en Roumanie et dissolution de celle des États-Unis," *Bulletin international des sociétés de secours aux militaires blessés* 7 (1876): 159–161.

64. Clyde Buckingham, *Clara Barton: A Broad Humanity* (Alexandria, VA: Mt. Vernon, 1977).

65. Clara Barton, *A Story of the Red Cross: Glimpses of Field Work* (New York: Appleton and Co., 1904), 13.

66. There were numerous clashes between Barton and competitor humanitarian organizations in the U.S., particularly because Barton claimed she had the U.S. government's support in various relief operations and was adamant about taking full charge of them. See Heather D. Curtis, *Holy Humanitarians: American Evangelicals and Global Aid* (Cambridge, MA: Harvard Univ. Press, 2018), 102–103.

67. Clara Barton, *The Red Cross: A History of This Remarkable International Movement in the Interest of Humanity* (Washington, DC: American National Red Cross, 1898). See also Marian Moser Jones, *The American Red Cross from Clara Barton to the New Deal* (Baltimore, MD: Johns Hopkins Univ. Press, 2013).

68. Barton, *The Red Cross in Peace and War*, 347. As Julia Irwin shows, as the twentieth century progressed, the U.S. government realized the national Red Cross society's potential for promoting U.S. international interests and made use of the ANRC in its foreign policy. See Julia Irwin, *Making the World Safe: The American Red Cross and a Nation's Humanitarian Awakening* (New York: Oxford Univ. Press, 2013).

69. Letter from Henry W. Bellows to Henry Dunant, June 7, 1866, New York, Bibliothèque de Genève, ms fr 2110.

70. Letter from Dr. W. Schlesinger to Gustave Moynier, November 14, 1869, Vienna, ICRC Archive, Anciens fonds 1,3/30(T).

71. Geneviève Zubrzycki has demonstrated the resilience and potency of "national sensoriums," the material culture manifestations of national mythologies and their expression in practices and performances. The national sensorium crystalizes abstract ideas of national character and values for national subjects. See Geneviève Zubrzycki,

"History and the National Sensorium: Making Sense of Polish Mythology," *Qualitative Sociology* 34 (2011): 21–57. See also Geneviève Zubrzycki, *Beheading the Saint: Nationalism, Religion, and Secularism in Quebec* (Chicago: Univ. of Chicago Press, 2016).

72. Comité central allemand, "Communication du Comité central allemand," *Bulletin international des sociétés de secours aux militaires blessés* 2 (1871): 8–14.

73. Comité central allemand, "Le Comité central allemand," *Bulletin international des sociétés de secours aux militaires blessés* 2 (1871): 202–203.

74. János Hantos, "Centenary of the Hungarian Red Cross," *International Review of the Red Cross* 21 (1981), 175–180.

75. Richard S. Horowitz, "International Law and State Transformation in China, Siam, and the Ottoman Empire during the Nineteenth Century," *Journal of World History* 15, no. 4 (2004): 445–486.

76. Comité central, "L'ambassade japonaise," *Bulletin international des sociétés de secours aux militaires blessés* 5 (1873): 11.

77. Ibid., 13.

78. Checkland, *Humanitarianism and the Emperor's Japan.*

79. Siamese Red Cross Society, *The Siamese Red Cross Society: Its Origin and Activities* (Bangkok: Siamese Red Cross Society, 1934).

80. See Jonathan Benthall, "The Red Cross and Red Crescent Movement and Islamic Societies, with Special Reference to Jordan," *British Journal of Middle Eastern Studies* 24 (1977): 160, and François Bugnion, *The Emblem of the Red Cross: A Brief History* (Geneva: International Committee of the Red Cross, 1977), 15–19, 29–31.

81. Chicago Daily Tribune, "Story of a Red Cross," *Chicago Daily Tribune*, January 19, 1896, 34, accessed October 6, 2014.

82. Comité central belge, "Journal d'une infirmière, par Mme la baronne de Crombrugghe," *Bulletin international des sociétés de secours aux militaires blessés* 2 (1871): 18.

83. Zdenko Löwenthal, "Anglo-Yugoslav Medical Relations in Peace and War," *British Medical Journal* 2 (1961): 1634–1637.

84. However, aid societies that were not officially related to the Red Cross remained active and, oftentimes, quite powerful (the Order of St. John of Jerusalem in Germany and the Knights of Malta in numerous Catholic states, for example).

85. Moynier, *Rappel succinct*, 11.

86. Such benefits are common to network forms of organizations. See Walter W. Powell, "Neither Market nor Hierarchy: Network Forms of Organization," in *Research in Organizational Behavior*, ed. Barry Staw and Larry L. Cummings (Greenwich, CT: JAI, 1990), 295–336; Brian Uzzi, "Networks and the Paradox of Embeddedness," *Administrative Science Quarterly* 42 (1990): 35–67.

87. At present, inclusion as part of the movement requires the approval of both the ICRC and the IFRC (International Federation of the Red Cross); it remains contentious grounds, with NGOs such as the North Cyprus Red Crescent Society and the Taipei-based Red Cross Society of the Republic of China achieving only limited recognition.

88. Indeed, social fields often create the conditions for the emergence of social networks. See Sourabh Singh, "What Is Relational Structure? Introducing History to the Debates on the Relation between Fields and Social Networks," *Sociological Theory* 34 (2016): 128–150.

89. Alfred Gautier, *Résultat du Concours relatif à l'emploi abusif du signe et du nom de la Croix-Rouge* (Geneva: Imprimerie B. & I. Soullier, 1890).

90. Comité international de la Croix-Rouge, *La Conférence Internationale*, 29.

91. Letter from Thomas Longmore to Gustave Moynier, April 14, 1872, Wortley, ICRC Archive, Anciens fonds 8,2 (116).
92. Letter from C. Burgess to Gustave Ador, January 17, 1877, London, ICRC Archive, Anciens fonds 8,2 (190).
93. Comité central—France, "L'œuvre française pendant la dernière guerre," *Bulletin international des sociétés de secours aux militaires blessés* 3, no. 12 (1872): 206–214.
94. In Prussia (and later Germany), the NRC enjoyed the strong support and, to a large extent, the cooperation of hundreds of local volunteer societies. Charlotte von Itzenplitz, "Association patriotique de dames à Berlin," *Bulletin international des sociétés de secours aux militaires blessés* 1, no. 2 (1870): 68–69.
95. Comité international [de la Croix-Rouge], "Progrès de l'œuvre de la Croix Rouge," *Bulletin international des sociétés de secours aux militaires blessés* 1 (1870): 173.
96. Andrew Fitzmaurice, "The Justification of King Leopold II's Congo Enterprise by Sir Travers Twiss," in *Law and Politics in British Colonial Thought: Transpositions of Empire*, ed. Shaunnagh Dorsett and Ian Hunter (New York: Palgrave Macmillan, 2010), 112–114.
97. L'Association congolaise et africaine, "Le drapeau congolais," *Bulletin international des sociétés de la Croix-Rouge* 30 (1899): 87.
98. Martti Koskenniemi, *The Gentle Civilizer of Nations: The Rise and Fall of International Law 1870–1960* (Cambridge: Cambridge Univ. Press, 2002), 156–165. Notably, Belgian international lawyers stayed silent during the heat of the Congo Free State debate, except for several Leopold apologists like Ernest Nys and Edouard Descamps. See Benjamin Allen, *Legalist Empire: International Law and American Foreign Relations in the Early Twentieth Century* (Oxford: Oxford Univ. Press, 2016), 23; Mark Lewis, *The Birth of the New Justice: The Internationalization of Crime and Punishment, 1919–1950* (Oxford: Oxford Univ. Press, 2014), 83.
99. Gustave Moynier, *La fondation de l'état indépendant du Congo au point de vue juridique* (Paris: l'Académie des sciences morales et politiques, 1887), 34–35.
100. Ringier Hammer, "Adhésion à la Convention de Genève," *Bulletin international des sociétés de la Croix-Rouge* 20 (1889): 100–101.
101. Gustave Moynier and Edouard Odier, "Formation d'une Société congolaise et africaine de la Croix-Rouge," *Bulletin international des sociétés de la Croix-Rouge* 20 (1889): 76–80.
102. Quoted in La Belgique coloniale, "l'Association congolaise et africaine de la Croix-Rouge," *Belgique coloniale* 2 (1896): 220.
103. Army Medical Department, *Report for the Year 1897* (London: Harrison and Sons, 1898), 413.
104. La Belgique Coloniale, "L'Association congolaise," 221.
105. L'Association congolaise et africaine, "L'avenir de la Croix-Rouge au Congo," *Bulletin international des sociétés de la Croix-Rouge* 34 (1903): 220.
106. Martin Ewans, *European Atrocity, African Catastrophe: Leopold II, the Congo Free State, and Its Aftermath* (London: Routledge, 2002).
107. Adam Hochschild, *King Leopold's Ghost: A Story of Greed, Terror, and Heroism in Colonial Africa* (Boston: Houghton Mifflin, 1999).
108. L'Association congolaise et africaine, "L'Association congolaise et africaine de la Croix-Rouge de 1888–1908," *Bulletin international des sociétés de la Croix-Rouge* 40 (1909): 96.
109. Comité international [de la Croix-Rouge], "Dissolution de l'Association congolaise et africaine," *Bulletin international des sociétés de la Croix-Rouge* 40 (1909): 143–144.

110. Allen Guttmann, *The Olympics: A History of the Modern Games* (Urbana: Univ. of Illinois Press, 2002).

111. David I. Macleod, *Building Character in the American Boy: The Boy Scouts, YMCA, and Their Forerunners, 1870–1920* (Madison: Univ. of Wisconsin Press, 2004).

112. The American Red Cross, for example, is chartered by Congress and holds much of the U.S. blood bank.

113. For extended discussion of transnational fields, see Julian Go and Monika Krause, "Fielding Transnationalism: An Introduction," *Sociological Review Monographs* 64 (2016): 6–30.

114. Geoffrey F. Best, *Humanity in Warfare* (London: Methuen, 1983); Didier Fassin, *Humanitarian Reason: A Moral History of the Present* (Berkeley: Univ. of California Press, 2011).

115. For more on the struggles over the field-specific capital of the transnational humanitarian field and how they evolved over the twentieth century, see Monika Krause, *The Good Project: Humanitarian Relief NGOs and the Fragmentation of Reason* (Chicago: Univ. of Chicago Press, 2014).

116. Respectively Larissa Buchholz, "What Is a Global Field? Theorizing Fields beyond the Nation-State," *Sociological Review Monographs* 64 (2016): 31–60, and Martin Petzke, "Taken In by the Numbers Game: The Globalization of a Religious 'Illusio' and 'Doxa' in Nineteenth-Century Evangelical Missions to India," *Sociological Review Monographs* 64 (2016): 124–145.

117. Notably, Bourdieu saw national distinction as a barrier to the international circulation of ideas, and he focused on their distortion and misunderstanding as they cross national contexts. Bourdieu was skeptical about the possibility of transnational fields altogether. Pierre Bourdieu, "The Social Conditions of the International Circulation of Ideas," in *Bourdieu: A Critical Reader*, ed. Richard Shusterman (Oxford: Blackwell Publishers, 1999), 220–228; Pierre Bourdieu, "On the Possibility of a Field of World Sociology," in *Social Theory for a Changing Society*, ed. Pierre Bourdieu and James S. Coleman (New York: Russell Sage Foundation, 1991), 374.

118. Eleanor Davey, "Famine, Aid, and Ideology: The Political Activism of Médecins sans Frontières in the 1980s," *French Historical Studies* 34 (2011): 529–558; Martha C. Nussbaum, "Patriotism and Cosmopolitanism," in *For Love of Country: Debating the Limits of Patriotism*, by Martha C. Nussbaum, ed. Joshua Cohen (Boston: Beacon Press, 1996), 2–29; Bryan S. Turner, *Vulnerability and Human Rights* (University Park: Pennsylvania State Univ. Press, 2006); Alison Brysk, *Speaking Rights to Power: Constructing Political Will* (New York: Oxford Univ. Press, 2013); Fuyuki Kurasawa, "L'humanitaire, manifestation du cosmopolitisme?" *Sociologie et sociétés* 44 (2012): 217–237; Étienne Balibar, "On the Politics of Human Rights," *Constellations* 20 (2013): 18–26; Renee Fox, *Doctors without Borders: Humanitarian Quests, Impossible Dreams of Médecins sans Frontières* (Baltimore, MD: Johns Hopkins Univ. Press, 2014).

119. Peter Redfield, *Life in Crisis: The Ethical Journey of Doctors without Borders* (Berkeley: Univ. of California Press, 2013); Johanna Siméant, "What Is Going Global? The Internationalization of French NGOs 'Without Borders,'" *Review of International Political Economy* 12, no. 5 (2005): 851–883; Sarah S. Stroup, *Borders among Activists: International NGOs in the United States, Britain, and France* (Ithaca, NY: Cornell Univ. Press, 2012).

120. Jackie Smith and Dawn Wiest, "The Uneven Geography of Global Civil Society: National and Global Influences on Transnational Association," *Social Forces* 84

(2005): 621–651; Sarah S. Stroup and Amanda Murdie, "There's No Place like Home: Explaining International NGO Advocacy," *Review of International Organizations* 7 (2012): 425–448; Marcel Hanegraaff et al., "The Domestic and Global Origins of Transnational Advocacy Explaining Lobbying Presence during WTO Ministerial Conferences," *Comparative Political Studies* 48 (2015): 1591–1621.

121. Annika Arnold, "Towards a Transcultural Community of Climate Change: Adapting Max Weber's Distinction of Vergemeinschaftung and Vergesellschaftung," in *Europe and America in the Mirror: Culture, Economy, and History*, ed. Maik Arnold and Przemysław Łukasik (Kraków: NOMOS, 2012), 107–123; Kari Marie Norgaard, *Living in Denial: Climate Change, Emotions, and Everyday Life* (Cambridge, MA: MIT Press, 2011); Liron Shani, *Nationalism between Land and Environment: The Conflict between "Oranges" and "Greens" over Settling in the East Lakhish Area* (Baltimore: Univ. of Maryland Institute for Israel Studies Research Papers Series, 2011).

122. Bart Bonikowski, "Nationalism in Settled Times," *Annual Review of Sociology* 42 (2016): 427–449.

123. Jeffrey C. Alexander, "'Globalization' as Collective Representation: The New Dream of a Cosmopolitan Civil Sphere," *International Journal of Politics, Culture, and Society* 19 (2005): 81–90; Craig J. Calhoun, "Nationalism and Civil Society: Democracy, Diversity, and Self-determination," in *Nations Matter: Culture, History, and the Cosmopolitan Dream*, by Craig Calhoun (London: Routledge, 2007), 77–101.

124. Philip S. Gorski and William McMillan, "Barack Obama and American Exceptionalism," *Review of Faith and International Affairs* 20 (2012): 41–50; Philip S. Gorski, *American Covenant: A History of Civil Religion from the Puritans to the Present* (Princeton, NJ: Princeton Univ. Press, 2017).

CHAPTER 4

1. Bourdieu provided many examples of field openness, in particular in his work on knowledge production fields. See Charles Camic, "Bourdieu's Two Sociologies of Knowledge," in *Bourdieu and Historical Analysis*, ed. Philip S. Gorski (Durham, NC: Duke Univ. Press, 2013), 196–198.

2. This was, of course, not uniform across all NRCs, as some exhibited a more explicit religious character. In the predominantly Catholic Red Cross society of Baden, volunteers were often referred to using the religiously connotative term "sister" rather than "nurse." See Jean H. Quataert, *Staging Philanthropy: Patriotic Women and the National Imagination in Dynastic Germany, 1813–1916* (Ann Arbor: Univ. of Michigan Press, 2001), 192.

3. Comité international [de la Croix-Rouge], "Les dix premières années de la Croix-Rouge," *Bulletin international des sociétés de secours aux militaires blessés* 16 (1873): 165–243. Why the "Red Cross" flag was chosen and to what extent it represents either Christianity or Switzerland remains unclear. In retrospect some parties denied its religious inspiration and claimed that the Swiss flag inversed was chosen in order to honor Switzerland as the host of the Geneva Convention. See John F. Hutchinson, *Champions of Charity: War and the Rise of the Red Cross* (Boulder, CO: Westview Press, 1996), 35.

4. Letter from M. Ristich to British Consul-General White, Belgrade, September 6, 1876, *Accounts and papers of the House of Commons, State Papers—Turkey* (vol. XC).

5. The Iranian national society used a Red Lion with Sun symbol, drawn from pre-Islamic Persian imagery, from 1924 to 1980, until the postrevolutionary government

adopted the crescent instead. The ICRC continues to recognize the Red Lion with Sun as one of the emblems of the movement.

6. Comité international [de la Croix-Rouge], "Les dix premières années de la Croix-Rouge," 242.

7. Gustave Moynier, *La Croix-Rouge: son passé et son avenir* (Paris: Sandoz & Thuillier, 1882), 6.

8. Société française de secours aux blessés militaires, "Assemblée générale de la société française et rapport annuel," *Bulletin International des Sociétés de la Croix-Rouge* 42, no. 168 (1911): 228–229.

9. Henry Dunant personal files, n.d., Bibliothèque de Genève MS Fr 2115N 5-1.

10. Letter from Rev. Henry W. Bellows, president of the U.S. Sanitary Commission and of the American Association for the Relief of the Misery of Battle Fields, to Henry Dunant, New York, June 7, 1866.

11. Letter from Bishop Augustin Egger, Roman Catholic Diocese of Saint Gallen, to Henry Dunant, St. Gallen, May 24, 1896, Bibliothèque de Genève, ms fr 5102 (54).

12. Bertrand Taithe, *Defeated Flesh: Welfare, Warfare, and the Making of Modern France* (Manchester: Manchester Univ. Press, 1999), 172.

13. "Red Cross Sunday," *Hartford Courant*, July 11, 1898, 10.

14. Caroline Moorehead, *Dunant's Dream: War, Switzerland, and the History of the Red Cross* (New York: Carroll & Graf Publishers, 1999), 34.

15. Ibid., 58.

16. "Current Paragraphs," *Boston Recorder*, October 6, 1865, 158.

17. Letter from Cornelia Steketee Hulst to Henry Dunant, Grand Rapids, Michigan, November 19, 1905, Bibliothèque de Genève.

18. Letter from Florence Nightingale to Henry Dunant, London, September 4, 1892, Bibliothèque de Genève, ms 2115 n82.

19. It is important to note that, at that time, the fact that Red Cross societies kept some distance from Evangelical circles helped make them seem more trustworthy. In the U.S., the American National Red Cross appealed to many supporters who balked at supporting more openly Evangelical aid organizations. See Heather D. Curtis, *Holy Humanitarians: American Evangelicals and Global Aid* (Cambridge, MA: Harvard Univ. Press, 2018), 227.

20. Clara Barton, *The Red Cross* (Washington, DC: American Historical Press, 1904), 28.

21. Monserrat Cabré, "Women or Healers? Household Practices and the Categories of Health Care in Late Medieval Iberia," *Bulletin of the History of Medicine* 82 (2008): 18–51; Margaret Pelling, "Nurses and Nursekeepers: Problems of Identification in the Early Modern Period," in *The Common Lot: Sickness, Medical Occupations, and the Urban Poor in Early Modern England*, ed. Margaret Pelling (London: Longmans, 1998), 179–202.

22. Morning Post, "Sketches in the Basque Provinces," *Morning Post*, February 27, 1837, 2.

23. For an overview of women's work on the battlefields of the mid-nineteenth century, see Renée Lelandais, "Les Filles de la Charité sur les champs de bataille, 1847–1863," in *Préludes et pionniers: Les précurseurs de la Croix-Rouge, 1840–1860*, eds. Roger Durand and Jacques Meurant (Geneva: Société Henry Dunant, 1991), 299–319.

24. Agnes Jones wrote in her diary, published by her sister in a memorial volume: "When this time two years ago, I left Kaiserswerth, my wish and prayer were that I might some time return there to be fitted and trained for active work in my Father's service." J. Jones, *"Una and Her Paupers": Memorials of Agnes Elizabeth Jones*, 2d ed. (New York: G. Routledge and Sons, 1872), 40.

25. Mark Bostridge, *Florence Nightingale: The Woman and Her Legend* (New York: Viking, 2008), 155–159.

26. For more on the nursing field, and the role of "femaleness" therein, see Kate Huppatz, "Reworking Bourdieu's 'Capital': Feminine and Female Capitals in the Field of Paid Caring Work," *Sociology* 43 (2009): 45–66.

27. Janet L. Bryant and Kathleen Byrne Colling, "Broken Wills and Tender Hearts: Religious Ideology and the Trained Nurse of the Nineteenth Century," in *Florence Nightingale and Her Era: A Collection of New Scholarship*, ed. Vern Bullough, Bonnie Bullough, and Marietta P. Stanton (New York: Garland Publishing, Inc., 1990), 154.

28. Florence Nightingale, *Notes on Nursing: What It Is, and What It Is Not* (Boston: Carter, 1860).

29. Much of the literature on gender and war has portrayed women as victims, rather than active participants. For further critiques, see Jocelyn Viterna, *Women in War: The Micro-Processes of Mobilization in El Salvador* (New York: Oxford Univ. Press, 2014).

30. "Military Sanitary Matters, and Statistics," *American Journal of the Medical Sciences* 50, no. 99 (1865): 171–180.

31. Caroline Moorehead, *Dunant's Dream: War, Switzerland, and the History of the Red Cross* (New York: Carroll & Graf Publishers, 1999), 56.

32. Ian McAllister, *Sustaining Relief with Development: Strategic Issues for the Red Cross and Red Crescent* (Dordrecht: Martinus Nijhoff Publishers, 1993), 112.

33. A sore point between German empress Victoria and her successor, Augusta Victoria, was the appointment of the latter as head of the German Red Cross, when the former had a longtime personal involvement with the society.

34. Her biography recounted some of this activity. Alice, Grand Duchess, Consort of Ludwig IV, *Alice, Grand Duchess of Hesse, Princess of Great Britain and Ireland: Biographical Sketch and Letters* (New York: G. P. Putnam's Sons, 1884). Louise, Grand Duchess of Baden, was similarly inspired by a longtime friendship with Clara Barton and a longstanding correspondence with Florence Nightingale.

35. Comité central allemand, "Allemagne," *Bulletin international des sociétés de secours aux militaires blessés* 2 (1871): 8–14.

36. Jean H. Quataert, *Staging Philanthropy: Patriotic Women and the National Imagination in Dynastic Germany, 1813–1916* (Ann Arbor: Univ. of Michigan Press, 2001), 6.

37. Ibid.

38. Barton, *The Red Cross*, 30.

39. Martha Finnemore, "Rules of War and Wars of Rules: The International Red Cross and the Restraint of State Violence," in *Constructing World Culture: International Nongovernmental Organizations since 1875*, ed. John Boli and George M. Thomas (Stanford, CA: Stanford Univ. Press, 1999), 161.

40. "Review of *First Aid to the Injured. Five Ambulance Lecture*. By Dr. Frederick Esmarch," *Glasgow Medical Journal* 19 (January–June 1883): 152.

41. Letter from Emilio R. Coni to the ICRC, February 25, 1885, Buenos Aires, ICRC Archive, ARG Anciens fonds 1,2 (2).

42. David H. Burton, *Clara Barton: In the Service of Humanity* (Westport, CT: Greenwood Press, 1995); Drew Gilpin Faust, *This Republic of Suffering: Death and the American Civil War* (New York: Alfred A. Knopf, 2008).

43. Comité central allemande, "Allemagne."

44. Jay Winter, *Sites of Memory, Sites of Mourning: The Great War in European Cultural History* (Cambridge: Cambridge Univ. Press, 1995), 38.

45. Peter Duckers, *British Orders and Decorations* (Shire: Princes Risborough, 2004).
46. New York Herald, "Foreign Club Talk," *New York Herald*, July 23, 1883: 5.
47. "The German Red Cross Medal," *British Medical Journal* 1 (1899), 582.
48. War Office, "The Decoration of 'the Royal Red Cross,'" *Illustrated Naval and Military Magazine* 4 (1884): 253.
49. Emma M. Pearson, "The Anglo-American Ambulance," *Times*, November 4, 1870, 6.
50. Emma M. Pearson, "A Voice from Orleans," *Times*, February 22, 1871, 10.
51. "Red Cross Decorations," *British Medical Journal*, August 17, 1872, 200.
52. Clara Barton, *The Red Cross: A History of This Remarkable International Movement in the Interest of Humanity* (Washington, DC: American National Red Cross, 1898), 89.
53. Clyde Buckingham, *Clara Barton: A Broad Humanity* (Alexandria, VA: Mt. Vernon, 1977).
54. David A. Bell, *The First Total War: Napoleon's Europe and the Birth of Warfare as We Know It* (Boston: Mariner Books, 2007).
55. This varied dramatically between states, as unlike the relative freedom British journalists enjoyed, censorship was employed in France under Napoleon III. This did not completely stifle French critical voices, but it considerably limited the reports they were receiving, especially during the Franco-Prussian War.
56. Martin Conboy, *Journalism: A Critical History* (London: Sage Publications, 2004).
57. Aryeh Neier, "War and War Crimes: A Brief History," in *Crimes of War: Guilt and Denial in the Twentieth Century*, ed. Omer Bartov, Atina Grossmann, and Mary Nolan (New York: New Press, 2003), 1–7.
58. In fact, London newspapers unwittingly supplied the Russians with all-too-accurate information about conditions and plans on the British side in the Crimean War. Yakup Bektas, "The Crimean War as a Technological Enterprise," *Notes and Records* 71 (2017): 244.
59. Alan Hankinson, *Man of Wars: William Howard Russell of the Times* (London: Heineman, 1982).
60. Ilana D. Miller, *Reports from America: William Howard Russell and the Civil War* (Stroud, UK: Sutton, 2001).
61. William Howard Russell, *Complete History of the Russian War, from Its Commencement to Its Close: Giving a Graphic Picture of the Great Drama of War* (New York: J. G. Wells, 1857), 107.
62. Russell, *Complete History of the Russian War*, 63–64.
63. Matthias Schulz, "The Guarantee of Humanity: The Concert of Europe and the Origins of the Russo-Ottoman War of 1877," in *Humanitarian Intervention: A History*, ed. Brendan Simms and David J. B. Trim (Cambridge: Cambridge Univ. Press, 2011), 192–193.
64. Dale L. Walker, *Januarius MacGahan: The Life and Campaigns of an American War Correspondent* (Athens: Ohio Univ. Press, 1988), 169.
65. Faust, *This Republic of Suffering*, 131.
66. Emma Maria Pearson and Louisa Elisabeth MacLaughlin, *Service in Servia under the Red Cross* (London: Tinsley Brothers, 1877).
67. "War Artists," *The Graphic*, December 1890, 643.
68. Clara Barton, *A Story of the Red Cross: Glimpses of Field Work* (New York: Appleton and Co., 1904), 31.
69. Ibid., 70.
70. Ibid., 13.

71. Daily News, *The War Correspondence of the "Daily News" 1877–8 . . . Forming a Continuous History of the War between Russia and Turkey* (London: Macmillan and Co., 1878), 281.

72. "The Care of the Wounded in the War," *The Sphere*, May 28, 1904: b2.

73. "Red Cross Aid at Siboney," *JAMA* 32 (1898): 995–996.

74. Much like humanitarian activists, many of these war journalists shared the attraction to danger. MacGahan was described as having "almost no discernible self-preservation instincts" as he rode alone into Bulgaria. Gary J. Bass, *Freedom's Battle: The Origins of Humanitarian Intervention* (New York: Alfred A. Knopf, 2008), 235.

75. Januarius A. MacGahan and Eugene Schuyler, *Turkish Atrocities in Bulgaria* (London: Bradbury, Agnew & Co., 1876), 43.

76. "Missionaries of Civilization," *Pall Mall Gazette*, August 15, 1876, 10.

77. "The War," *Birmingham Daily Post*, September 27, 1877, 8.

78. John F. Hutchinson, *Champions of Charity: War and the Rise of the Red Cross* (Boulder, CO: Westview Press, 1996).

79. Pierre Boissier, *From Solferino to Tsushima: History of the International Committee of the Red Cross* (Geneva: Henry Dunant Institute, 1985), 251.

80. "The Geneva Convention," *Liverpool Mercury*, April 26, 1865: 6.

81. Louis P. Smith, "The Medical Department of the Army," *Journal of the American Medical Association* 31 (1898): 477–478.

82. *Protocol Additional to the Geneva Conventions of 12 August 1949, and Relating to the Protection of Victims of International Armed Conflicts (Protocol I)*, June 8, 1977, art. 5(4).

83. Ibid., art. 81(1).

84. *Geneva Convention Relative to the Treatment of Prisoners of War*, August 12, 1949, pt. III, sec. V, art. 72.

85. *Protocol Additional to the Geneva Conventions of 12 August 1949, and Relating to the Adoption of an Additional Distinctive Emblem (Protocol III)*, December 8, 2005, art. 3(1(b)) and art. 13(1).

86. *Geneva Convention for the Amelioration of the Condition of the Wounded and Sick in Armed Forces in the Field*, August 12, 1949, chap. I, art. 9.

87. *Protocols Additional to the Geneva Conventions of 12 August 1949: Resolutions of the Diplomatic Conference: Extracts from the Final Act of the Diplomatic Conference* (Geneva: International Committee of the Red Cross, 1977), resolution 11.

88. *Geneva Convention Relative to the Treatment of Prisoners of War of 12 August 1949*, pt. V, art. 125.

89. Geoffrey Best, *Humanity in Warfare: The Modern History of the International Law of Armed Conflicts* (London: Methuen, 1983), 144.

90. The appearance of public international law was not new to the era, however. It had been developing in Europe since at the very least the Peace of Westphalia (and even before, with Dutch jurist Hugo Grotius's 1625 treatise on the subject).

91. Stephen C. Neff, "A Short History of International Law," in *International Law*, ed. Malcolm Evans (Oxford: Oxford Univ. Press, 2006), 29–55.

92. Jack Donnelly, "Human Rights: A New Standard of Civilization?" *International Affairs* 74, no. 1 (1998): 1–24.

93. Comité international [de la Croix-Rouge], "La société prussienne et la nouvelle instruction pour le service sanitaire de l'armée en campagne," *Bulletin des sociétés de secours aux militaires blessés* 1 (1870): 165–168.

94. Comité international [de la Croix-Rouge], "Législation militaire," *Bulletin international des sociétés de secours aux militaires blessés* 1 (1870): 108–119.

95. Comité de Madrid, "La charité dans les guerres civiles," *Bulletin international des sociétés de secours aux militaires blessés* 1 (1870): 175–178, 175–176. See also Eduardo de No Louis, "Reflections on Spain's Contribution to the Application of Humanitarian Law in War," *International Review of the Red Cross* 70 (1967): 3–12.

96. Letter included in Charles S. P. Bowles, *Report of Charles S. P. Bowles, Foreign Agent of the United States Sanitary Commission, upon the International Congress of Geneva: for the Amelioration of the Condition of the Sick and Wounded Soldiers of Armies in the Field, Convened at Geneva, 8th August, 1864* (London: R. Clay, and Taylor, 1864), 25.

97. Dietrich Schindler, "J. C. Bluntschli's Contribution to the Law of War," in *Promoting Justice, Human Rights, and Conflict Resolution through International Law*, ed. Marcelo Kohen (Boston, MA: Brill, 2006), 437–454.

98. Frank Freidel, "Francis Lieber and the Codification of the International Law of War," in *Préludes et pionniers: Les précurseurs de la Croix-Rouge, 1840–1860*, ed. Roger Durand and Jacques Meurant (Geneva: Société Henry Dunant, 1999), 43.

99. Johann Caspar Bluntschli, *Le droit international codifié*, trans. C. Lardy (Paris: Guillaumin et cie, 1870), 305.

100. Schindler, "J. C. Bluntschli's Contribution to the Law of War."

101. Contemporary multilateral human rights institutions still lack power and truly binding judicial arrangements for the enforcement of international humanitarian law are yet to be seen in the global arena. See Donnelly, "Human Rights," 19.

102. Moynier was inspired by the successful arbitration of the Alabama Claims, a series of damages claims by the United States against Great Britain in 1869. The two sides signed the 1871 Treaty of Washington, agreeing to establish an international tribunal in Geneva in order to arbitrate between them. Gustave Moynier, "Note sur la création d'une institution judiciaire internationale propre à prévenir et à réprimer les infractions à la convention de Genève," *Bulletin international des sociétés de secours aux militaires blessés* 3, no. 11 (1872): 122–131.

103. Gustave Rolin-Jaequemyns, "Chronique du droit international: Étude complémentaire sur la guerre franco-allemande, dans ses rapports avec le droit international: De la conduite respective des belligérants par rapport aux lois de la guerre," *Revue de droit international et de législation comparée* 3 (1871): 329.

104. Francis Lieber's letter to General Dufour of April 10, 1872, was published in Gustave Rolin-Jaequemyns, "Note sur le projet de M. Moynier, relatif à l'établissement d'une institution judiciaire internationale, protectrice de la Convention, avec lettres de MM. Lieber, Ach, Morin, de Holtzendorff et Westlake," *Revue de droit international et de législation comparée* 4 (1872): 330–332.

105. André Durand, "The Role of Gustave Moynier in the Founding of the Institute of International Law (1873)," *International Review of the Red Cross* 34 (1994): 548.

106. Gustave Moynier, "Le congrès de Bruxelles et la révision de la Convention de Genève: trentième circulaire à Messieurs les Présidents et les Membres des Comités centraux de secours aux militaires blessés," *Bulletin international des sociétés de secours aux militaires blessés* 17 (1873): 197–201.

107. Gustave Moynier, "Ma contribution aux progrès du droit international," undated manuscript, ICRC Archive, GM.

108. George Halstead Boyland, *Six Months under the Red Cross, with the French Army* (Cincinnati, OH: Robert Clarke & Co., 1873), 28.

109. Ibid., 25.

110. Gorski notes that field boundaries may be porous to various extents, and that they may facilitate either the import or export of symbolic goods. See Philip S. Gorski,

"Bourdieusian Theory and Historical Analysis: Maps, Mechanisms, and Methods," in *Bourdieu and Historical Analysis*, ed. Philip S. Gorski (Durham, NC: Duke Univ. Press, 2013), 332, 340.

111. See chapter 3 for examples.

CHAPTER 5

1. Tim Allen and David Styan, "A Right to Interfere? Bernard Kouchner and the New Humanitarianism," *Journal of International Development* 12 (2000): 825–842; Philip Hammond, "Moral Combat: Advocacy Journalists and the New Humanitarianism," in *Rethinking Human Rights: Critical Approaches to International Politics*, ed. David Chandler (Basingstoke: Palgrave Macmillan, 2002), 176–195.

2. Peter Redfield, "Doctors, Borders, and Life in Crisis," *Cultural Anthropology* 20 (2005): 329.

3. Jonathan Benthall, "Le sans-frontiérisme," *Anthropology Today* 7 (1991): 1–3. With the rise of MSF as a movement focusing on medical aid, other NGOs transposed the model of *sans-frontiérisme* onto their own areas of work in organizations such as Reporters without Borders, Écoles sans Frontières, Télécoms sans Frontières, and Avocats sans Frontières.

4. François Jean, ed., *Life, Death, and Aid: The Médecins sans Frontières Report on World Crisis Intervention* (London: Routledge, 1993); Étienne Balibar, "On the Politics of Human Rights," *Constellations* 20 (2013): 18–26.

5. Referring to MSF as a singular movement is somewhat misleading since MSF members have often expressed different opinions on matters of intervention ethics. MSF today has five operational centers, spread around Europe, each of which is independent in its decision making process and possesses its own distinctive organizational culture. For this reason, this chapter focuses on the actions of specific key founding members or on specific chapters of the movement, rather than attempt to capture the movement with all of its diversity.

6. Monika Krause suggests that the humanitarian field only came into existence with the appearance of MSF in 1971, because until then there were no international actors struggling over field-specific capital. Indeed, there is no question that 1971 was the sharpest breaking point in the history of the humanitarian sector, and that MSF introduced a radically different view on humanitarian work than previously held. However, the ICRC was not alone in the international humanitarian arena before 1971. As the next section will show, important challenges to the primacy of the ICRC came from the American Red Cross and the International Federation of the Red Cross (IFRC). These organizations were acting internationally and modeling different iterations of the original framework the ICRC established for the movement. See Monika Krause, *The Good Project: Humanitarian Relief NGOs and the Fragmentation of Reason* (Chicago: Univ. of Chicago Press, 2014), 99–110.

7. As Bourdieu put it, "Someone who wants to achieve a revolution in the cinema . . . says [about his rival:] 'That is not *real* cinema.' . . . He pronounces anathemas, but in the name of a purer, more authentic definition of the *principles in whose name the dominant dominate*." Pierre Bourdieu, *The Field of Cultural Production: Essays on Art and Literature* (New York: Columbia Univ. Press, 1993), 134, italics added.

8. Jaquez Charl de Villiers, *Healers, Helpers and Hospitals: A History of Military Medicine in the Anglo-Boer War*, vol. 1 (Pretoria: Protea Book House, 2008).

9. Elizabeth van Heyningen, "The South African War as Humanitarian Crisis," *International Review of the Red Cross* 97 (2015): 999–1028.

10. Julia Irwin, *Making the World Safe: The American Red Cross and a Nation's Humanitarian Awakening* (New York: Oxford Univ. Press, 2013).

11. Matthew Stibbe, "The Internment of Civilians by Belligerent States during the First World War and the Response of the International Committee of the Red Cross," *Journal of Contemporary History* 41 (2006): 5–19.

12. See also André Durand, *From Sarajevo to Hiroshima: History of the International Committee of the Red Cross* (Geneva: Henry Dunant Institute, 1984).

13. John F. Hutchinson, *Champions of Charity: War and the Rise of the Red Cross* (Boulder, CO: Westview Press, 1996), 280.

14. *Christian Advocate*, February 26, 1914, 288.

15. For specifics about the split and about the orientation of the League of Red Cross Societies, see Bridget Towers, "Red Cross Organisational Politics, 1918–1922: Relations of Dominance and the Influence of the United States," in *International Health Organisations and Movements: 1918–1939*, ed. Paul Weindling (New York: Cambridge Univ. Press, 1995), 36–55. For details about the creation of the League and the ICRC's responses to it, see André Durand, *From Sarajevo to Hiroshima: History of the International Committee of the Red Cross* (Geneva: Henry Dunant Institute, 1984), 143–162.

16. Conference agreements included the 1928 establishment of the Standing Commission of the Red Cross and Red Crescent, which would coordinate between the league and the ICRC, as well as the adoption of the Statutes of the International Red Cross.

17. Caroline Moorehead, *Dunant's Dream: War, Switzerland, and the History of the Red Cross* (New York: Carroll & Graf Publishers, 1999), 349–350.

18. Moorehead claims that it is hard to know based on the reports whether the delegates were misled or simply ignored some evidence to the severity of the conditions at the camp. Moorehead, *Dunant's Dream*, 360–361.

19. Jean-Claude Favez, *The Red Cross and the Holocaust* (New York: Cambridge Univ. Press, 1999); David P. Forsythe, "Naming and Shaming: The Ethics of ICRC Discretion," *Millennium* 34 (2006): 461–474; Arieh Ben-Tov, *Facing the Holocaust in Budapest: The International Committee of the Red Cross and the Jews in Hungary, 1943–1945* (Norwell, MA: Kluwer, 1988).

20. Joachim J. Savelsberg, *Representing Mass Violence: Conflicting Responses to Human Rights Violations in Darfur* (Berkeley: Univ. of California Press, 2015), 106.

21. In a videotaped interview with Claude Lanzmann, Rossel claimed that although he had a suspicion that the camp had been prearranged for his visit, he was obliged to include only objective observations in his report. Having seen the camp in relatively good condition, his report was positive. "Maurice Rossel's ICRC visit to Theresienstadt and Auschwitz," United States Holocaust Memorial Museum, https:// collections.ushmm.org/search/catalog/irn1004374, accessed March 27, 2018.

22. ICRC delegates Charles Kolb and Vladimir de Steiger also worked in Bucharest and attempted to obtain permissions for Romanian Jews to emigrate to Turkey. Favez, *The Red Cross and the Holocaust*, 214.

23. Sébastien Farré, "The ICRC and the Detainees in Nazi Concentration Camps (1942–1945)," *International Review of the Red Cross* 94 (2012): 1381–1408.

24. For more on ICRC activities during World War II, see also François Bugnion, *The International Committee of the Red Cross and the Protection of War Victims* (Geneva: ICRC; Oxford: Macmillan Education, 2003), 167–243, and Gradimir Djurovic, *The Central Tracing Agency of the International Committee of the Red Cross* (Geneva: Henry Dunant Institute, 1986).

25. Gerald Steinacher, *Humanitarians at War: The Red Cross in the Shadow of the Holocaust* (Oxford: Oxford Univ. Press., 2017).

26. Ben-Tov, *Facing the Holocaust in Budapest*.

27. Walter Laqueur, *The Terrible Secret: Suppression of the Truth about Hitler's "Final Solution"* (Paris: Gallimard, 1981).

28. Jakob Kellenberger, "Speaking Out or Remaining Silent in Humanitarian Work," *International Review of the Red Cross* 86 (2004): 594.

29. Ibid., 600.

30. See also on this Jonathan Benthall, *Disasters, Relief, and the Media* (London: I. B. Tauris, 1993); Michael Ignatieff, "The Stories We Tell: Television and Humanitarian Aid," in *Hard Choices: Moral Dilemmas in Humanitarian Intervention*, ed. Jonathan Moore (Lanham, MD: Rowman & Littlefield Publishers, 1998), 287–302.

31. David P. Forsythe, *The Humanitarians: The International Committee of the Red Cross* (Cambridge: Cambridge Univ. Press, 2005), 46–48.

32. Ibid.

33. David Rieff, *A Bed for the Night: Humanitarianism in Crisis* (New York: Simon & Schuster, 2002), 148–149.

34. Alberto Melucci, "Social Movements and the Democratization of Everyday Life," in *Civil Society and the State: New European Perspectives*, ed. John Keane (London: Verso, 1988), 245–260; Jean Cohen and Andrew Arato, *Civil Society and Political Theory* (Cambridge, MA: MIT Press, 1992); Alain Touraine, "An Introduction to the Study of Social Movements," *Social Research* 52 (1985): 749–88.

35. Claus Offe, "New Social Movements: Challenging the Boundaries of Institutional Politics," *Social Research* 52 (1985): 826.

36. Craig J. Calhoun, "'New Social Movements' of the Early Nineteenth Century," *Social Science History* 17 (1993): 385–427.

37. On this, see also Michal Givoni, "Humanitarian Governance and Ethical Cultivation: Médecins sans Frontières and the Advent of the Expert-Witness," *Millennium* 40 (2011): 43–63.

38. Kevin P. Q. Phelan, "From an Idea to Action: The Evolution of *Médecins sans Frontières*," in *The New Humanitarians: Inspiration, Innovations, and Blueprints for Visionaries*, ed. Chris E. Stout (Westport, CT: Praeger Publishers, 2009), 8.

39. Ibid.

40. Historian Eleanor Davey demonstrates that the emergence of MSF and *sans-frontiérisme* in the 1970s was precipitated by a French preoccupation with the Third World (in particular with 1950s and 1960s *tiers-mondiste* ideas). See Eleanor Davey, *Idealism beyond Borders: The French Revolutionary Left and the Rise of Humanitarianism 1954–1988* (Cambridge: Cambridge Univ. Press, 2015).

41. Françoise Pradier, "Médecins sans Frontières, au service de la médecine des catastrophes," *Le Quotidien du Médecins*, December 16, 1971, 5.

42. Chibuike Uche, "Oil, British Interests, and the Nigerian Civil War," *Journal of African History* 49 (2008): 111–135.

43. See further discussion of the war and its consequences in Marc-Antoine Perouse de Montclos, "Humanitarian Aid and the Biafra War: Lessons Not Learned," *Africa Development* 34 (2009): 69–82.

44. Marie-Luce Desgrandchamps, "'Organising the Unpredictable': The Nigeria-Biafra War and Its Impact on the ICRC," *International Review of the Red Cross* 94 (2012): 1409–1432.

45. Renée C. Fox, *Doctors without Borders: Humanitarian Quests, Impossible Dreams of Médecins sans Frontières* (Baltimore, MD: Johns Hopkins Univ. Press, 2014).

46. Claudine Vidal, "Natural Disasters: 'Do Something!'" (interview with Rony Brauman), in *Humanitarian Negotiations Revealed: The MSF Experience*, ed. Claire Magone, Michaël Neuman, and Fabrice Weissman (London: Hurst & Co., 2011), 219–238.

47. Renée C. Fox, "Medical Humanitarianism and Human Rights: Reflections on Doctors without Borders and Doctors of the World," *Social Science and Medicine* 41 (1995): 1607–1616.

48. For more on the differences between ICRC and MSF conceptions of speaking out, see Fiona Terry, *Condemned to Repeat? The Paradox of Humanitarian Action* (Ithaca: Cornell Univ. Press, 2002), 22.

49. "Chantilly Principles," Médecins sans Frontières, http://association.msf.org/sites/default/files/documents/Principles%20Chantilly%20EN.pdf/, accessed March 27, 2018.

50. See Comité International de la Croix-Rouge, "Au secours des victimes du conflit du Nigéria," *Revue internationale de la Croix-Rouge* 51 (1969): 5–21.

51. Some have noted that the French doctors' publication of their experience in Biafra has been overdramatized, and that the gravity of the split between the Red Cross and the doctors has been overstated by the media and some historians. In fact, some of the doctors returned to Biafra with the Red Cross after publishing their articles. See Marie-Luce Desgrandchamps, "Revenir sur le mythe fondateur de Médecins sans Frontières: les relations entre les médecins français et le CICR pendant la guerre du Biafra (1967–1970)," *Relations internationales* 146 (2011): 95–108.

52. "MSF Financial Report 2012," Médecins sans Frontières, http://www.msf.org/sites/msf.org/files/msf_financial_report_interactive_2012_final.pdf/, accessed March 27, 2018.

53. "MSF International Activity Report 2012—Syria," Médecins sans Frontières, http://www.msf.org/international-activity-report-2012-syria/, accessed March 27, 2018.

54. Rony Brauman and Joelle Tanguy, "The MSF Experience," Médecins sans Frontières, 1998, https://www.doctorswithoutborders.org/msf-experience/, accessed March 27, 2018.

55. Bernard Kouchner, "Vive la vie," *Le Monde*, December 11, 1999.

56. Fabrice Weissman, "Silence Heals . . . From the Cold War to the War on Terror, MSF Speaks Out: A Brief History," in *Humanitarian Negotiations Revealed: The MSF Experience*, ed. Claire Magone, Michaël Neuman, and Fabrice Weissman, trans. Nina Friedman (London: Hurst & Co., 2011), 179.

57. *Libération*, "Le nouvel horizon humanitaire," December 10, 1999.

58. Dan Bortolotti, *Hope in Hell: Inside the World of Doctors without Borders* (Buffalo, NY: Firefly Books, 2004), 13.

59. Elliott Leyton, *Touched by Fire: Doctors without Borders in a Third World Crisis* (Toronto: McClelland & Stewart Inc., 1998), 58.

60. Ibid., 53.

61. Emmanuelli, quoted in Michal Givoni, *The Care of the Witness: A Contemporary History of Testimony in Crises* (New York: Cambridge Univ. Press, 2016), 193.

62. Leyton, *Touched by Fire*, 72.

63. Jeffrey C. Alexander, "Modern, Anti, Post, and Neo: How Intellectuals Explain 'Our Time,'" in *The Meanings of Social Life: A Cultural Sociology*, by Jeffrey C. Alexander (Oxford: Oxford Univ. Press, 2003), 193–228.

64. Jean, *Life, Death, and Aid*, 7.

65. Guy Hermet, "The Human Rights Challenge to Sovereignty," in *Life, Death, and Aid: The Médecins sans Frontières Report on World Crisis Intervention*, ed. François Jean (London: Routledge, 1993), 133.

66. See Sarah S. Stroup, *Borders among Activists: International NGOs in the United States, Britain, and France* (Ithaca, NY: Cornell Univ. Press, 2012), 71–134.

67. Terry, *Condemned to Repeat?*, 101.

68. Marie-Pierre Allié, "Introduction: Acting at Any Price?" in *Humanitarian Negotiations Revealed: The MSF Experience*, ed. Claire Magone, Michaël Neuman, and Fabrice Weissman (London: Hurst & Co., 2011), 1–14.

69. Laurence Binet, *MSF Speaks Out: Famine* and *Forced Relocations in Ethiopia 1984–1986* (Paris: Médecins Sans Frontières, 2005), 67.

70. Susan L. Woodward, *Balkan Tragedy: Chaos and Dissolution after the Cold War* (Washington, DC: Brookings Institution, 1995), 325.

71. Terry, *Condemned to Repeat?*, 89–105.

72. Laurence Binet, "Famine and Forced Relocations in Ethiopia 1984–1986," MSF-CRASH, November 13, 2013, https://www.msf-crash.org/en/publications/humanitarian-actors-and-practice/famine-and-forced-relocations-ethiopia-1984-1986/, accessed March 27, 2018; Weissman, "Silence Heals."

73. Terry, *Condemned to Repeat?*, 20.

74. Peter Moszynski, "Medical Charity Is Expelled from Darfur," *British Medical Journal* 342 (2011): 464; Fabrice Weissman, *Humanitarian Aid and the International Criminal Court: Grounds for Divorce* (Paris: CRASH, 2009).

75. Craig J. Calhoun, "The Imperative to Reduce Suffering: Charity, Progress, and Emergencies in the Field of Humanitarian Action," in *Humanitarianism in Question: Politics, Power, Ethics*, ed. Michael Barnett and Thomas Weiss (Ithaca, NY: Cornell Univ. Press, 2008), 73–97.

76. Rony Brauman, "Médecins Sans Frontières and the ICRC: Matters of Principle," *International Review of the Red Cross* 94 (2012): 1532 (emphasis in original).

77. See, e.g., "Syria: Aid Reaches Beleaguered Population in Homs and Harasta (Operational Update No. 14/2012)," ICRC, October 25, 2012, www.icrc.org/eng/resources/documents/update/2012/syriaupdate-2012-10-25.htm/, accessed March 27, 2018; "Syria: Assistance Reaches People in Old City of Homs (News Release No. 12/213)," ICRC, November 4, 2012, accessed March 27, 2018, http://www.icrc.org/eng/resources/documents/news-release/2012/11-04-syria-homs.htm/, accessed March 27, 2018; "Syria: Humanitarian Situation Catastrophic," ICRC, February 19, 2013, http://www.icrc.org/eng/resources/documents/press-briefing/2013/02-15-syria-humanitarian-situation.htm/, accessed March 27, 2018. For a broader policy overview, see Pierre Krähenbühl, "There Are No 'Good' or 'Bad' Civilians in Syria—We Must Help All Who Need Aid," *The Guardian*, March 3, 2013, https://www.theguardian.com/commentisfree/2013/mar/03/red-cross-aid-inside-syria/, accessed March 27, 2018.

78. Krause, *The Good Project*, 112–113.

CONCLUSION

1. A recent review of the state of the research on the closely related field of development demonstrated considerable limitations to existing knowledge. See Jennifer N. Brass, Wesley Longhofer, Rachel S. Robinson, and Allison Schnable, "NGOs and International Development: A Review of Thirty-Five Years of Scholarship," *World Development* 112 (2018): 136–149.

2. Richard Dawkins, *The God Delusion* (London: Bantam Press, 2006); Daniel C. Dennett, *Breaking the Spell: Religion as a Natural Phenomenon* (New York: Viking, 2006); Sam Harris, *The End of Faith: Religion, Terror, and the Future of Reason* (New York: W. W. Norton & Co., 2005); Christopher Hitchens, *God Is Not Great: How Religion Poisons Everything* (New York: Twelve [Hachette, Warner], 2007).

3. Yiyang Wu, "Pinker: No Scientific Evidence for God," *Harvard Crimson*, April 21, 2004, http://www.thecrimson.com/article/2004/4/21/pinker-no-scientific-evidence-for-god/, accessed April 9, 2018. See more in Steven Pinker, *Enlightenment Now: The Case for Reason, Science, Humanism, and Progress* (New York: Viking, 2018).

4. Steven Pinker, *The Better Angels of Our Nature: Why Violence Has Declined* (New York: Penguin Books, 2011), 677.

5. Peter Redfield, "A Less Modest Witness," *American Ethnologist* 33 (2006): 7. See similar sentiments in Peter Redfield, "Secular Humanitarianism and the Value of Life," in *What Matters? Ethnographies of Value in a Not So Secular Age*, ed. Courtney Bender and Ann Taves (New York: Columbia Univ. Press, 2012), 145.

6. Quoted in Caroline Abu-Sada, "Themes from the Project, Part 1," Médecins sans Frontières, https://www.doctorswithoutborders.org/themes-project-part-1/, accessed April 9, 2018.

7. Polly Markandya, "Secular Aid Reaches Those in Most Need," *The Guardian*, September 24, 2010, https://www.theguardian.com/commentisfree/belief/2010/sep/24/secular-aid-medecins-sans-frontires/, accessed April 9, 2018.

8. Monika Krause, *The Good Project: Humanitarian Relief NGOs and the Fragmentation of Reason* (Chicago: Univ. of Chicago Press, 2014), 119–120; see also Elizabeth Ferris, "Faith-based and Secular Humanitarian Organizations," *International Review of the Red Cross* 87 (2005): 311–325.

9. "Lutheran World Relief," Charity Navigator, https://www.charitynavigator.org/index.cfm?bay=search.history&orgid=4031/, accessed April 29, 2018; "Catholic Relief Services," Charity Navigator, https://www.charitynavigator.org/index.cfm?bay=search.history&orgid=5934/, accessed April 29, 2018; "Samaritan's Purse," Charity Navigator, https://www.charitynavigator.org/index.cfm?bay=search.history&orgid=4423/, accessed April 29, 2018.

10. See also Alastair Ager and Joey Ager, "Faith and the Discourse of Secular Humanitarianism," *Journal of Refugee Studies* 24 (2011–2013): 456–472; Alastair Ager and Joey Ager, *Faith, Secularism, and Humanitarian Engagement: Finding the Place of Religion in the Support of Displaced Communities* (New York: Palgrave Macmillan, 2015). For broader debates on the topic, see Elena Fiddian-Qasmiyeh, "Introduction: Faith-Based Humanitarianism in Contexts of Forced Displacement," *Journal of Refugee Studies* 24 (2011): 429–439.

11. David Skeel, "How Churches Are Helping Puerto Rico," *Wall Street Journal*, November 9, 2017, https://www.wsj.com/articles/how-churches-are-helping-puerto-rico-1510274035/, accessed April 29, 2018.

12. The same is true for international development organizations working on AIDS intervention: while some have been shown to partner successfully with religious organizations, many AIDS organizations see local religious leaders as primarily a source of misinformation. See Terence E. McDonnell, *Best Laid Plans: Cultural Entropy and the Unraveling of AIDS Media Campaigns* (Chicago: Univ. of Chicago Press, 2016), chap. 2.

13. Ann Swidler and Susan Cotts Watkins, *A Fraught Embrace: The Romance and Reality of AIDS Altruism in Africa* (Princeton, NJ: Princeton Univ. Press, 2017); Arland Thornton, *Reading History Sideways: The Fallacy and Enduring Impact of the Developmental Paradigm*

on Family Life (Chicago: Univ. of Chicago Press, 2005); Arland Thornton, Shawn F. Dorius, and Jeffrey Swindle, "Developmental Idealism: The Cultural Foundations of World Development Programs," *Sociology of Development* 1 (2015): 277–320.

14. Martin Ceadel, "The Quaker Peace Testimony and Its Contribution to the British Peace Movement: An Overview," *Quaker Studies* 7 (2003): 9–29; Martin Ceadel, *The Origins of War Prevention: The British Peace Movement and International Relations, 1730–1854* (Oxford: Clarendon, 1996); Martin Ceadel, *Semi-detached Idealists: The British Peace Movement and International Relations, 1854–1945* (Oxford: Oxford Univ. Press, 2000).

15. The committee is the author of *Speak Truth to Power: A Quaker Search for an Alternative to Violence*, one of the best known contemporary statements of Christian pacifism. About FBI involvement, see American Civil Liberties Union, "Documents Shed New light on Pentagon Surveillance of Peace Activists," ACLU, October 12, 2006, https://www.aclu.org/news/documents-shed-new-light-pentagon-surveillance-peace-activists/, accessed April 29, 2018.

16. See, for example, "Volunteers Lead by Example in the Promotion of Peace," IFRC, November 26, 2011, http://www.ifrc.org/fr/nouvelles/nouvelles/common/volunteers-lead-by-example-in-the-promotion-of-peace/, accessed April 23, 2018.

17. Baur and Schmitz usefully distinguish between "upward" accountability, toward donors and business partners, and "bottom-up" accountability, toward beneficiaries of INGO aid. See Dorothea Baur and Hans Peter Schmitz, "Corporations and NGOs: When Accountability Leads to Co-optation," *Journal of Business Ethics* 106 (2012): 9–21. For a broad overview of NGO accountability, see L. David Brown and Mark H. Moore, "Symposium: New Roles and Challenges for NGOs: Accountability, Strategy, and International Nongovernmental Organizations," *Nonprofit and Voluntary Sector Quarterly* 30 (2001): 569–587.

18. Anthony Bebbington, "Donor-NGO Relations and Representations of Livelihood in Nongovernmental Aid Chains," *World Development* 33 (2005): 937–950.

19. Greg Beckett, "A Dog's Life: Suffering Humanitarianism in Port-au-Prince, Haiti," *American Anthropologist* 119 (2017): 35–45.

20. Hugo Slim, "Not Philanthropy but Rights: The Proper Politicisation of Humanitarian Philosophy," *International Journal of Human Rights* 6 (2002): 1–22.

21. Mary Mostafanezhad, "Volunteer Tourism and the Popular Humanitarian Gaze," *Geoforum* 54 (July 2014): 111–118.

22. Hugo Slim, "Dissolving the Difference between Humanitarianism and Development: The Mixing of a Rights-based Solution," *Development in Practice* 10 (2000): 491–494.

23. Oxfam America, *Annual Report 2017* (Boston, MA: Oxfam America, 2018), 9.

24. Christian Captier, "What Does Humanitarian Protection Really Mean?" *Humanitarian Exchange Magazine* 23 (2003): 15–19.

25. Lin Cotterell, *Human Rights and Poverty Reduction Approaches to Human Rights in Humanitarian Crises* (London: Overseas Development Institute, 2005).

APPENDIX: SOURCES AND METHODOLOGY

1. The journal was renamed in 1885 *Bulletin international des sociétés de la Croix-Rouge*. It exists today as *Revue internationale de la Croix-Rouge*.

BIBLIOGRAPHY

Aaronson, Michael. "The Nigerian Civil War and 'Humanitarian Intervention.'" In *The History and Practice of Humanitarian Intervention and Aid in Africa*, edited by Bronwen Everill and Josiah Kaplan, 176–196. London: Palgrave Macmillan, 2013.

Abu-Sada, Caroline. "Themes from the Project, Part 1." *Médecins sans Frontières*. n.d. https://www.doctorswithoutborders.org/themes-project-part-1 (accessed April 9, 2018).

Acuto, Michele, ed. *Negotiating Relief: The Dialectic of Humanitarian Space*. London: C. Hurst, 2006.

Ador, Gustave, and Gustave Moynier. "Fondation d'une société en Roumanie et dissolution de celle des États-Unis." *Bulletin international des sociétés de secours aux militaires blessés* 7, no. 28 (1876): 159–161.

"Afghanistan: UN Strongly Condemns 'Tragic, Inexcusable' Kunduz Hospital Airstrike." *UN News*. October 3, 2015. https://news.un.org/en/story/2015/10/511652-afghanistan-un-strongly-condemns-tragic-inexcusable-kunduz-hospital-airstrike (accessed November 15, 2018).

Ager, Alastair, and Joey Ager. "Faith and the Discourse of Secular Humanitarianism." *Journal of Refugee Studies* 24, no. 3 (2011): 456–472.

Ager, Alastair, and Joey Ager. *Faith, Secularism, and Humanitarian Engagement: Finding the Place of Religion in the Support of Displaced Communities*. New York: Palgrave Macmillan, 2015.

Agier, Michel. "Humanity as an Identity and Its Political Effects (a Note on Camps and Humanitarian Government)." *Humanity* 1, no. 1 (2010): 29–45.

Alcott, Louisa May. *The Journals of Louisa May Alcott*. Edited by Joel Myerson and Daniel Shealy. Boston, MA: Little, Brown, 1989.

Alexander, Jeffrey C. *The Civil Sphere*. New York: Oxford Univ. Press, 2006.

Alexander, Jeffrey C. "'Globalization' as Collective Representation: The New Dream of a Cosmopolitan Civil Sphere." *Sociological Inquiry* 19, no. 1 (2005): 81–90.

Alexander, Jeffrey C. "Modern, Anti, Post, and Neo: How Intellectuals Explain 'Our Time.'" In *The Meanings of Social Life: A Cultural Sociology*, by Jeffrey C. Alexander, 193–228. Oxford: Oxford Univ. Press, 2003.

Alexander, Jeffrey C. "The Reality of Reduction: The Failed Synthesis of Pierre Bourdieu." In *Fin-de-Siècle Social Theory: Relativism, Reduction, and the Problem of Reason*, 128–217. London: Verso, 1995.

Alexander, Jeffrey C., and Philip Smith. "The Strong Program in Cultural Sociology: Elements of a Structural Hermeneutics." In *The Meanings of Social Life: A Cultural Sociology*, by Jeffrey C. Alexander, 11–26. Oxford: Oxford Univ. Press, 2003.

Alice, Grand Duchess, consort of Ludwig IV. *Alice, Grand Duchess of Hesse, Princess of Great Britain and Ireland: Biographical Sketch and Letters*. New York: G. P. Putnam's Sons, 1884.

Allen, Benjamin. *Legalist Empire: International Law and American Foreign Relations in the Early Twentieth Century*. Oxford: Oxford Univ. Press, 2016.

Allen, Tim, and David Styan. "A Right to Interfere? Bernard Kouchner and the New Humanitarianism." *Journal of International Development* 12, no. 6 (2000): 825–842.

Allié, Marie-Pierre. "Introduction: Acting at Any Price?" In *Humanitarian Negotiations Revealed: The MSF Experience*, edited by Claire Magone, Michaël Nerman, and Fabrice Weissman, 1–14. London: Hurst & Co., 2011.

Altay, Nezih, and Melissa Labonte. "Challenges in Humanitarian Information Management and Exchange: Evidence from Haiti." *Disasters* 38, no. S1 (2014): S50–S72.

American Civil Liberties Union. "Documents Shed New Light on Pentagon Surveillance of Peace Activists." *ACLU*. October 12, 2006. https://www.aclu.org/news/documents-shed-new-light-pentagon-surveillance-peace-activists (accessed April 29, 2018).

Anheier, Helmut K., Jürgen Gerhards, and Frank P. Romo. "Forms of Capital and Social Structure in Cultural Fields: Examining Bourdieu's Social Topography." *American Journal of Sociology* 100, no. 4 (1995): 859–903.

Appia, Louis Paul. *Les blessés dans le Schleswig pendant la guerre de 1864: rapport présenté au Comité international de Genève*. Geneva: Jules-Guillaume Fick, 1864.

Ariga, Nagao. *La Croix-Rouge en Extrême-Orient: Exposé de l'organisation et du fonctionnement*. Paris: A. Pedone, 1900.

Army Medical Department. *Report for the Year 1897*. London: Harrison and Sons, 1898.

Arnold, Annika. "Towards a Transcultural Community of Climate Change: Adapting Max Weber's Distinction of Vergemeinschaftung and Vergesellschaftung." In *Europe and America in the Mirror: Culture, Economy, and History*, edited by Maik Arnold and Przemysław Łukasik, 107–123. Krakow: NOMOS, 2012.

Arrault, Henri. *Notice sur le perfectionnement du matériel des ambulances volantes*. Paris: Victor Rozier, 1861.

Association congolaise et africaine. "L'Association congolaise et africaine de la Croix-Rouge de 1888–1908." *Bulletin international des sociétés de la Croix-Rouge* 40, no. 158 (1909): 93–96.

Association congolaise et africaine. "L'Avenir de la Croix-Rouge au Congo." *Bulletin international des sociétés de la Croix-Rouge* 34, no. 136 (1903): 219–224.

Association congolaise et africaine. "Le drapeau congolais." *Bulletin international des sociétés de la Croix-Rouge* 30, no. 118 (1899): 86–87.

Baer, Susanne. "Privatizing Religion, Legal Groupism, No-Go-Areas, and the Public-Private-Ideology in Human Rights Politics." *Constellations* 20, no. 1 (2013): 68–84.

Balibar, Étienne. "On the Politics of Human Rights." *Constellations* 20, no. 1 (2013): 18–26.

Baly, Monica E. *Nursing and Social Change*. London: Heinemann Medical, 1973.

Barnett, Michael N. *Empire of Humanity: A History of Humanitarianism*. Ithaca, NY: Cornell Univ. Press, 2011.

Barnett, Michael N. "Humanitarian Governance." *Annual Review of Political Science* 16 (2013): 379–398.

Barton, Clara. *The Red Cross*. Washington, DC: American Historical Press, 1906.

Barton, Clara. *The Red Cross: A History of This Remarkable International Movement in the Interest of Humanity*. Washington, DC: American National Red Cross, 1898.

Barton, Clara. *The Red Cross in Peace and War*. Washington, DC: American Historical Press, 1904.

Barton, Clara. *The Red Cross of the Geneva Convention: What It Is*. Washington, DC: Rufus H. Darby, 1878.

Barton, Clara. *A Story of the Red Cross: Glimpses of Field Work*. New York: Appleton and Co., 1904.

Bass, Gary J. *Freedom's Battle: The Origins of Humanitarian Intervention*. New York: Alfred A. Knopf, 2008.

Baur, Dorothea, and Hans Peter Schmitz. "Corporations and NGOs: When Accountability Leads to Co-optation." *Journal of Business Ethics* 106, no. 1 (2012): 9–21.

Beaufort, Comte de. "Déclaration du conseil de la Société française de secours aux blessés des armées de terre et de mer." *Bulletin international des sociétés de secours aux militaires blessés* 2, no. 7–8 (1871): 208–212.

Bebbington, Anthony. "Donor-NGO Relations and Representations of Livelihood in Non-governmental Aid Chains." *World Development* 33, no. 6 (2005): 937–950.

Beckett, Greg. "A Dog's Life: Suffering Humanitarianism in Port-au-Prince, Haiti." *American Anthropology* 119, no. 1 (2017): 35–45.

Bektas, Yakup. "The Crimean War as a Technological Enterprise." *Notes and Records* 71 (2017): 233–262.

Bell, David A. *The First Total War: Napoleon's Europe and the Birth of Warfare as We Know It*. Boston: Mariner Books, 2007.

Benthall, Jonathan. *Disasters, Relief, and the Media*. London: I. B. Tauris, 1993.

Benthall, Jonathan. "Le sans-frontiérisme." *Anthropology Today* 7, no. 6 (1991): 1–3.

Benthall, Jonathan. "The Red Cross and Red Crescent Movement and Islamic Societies, with Special Reference to Jordan." *British Journal of Middle Eastern Studies* 24, no. 2 (1977): 157–177.

Ben-Tov, Arieh. *Facing the Holocaust in Budapest: The International Committee of the Red Cross and the Jews in Hungary, 1943–1945*. Norwell, MA: Kluwer, 1988.

Berry, Nicholas O. *War and the Red Cross: The Unspoken Mission*. New York: St. Martin's Press, 1997.

Best, Geoffrey. *Humanity in Warfare: The Modern History of the International Law of Armed Conflicts*. London: Methuen, 1983.

Biéler, Blanche. *Un fils du refuge, Jean-Henri Merle d'Aubigné: ses origines, sa vie, son œuvre*. Geneva: Éditions Labor, 1934.

Biernacki, Richard. "Cultural Coherence in Early Modern England: The Invention of Contract." *American Journal of Cultural Sociology* 2, no. 3 (2014): 277–299.

Binet, Laurence. "Famine and Forced Relocations in Ethiopia 1984–1986." *MSF-CRASH*. November 13, 2013. https://www.msf-crash.org/en/publications/humanitarian -actors-and-practice/famine-and-forced-relocations-ethiopia-1984-1986 (accessed March 27, 2018).

Binet, Laurence. *MSF Speaks Out: Famine and Forced Relocations in Ethiopia 1984–1986*. Paris: Médecins sans Frontières, 2005.

Birmingham Daily Post. "The War." September 27, 1877: 8.

Blake, Debbie. *Daughters of Ireland: Pioneering Irish Women*. Dublin: History Press Ireland, 2015.

Bluntschli, Johann Caspar. *Le droit international codifié*. Translated by C. Lardy. Paris: Guillaumin et cie, 1870.

Boardman, Mabel Thorp. *Under the Red Cross Flag at Home and Abroad*. Philadelphia: J. B. Lippincott Co., 1917.

Bodart, Gaston. *Losses of Life in Modern Wars: Austria-Hungary, France.* Oxford: Clarendon Press; New York: H. Milford, 1916.

Boissier, Pierre. *From Solferino to Tsushima: History of the International Committee of the Red Cross.* Geneva: Henry Dunant Institute, 1985.

Boissier, Pierre. *Henry Dunant.* Geneva: Henry Dunant Institute, 1974.

Boissier, Pierre. "Les premières années de la Croix-Rouge." *Revue Internationale de la Croix-Rouge* 45, no. 531 (1963): 114–132.

Boli, John, and George M. Thomas, eds. *Constructing World Culture: International Nongovernmental Organizations since 1875.* Stanford, CA: Stanford Univ. Press, 1999.

Boli, John, and George M. Thomas. "INGOs and the Organization of World Culture." In *Constructing World Culture: International Nongovernmental Organizations since 1875,* edited by John Boli and George M. Thomas, 13–49. Stanford, CA: Stanford Univ. Press, 1999.

Boltanski, Luc. *Distant Suffering: Morality, Media, and Politics.* Cambridge: Cambridge Univ. Press, 1999.

Bond, Brian. *War and Society in Europe, 1870–1970.* Montreal: McGill-Queen's Univ. Press, 1998.

Bonikowski, Bart. "Nationalism in Settled Times." *Annual Review of Sociology* 42 (2016): 427–449.

Bortolotti, Dan. *Hope in Hell: Inside the World of Doctors without Borders.* Buffalo, NY: Firefly Books, 2004.

Bost, Ami. *Mémoires pouvant servir à l'histoire du réveil religieux des Églises protestantes de la Suisse et de la France: et à l'intelligence des principales questions théologiques et ecclésiastiques du jour.* Paris: C. Meyrueis, 1854–1855.

Boston Recorder. "Current Paragraphs." October 6, 1865, 158.

Bostridge, Mark. *Florence Nightingale: The Woman and Her Legend.* New York: Viking, 2008.

Bourdieu, Pierre. *The Field of Cultural Production: Essays on Art and Literature.* New York: Columbia Univ. Press, 1993.

Bourdieu, Pierre. "The Force of Law: Toward a Sociology of the Juridical Field." *Hastings Law Journal* 38, no. 3 (1987): 805–1297.

Bourdieu, Pierre. "On the Possibility of a Field of World Sociology." In *Social Theory for a Changing Society,* edited by Pierre Bourdieu and James S. Coleman, 373–387. New York: Russell Sage Foundation, 1991.

Bourdieu, Pierre. *Practical Reason.* Cambridge: Polity Press, 1998 [1994].

Bourdieu, Pierre. "Rethinking the State: Genesis and Structure of the Bureaucratic Field." In *State/Culture: State Formation after the Cultural Turn,* edited by George Steinmetz, translated by Loïc J. D. Wacquant and Samar Farage, 53–94. Ithaca, NY: Cornell Univ. Press, 1999.

Bourdieu, Pierre. *The Rules of Art: Genesis and Structure of the Literary Field.* Cambridge: Polity Press, 1996.

Bourdieu, Pierre. "The Social Conditions of the International Circulation of Ideas." In *Bourdieu: A Critical Reader,* edited by Richard Shusterman, 220–228. Oxford: Blackwell Publishers, 1999.

Bourdieu, Pierre, Gisele Sapiro, and Brian McHale. "First Lecture. Social Space and Symbolic Space: Introduction to a Japanese Reading of Distinction." *Poetics Today* 12, no. 4 (1991): 627–638.

Bowles, Charles S. P. *Report of Charles S. P. Bowles, Foreign Agent of the United States Sanitary Commission, upon the International Congress of Geneva: For the Amelioration of the Condi-*

tion of the Sick and Wounded Soldiers of Armies in the Field, Convened at Geneva. London: R. Clay, and Taylor, 1864.

Boyland, George Halstead. Six Months Under the Red Cross, with the French Army. Cincinnati, OH: Robert Clarke & Co., 1873.

Brass, Jennifer N., Wesley Longhofer, Rachel S. Robinson, and Allison Schnable. "NGOs and International Development: A Review of Thirty-Five Years of Scholarship." World Development 112 (2018): 136–149.

Brauman, Rony. "Médecins sans Frontières and the ICRC: Matters of Principle." International Review of the Red Cross 94, no. 888 (2012): 1523–1535.

Brauman, Rony, and Joelle Tanguy. "The MSF Experience." Médecins sans Frontières. 1998. https://www.doctorswithoutborders.org/msf-experience (accessed March 27, 2018).

Breycha-Vauther, Arthur C., and Michael Potulicki. "The Order of St. John in International Law: A Forerunner of the Red Cross." American Journal of International Law 48 (1954): 554–563.

British Medical Journal. "Red Cross Decorations." August 17, 1872: 200.

Brown, L. David, and Mark H. Moore. "Symposium: New Roles and Challenges for NGOs: Accountability, Strategy, and International Nongovernmental Organizations." Nonprofit and Voluntary Sector Quarterly 30, no. 3 (2001): 569–587.

Brubaker, Rogers. Citizenship and Nationhood in France and Germany. Cambridge, MA: Harvard Univ. Press, 1991.

Bryant, Janet L., and Kathleen Byrne Colling. "Broken Wills and Tender Hearts: Religious Ideology and the Trained Nurse of the Nineteenth Century." In Florence Nightingale and Her Era: A Collection of New Scholarship, edited by Vern Bullough, Bonnie Bullough, and Marietta P. Stanton, 153–167. New York: Garland Publishing, Inc., 1990.

Brysk, Alison. Speaking Rights to Power: Constructing Political Will. New York: Oxford Univ. Press, 2013.

Buchholz, Larissa. "What Is a Global Field? Theorizing Fields beyond the Nation-State." Sociological Review Monographs 64, no. 2 (2016): 31–60.

Buckingham, Clyde. Clara Barton: A Broad Humanity. Alexandria, VA: Mt. Vernon, 1977.

Bugnion, François. "The Arrival of Bourbaki's Army at Les Verrières: The Internment of the First French Army in Switzerland on 1 February 1871." International Review of the Red Cross 36, no. 311 (1996): 181–193.

Bugnion, François. "Birth of an Idea: The Founding of the International Committee of the Red Cross and of the International Red Cross and Red Crescent Movement: From Solferino to the Original Geneva Convention (1859–1864)." International Review of the Red Cross 94, no. 888 (2012): 1299–1338.

Bugnion, François. "Geneva and the Red Cross." International Committee of the Red Cross. 2005. https://www.icrc.org/eng/assets/files/other/geneve_et_croix_rouge_anglais.pdf (accessed March 24, 2018).

Bugnion, François. The Emblem of the Red Cross: A Brief History. Geneva: International Committee of the Red Cross, 1977.

Bugnion, François. The International Committee of the Red Cross and the Protection of War Victims. Geneva: ICRC; Oxford: Macmillan Education, 2003.

Burton, David H. Clara Barton: In the Service of Humanity. Westport, CT: Greenwood Press, 1995.

Büyükokutan, Barış. "Toward a Theory of Cultural Appropriation: Buddhism, the Vietnam War, and the Field of U.S. Poetry." American Sociological Review 76, no. 4 (2011): 620–639.

Cabré, Monserrat. "Women or Healers? Household Practices and the Categories of Health Care in Late Medieval Iberia." *Bulletin of the History of Medicine* 82 (2008): 18–51.

Caglioti, Daniela L. "Waging War on Civilians: The Expulsion of Aliens in the Franco-Prussian War." *Past Present* 221, no. 1 (2013): 161–195.

Calhoun, Craig J. "For the Social History of the Present: Bourdieu as Historical Sociologist." In *Bourdieu and Historical Analysis*, edited by Philip S. Gorski, 36–66. Durham, NC: Duke Univ. Press, 2013.

Calhoun, Craig J. "The Idea of Emergency: Humanitarian Action and Global Disorder." In *Contemporary States of Emergency: The Politics of Military and Humanitarian Intervention*, edited by Didier Fassin and Mariella Pandolfi, 29–58. Cambridge, MA: Zone Books, 2010.

Calhoun, Craig J. "The Imperative to Reduce Suffering: Charity, Progress, and Emergencies in the Field of Humanitarian Action." In *Humanitarianism in Question: Power, Politics, Ethics*, edited by Michael Barnett and Thomas G. Weiss, 73–97. Ithaca, NY: Cornell Univ. Press, 2008.

Calhoun, Craig J. "Nationalism and Civil Society: Democracy, Diversity, and Self-determination." In *Nations Matter: Culture, History, and the Cosmopolitan Dream*, by Craig J. Calhoun, 77–101. London: Routledge, 2007.

Calhoun, Craig J. "'New Social Movements' of the Early Nineteenth Century." *Social Science History* 17, no. 3 (1993): 385–427.

Camic, Charles. "Bourdieu's Two Sociologies of Knowledge." In *Bourdieu and Historical Analysis*, edited by Philip S. Gorski, 183–211. Durham, NC: Duke Univ. Press, 2013.

Captier, Christian. "What Does Humanitarian Protection Really Mean?" *Humanitarian Exchange Magazine* 23 (2003): 15–19.

CARE. *CARE USA 2016 Annual Report*. Atlanta, GA: CARE USA, 2017.

Carnahan, Burrus M. "Lincoln, Lieber, and the Laws of War: The Origins and Limits of the Principle of Military Necessity." *American Journal of International Law* 92, no. 2 (1998): 213–31.

Casanova, José. *Public Religions in the Modern World*. Chicago: Univ. of Chicago Press, 1994.

"Catholic Relief Services." *Charity Navigator*. n.d. https://www.charitynavigator.org/index .cfm?bay=search.history&orgid=5934 (accessed April 29, 2018).

Ceadel, Martin. *The Origins of War Prevention: The British Peace Movement and International Relations, 1730–1854*. Oxford: Clarendon, 1996.

Ceadel, Martin. "The Quaker Peace Testimony and Its Contribution to the British Peace Movement: An Overview." *Quaker Studies* 7, no. 1 (2003): 9–29.

Ceadel, Martin. *Semi-detached Idealists: The British Peace Movement and International Relations, 1854–1945*. Oxford: Oxford Univ. Press, 2000.

"Chantilly Principles." *Médecins sans Frontières*. n.d. http://association.msf.org/sites /default/files/documents/Principles%20Chantilly%20EN.pdf (accessed March 27, 2018).

Chaponnière, Corinne. *Henry Dunant: La Croix d'un homme*. Paris: Perrin, 2010.

Chassay, Clancy. "I Was Still Holding My Grandson's Hand—The Rest Was Gone." *The Guardian*. December 15, 2008. https://www.theguardian.com/world/2008/dec/16 /afghanistan-taliban-us-foreign-policy (accessed November 29, 2018).

Checkland, Olive. *Humanitarianism and the Emperor's Japan, 1877–1977*. New York: St. Martin's, 1994.

Chenevière, Jean-Jacques-Caton. *Première lettre à un ami sur l'état actuel de l'église de Genève, et sur quelques-unes des accusations intentées contre ses pasteurs*. Geneva: J.-J. Paschoud, 1817.

Chenu, Jean-Charles. *Aperçu historique, statistique et clinique sur le service des ambulances et des hôpitaux de la Société française de secours aux blessés des armées de terre et de mer: pendant la guerre de 1870–1871*. Paris: Dumaine, 1874.

Chenu, Jean Charles. "La guerre et l'humanité au XIXme siècle, par M. L. de Cazenove." *Bulletin international des sociétés de secours aux militaires blessés* 1, no. 2 (1870): 88–91.

Chicago Daily Tribune. "Story of a Red Cross." January 19, 1896: 34.

Chrastil, Rachel. "The French Red Cross, War Readiness, and Civil Society, 1866–1914." *French Historical Studies* 31, no. 3 (2008): 445–476.

Christian Advocate. February 26, 1914: 288.

"Christian Work on the Battle-field; Being Incidents of the Labours of the United States 'Christian Commission." *British Quarterly Review* 52 (1870): 564.

Chung, King-Thom. *Women Pioneers of Medical Research: Biographies of 25 Outstanding Scientists*. Jefferson, NC: McFarland, 2010.

Clark, Ann Marie, Elisabeth J. Friedman, and Kathryn Hochstetler. "The Sovereign Limits of Global Civil Society: A Comparison of NGO Participation in UN World Conferences on the Environment, Human Rights, and Women." *World Politics* 51, no. 1 (1998): 1–35.

Clemens, Elisabeth S. "Toward a Historicized Sociology: Theorizing Events, Processes, and Emergence." *Annual Review of Sociology* 33 (2007): 527–549.

Cohen, Jean, and Andrew Arato. *Civil Society and Political Theory*. Cambridge, MA: MIT Press, 1992.

Collinson, Patrick. "England and International Calvinism 1558–1640." In *International Calvinism, 1541–1715*, edited by Menna Prestwich, 197–223. New York: Clarendon Press of Oxford Univ. Press, 1985.

Collinson, Sarah, and Samir Elhawary. *Humanitarian Space: A Review of Trends and Issues*. London: Overseas Development Institute, 2012.

Comité auxiliaire de Strasbourg. "Compte rendu des travaux du Comité auxiliaire de Strasbourg, du 26 juillet 1870 au 31 octobre 1871." *Bulletin international des sociétés de secours aux militaires blessés* 3, no. 11 (1872): 153–154.

Comité central. "L'ambassade japonaise." *Bulletin international des sociétés de secours aux militaires blessés* 5, no. 17 (1873): 11.

Comité central allemand. "Allemagne." *Bulletin international des sociétés de secours aux militaires blessés* 2, no. 9 (1871): 8–14.

Comité central allemand. "Assemblée de Nuremberg." *Bulletin international des sociétés de secours aux militaires blessés* 3, no. 10 (1872): 57–60.

Comité central allemand. "Communication du Comité central allemand." *Bulletin international des sociétés de secours aux militaires blessés* 2, no. 9 (1871): 8–14.

Comité central allemand. "Le Comité central allemand." *Bulletin international des sociétés de secours aux militaires blessés* 2, no. 7–8 (1871): 202–203.

Comité central belge. "Journal d'une infirmière, par Mme la baronne de Crombrugghe." *Bulletin international des sociétés de secours aux militaires blessés* 2, no. 9 (1871): 16–20.

Comité central espagnol. "La guerre civile." *Bulletin international des sociétés de secours aux militaires blessés* 3, no. 12 (1872): 196–203.

Comité central français. "France." *Bulletin international des sociétés de secours aux militaires blessés* 2, no. 9 (1871): 25.

Comité central–France. "L'œuvre française pendant la dernière guerre." *Bulletin international des sociétés de secours aux militaires blessés* 3, no. 12 (1872): 206–214.

Comité de Bade. "La Convention de Genève pendant la guerre de 1870–71." *Bulletin international des sociétés de secours aux militaires blessés* 2, no. 9 (1871): 15.

Comité de Berlin. *Les violations de la Convention de Genève par les Français en 1870–71: Dépêches, protocoles, rapports, etc.* Berlin: C. Heymons, 1871.

Comité de l'Asie française. "Japon." *Bulletin du comité de l'Asie française* 6, no. 69 December (1906): 504–506.

Comité de Madrid. "La charité dans les guerres civiles." *Bulletin international des sociétés de secours aux militaires blessés* 1, no. 4 (1870): 175–178.

Comité international [de la Croix-Rouge]. "Assemblée générale de la société néerlandaise." *Bulletin international des sociétés de secours* 1, no. 1 (1869): 31–35.

Comité international [de la Croix-Rouge]. "Association américaine." *Bulletin international des sociétés de secours aux militaires blessés* 1, no. 1 (1869): 24–25.

Comité international de la Croix-Rouge. "Au secours des victimes du conflit du Nigéria." *Revue internationale de la Croix-Rouge* 51, no. 601 (1969): 5–21.

Comité international [de la Croix-Rouge]. "Avant-propos." *Bulletin international des sociétés de secours aux militaires blessés* 1, no. 1 (1869): 2.

Comité international [de la Croix-Rouge]. "Comité international." *Bulletin international des sociétés de secours aux militaires blessés* 2, no. 5 (1870): 3–13.

Comité international [de la Croix-Rouge]. "De l'adoption par les diverses sociétés de secours d'une dénomination uniforme." *Bulletin international des sociétés de secours aux militaires blessés* 3, no. 12 (1872): 177–181.

Comité international [de la Croix-Rouge]. "Dissolution de l'Association congolaise et africaine." *Bulletin international des sociétés de la Croix-Rouge* 40, no. 159 (1909): 143–144.

Comité international [de la Croix-Rouge]. "Du double caractère, national et international, des sociétés de secours." *Bulletin internationale des sociétés de secours aux militaires blessés* 1, no. 4 (1870): 11–14.

Comité international de la Croix-Rouge. *La Conférence Internationale réunie à Genève les 26, 27, 28, et 29 Octobre 1863 pour étudier les moyens de pourvoir à l'insuffisance du service sanitaire dans les armées en campagne, deuxième édition.* Geneva: Comité international de la Croix-Rouge, 1904.

Comité international [de la Croix-Rouge]. "La société prussienne et la nouvelle instruction pour le service sanitaire de l'armée en campagne." *Bulletin des sociétés de secours aux militaires blessés* 1, no. 4 (1870): 165–168.

Comité international [de la Croix-Rouge]. "Législation militaire." *Bulletin international des sociétés de secours aux militaires blessés* 1, no. 3 (1870): 108–119.

Comité international [de la Croix-Rouge]. "Les dix premières années de la Croix-Rouge." *Bulletin international des sociétés de secours aux militaires blessés* 16, no. July (1873): 165–243.

Comité international [de la Croix-Rouge]. "Les prisonniers de guerre." *Bulletin international des sociétés de secours aux militaires blessés* 2, no. 6 (1871): 92–96.

Comité international [de la Croix-Rouge]. "Note sur le Comité de Lisbon." *Bulletin des sociétés de secours aux militaires blessés* 1, no. 3 (1870): 151–153.

Comité international [de la Croix-Rouge]. "Progrès de l'œuvre de la Croix Rouge." *Bulletin international des sociétés de secours aux militaires blessés* 1, no. 4 (1870): 173.

Comité international de la Croix-Rouge. *Résumé des travaux du Comité International de la Croix-Rouge de 1884–1890, lu à la séance du 14 Novembre 1890 par son président.* Geneva: B. Soullier, 1890.

Comité international [de la Croix-Rouge]. *Secours aux blessés: Communication du Comité international faisant suite au compte rendu de la conférence internationale de Genève.* Geneva: Imprimerie de Jules-Guillaume Fick, 1864.

Comité international [de la Croix-Rouge]. "Travaux du Comité international pendant le dernier trimestre de l'année 1870." *Bulletin international des sociétés de secours aux militaires blessés* 2, no. 6 (1871): 77–91.

Conboy, Martin. *Journalism: A Critical History.* London: Sage Publications, 2004.

Cotterell, Lin. *Human Rights and Poverty Reduction Approaches to Human Rights in Humanitarian Crises.* London: Overseas Development Institute, 2005.

Coupland, Robin M. "The Effects of Weapons and the Solferino Cycle: Where Disciplines Meet to Prevent or Limit the Damage Caused by Weapons." *British Medical Journal* 319, no. 7214 (1999): 864–865.

Curtis, Heather D. *Holy Humanitarians: American Evangelicals and Global Aid.* Cambridge, MA: Harvard Univ. Press, 2018.

Daily News. *The War Correspondence of the "Daily News" 1877–8 . . . Forming a Continuous History of the War between Russia and Turkey.* London: Macmillan and Co., 1878.

d'Arneth, F.-H. "Événements de Dalmatie." *Bulletin international des sociétés de secours aux militaires blessés* 1, no. 3 (1870): 123–124.

Davey, Eleanor. "Famine, Aid, and Ideology: The Political Activism of Médecins sans Frontières in the 1980s." *French Historical Studies* 34, no. 3 (2011): 529–558.

Davey, Eleanor. *Idealism beyond Borders: The French Revolutionary Left and the Rise of Humanitarianism 1954–1988.* Cambridge: Cambridge Univ. Press, 2015.

Davies, Thomas. "Rethinking the Origins of Transnational Humanitarian Organizations: The Curious Case of the International Shipwreck Society." *Global Networks* 18, no. 3 (2018): 461–478.

Davis, David Brion. *The Problem of Slavery in the Age of Revolution, 1770–1823.* Ithaca, NY: Cornell Univ. Press, 1975.

Davis, Norman H. "Preface." In *A Memory of Solferino,* by J. Henry Dunant, 5–16. Washington, DC: American National Red Cross, 1939.

Dawkins, Richard. *The God Delusion.* London: Bantam Press, 2006.

de Melun, Armand. "Société française de secours aux blessés militaires des armées de terre et de mer: Séance générale du 28 Décembre 1871." *Paris,* 1872: A. Le Clere.

de No Louis, Eduardo. "Reflections on Spain's Contribution to the Application of Humanitarian Law in War." *International Review of the Red Cross* 70, no. 1 (1967): 3–12.

de Senarclens, Jean. *Gustave Moynier le bâtisseur.* Geneva: Slatkine, 2000.

de Swaan, Abram. "Widening Circles of Identification: Emotional Concerns in Sociogenetic Perspective." *Theory, Culture, and Society* 12, no. 2 (1995): 25–39.

de Villiers, Jaquez Charl. *Healers, Helpers, and Hospitals: A History of Military Medicine in the Anglo-Boer War.* Vol. 1. Pretoria: Protea Book House, 2008.

De Waal, Alex. *Famine Crimes: Politics and the Disaster Relief Industry in Africa.* Bloomington: Indiana Univ. Press, 1997.

Dennett, Daniel C. *Breaking the Spell: Religion as a Natural Phenomenon.* New York: Viking, 2006.

Desgrandchamps, Marie-Luce. "'Organising the Unpredictable': The Nigeria–Biafra War and Its Impact on the ICRC." *International Review of the Red Cross* 94, no. 888 (2012): 1409–1432.

Desgrandchamps, Marie-Luce. "Revenir sur le mythe fondateur de Médecins sans Frontières: les relations entre les médecins français et le CICR pendant la guerre du Biafra (1967–1970)." *Relations internationales* 146, no. 2 (2011): 95–108.

Dezalay, Yves, and Bryant G. Garth. *The Internationalization of Palace Wars: Lawyers, Economists, and the Contest to Transform Latin American States.* Chicago: Univ. of Chicago Press, 2010.

Dictionnaire historique de la Suisse. January 25, 2018. http://www.hls-dhs-dss.ch/f/home.

Dixon, Peter, and Chris Tenove. "International Criminal Justice as a Transnational Field: Rules, Authority, and Victims." *International Journal of Transnational Justice* 7, no. 3 (2013): 393–412.

Djurovic, Gradimir. *The Central Tracing Agency of the International Committee of the Red Cross.* Geneva: Henry Dunant Institute, 1986.

Donnelly, Jack. "Human Rights: A New Standard of Civilization?" *International Affairs* 74, no. 1 (1998): 1–24.

Dromi, Shai M. "For Good and Country: Nationalism and the Diffusion of Humanitarianism in the Late Nineteenth Century." *Sociological Review Monographs* 64, no. 2 (2016): 79–97.

Dromi, Shai M. "Soldiers of the Cross: Calvinism, Humanitarianism, and the Genesis of Social Fields." *Sociological Theory* 34, no. 3 (2016): 196–219.

Duckers, Peter. *British Orders and Decorations.* Shire: Princes Risborough, 2004.

Duffield, Mark R. *Development, Security, and Unending War: Governing the World of Peoples.* Cambridge, UK: Polity Press, 2007.

Dunant, Henry. *A Memory of Solferino.* Washington, DC: American National Red Cross, 1939.

Durand, André. "The Development of the Idea of Peace in the Thinking of Henry Dunant." *International Review of the Red Cross* 26, no. 250 (1986): 16–51.

Durand, André. *From Sarajevo to Hiroshima: History of the International Committee of the Red Cross.* Geneva: Henry Dunant Institute, 1984.

Durand, André. "Gustave Moynier and the Peace Societies." *International Review of the Red Cross* 36, no. 314 (1996): 532–550.

Durand, André. "The Role of Gustave Moynier in the Founding of the Institute of International Law (1873)." *International Review of the Red Cross* 34, no. 303 (1994): 542–564.

Durand, Roger, and Jacques Meurant. *Préludes et pionniers: les précurseurs de la Croix-Rouge, 1840–1860.* Geneva: Société Henry Dunant, 1991.

Edgell, Penny. "A Cultural Sociology of Religion: New Directions." *Annual Review of Sociology* 38 (2012): 247–265.

Elliott, Michael A. "The Institutional Expansion of Human Rights, 1863–2003: A Comprehensive Dataset of International Instruments." *Journal of Peace Research* 48, no. 4 (2011): 537–546.

Ellis, John. *The Social History of the Machine Gun.* Baltimore, MD: Johns Hopkins Univ. Press, 1986.

Emirbayer, Mustafa, and Erik Schneiderhan. "Dewey and Bourdieu on Democracy." In *Bourdieu and Historical Analysis,* edited by Philip S. Gorski, 131–157. Durham, NC: Duke Univ. Press, 2013.

Entwistle, Joanne, and Agnès Rocamora. "The Field of Fashion Materialized: A Study of London Fashion Week." *Sociology* 40, no. 4 (2006): 735–751.

Ewans, Martin. *European Atrocity, African Catastrophe: Leopold II, the Congo Free State, and Its Aftermath.* London: Routledge, 2002.

Farré, Sébastien. "The ICRC and the Detainees in Nazi Concentration Camps (1942–1945)." *International Review of the Red Cross* 94, no. 888 (2012): 1381–1408.

Fassin, Didier. *Humanitarian Reason: A Moral History of the Present.* Berkeley: Univ. of California Press, 2012.

Faust, Drew Gilpin. *This Republic of Suffering: Death and the American Civil War.* New York: Alfred A. Knopf, 2008.

Favez, Jean-Claude. *The Red Cross and the Holocaust*. New York: Cambridge Univ. Press, 1999.

Ferris, Elizabeth. "Faith-based and Secular Humanitarian Organizations." *International Review of the Red Cross* 87, no. 858 (2005): 311–325.

Fiddian-Qasmiyeh, Elena. "Introduction: Faith-Based Humanitarianism in Contexts of Forced Displacement." *Journal of Refugee Studies* 24, no. 3 (2011): 429–439.

Finnemore, Martha. "Rules of War and Wars of Rules: The International Red Cross and the Restraint of State Violence." In *Constructing World Culture: International Nongovernmental Organizations since 1875*, edited by John Boli and George M. Thomas, 149–165. Stanford, CA: Stanford Univ. Press, 1999.

Fitzmaurice, Andrew. "The Justification of King Leopold II's Congo Enterprise by Sir Travers Twiss." In *Law and Politics in British Colonial Thought: Transpositions of Empire*, edited by Shaunnagh Dorsett and Ian Hunter, 109–128. New York: Palgrave Macmillan, 2010.

Florini, Ann M., ed. *Third Force: The Rise of Transnational Civil Society*. Washington, DC: Carnegie Endowment for International Peace, 2000.

Forsythe, David P. "Naming and Shaming: The Ethics of ICRC Discretion." *Millennium* 34, no. 1 (2006): 461–474.

Forsythe, David P. *The Humanitarians: The International Committee of the Red Cross*. Cambridge: Cambridge Univ. Press, 2005.

Forsythe, David P. "The Red Cross as Transnational Movement: Conserving and Changing the Nation State System." *International Organization* 30, no. 1 (1976): 607–630.

Fox, Renée C. *Doctors without Borders: Humanitarian Quests, Impossible Dreams of Médecins sans Frontières*. Baltimore, MD: Johns Hopkins Univ. Press, 2014.

Fox, Renée C. "Medical Humanitarianism and Human Rights: Reflections on Doctors Without Borders and Doctors of the World." *Social Science and Medicine* 41, no. 12 (1995): 1607–1616.

Freemon, Frank R. *Gangrene and Glory: Medical Care during the American Civil War*. Urbana: Univ. of Illinois Press, 2001.

Freidel, Frank. "Francis Lieber and the Codification of the International Law of War." In *Préludes et pionniers: Les précurseurs de la Croix-Rouge, 1840–1860*, edited by Roger Durand and Jacques Meurant, 31–52. Geneva: Société Henry Dunant, 1999.

Furley, John. *Struggles and Experiences of a Neutral Volunteer*. London: Chapman and Hall, 1872.

Gaussen, Louis. *Geneva and Rome: Rome Papal as Portrayed by Prophecy and History*. London: W. H. Dalton, 1844.

Gautier, Alfred. *Résultat du Concours relatif à l'emploi abusif du signe et du nom de la Croix-Rouge*. Geneva: Imprimerie B. & I. Soullier, 1890.

Geneva Convention for the Amelioration of the Condition of the Wounded and Sick in Armed Forces in the Field. August 12, 1949.

Geneva Convention Relative to the Treatment of Prisoners of War. August 12, 1949.

"German Red Cross Medal, The." *British Medical Journal* 1 (1899): 582.

Gharib, Malaka. "MSF Director Unsatisfied with Pentagon's 'Admission of Gross Negligence' Facebook Twitter Flipboard Email." *NPR*. November 25, 2015. https://www.npr.org/sections/goatsandsoda/2015/11/25/457393164/msf-director-unsatisfied-with-pentagons-admission-of-gross-negligence (accessed November 18, 2018).

Givoni, Michal. *The Care of the Witness: A Contemporary History of Testimony in Crises*. New York: Cambridge University Press, 2016.

Givoni, Michal. "Humanitarian Governance and Ethical Cultivation: Médecins sans Frontières and the Advent of the Expert-Witness." *Millennium* 40, no. 1 (2011): 43–63.

Go, Julian, and Monika Krause. "Fielding Transnationalism: An Introduction." *Sociological Review Monographs* 64, no. 2 (2016): 6–30.

Gordon, Bruce. *The Swiss Reformation.* Manchester: Manchester Univ. Press, 2002.

Gorski, Philip S. *American Covenant: A History of Civil Religion from the Puritans to the Present.* Princeton, NJ: Princeton Univ. Press, 2017.

Gorski, Philip S. "Bourdieusian Theory and Historical Analysis: Maps, Mechanisms, and Methods." In *Bourdieu and Historical Analysis,* edited by Philip S. Gorski, 327–366. Durham, NC: Duke Univ. Press, 2013.

Gorski, Philip S. *The Disciplinary Revolution: Calvinism and the Rise of the State in Early Modern Europe.* Chicago: Univ. of Chicago Press, 2003.

Gorski, Philip S. "The Return of the Repressed: Religion and the Political Unconscious of Historical Sociology." In *Remaking Modernity: Politics, History, and Sociology,* edited by Julia Adams, Elisabeth S. Clemens, and Ann Shola Orloff, 161–189. Durham, NC: Duke Univ. Press, 2005.

Gorski, Philip S., and Ateş Altınordu. "After Secularization?" *Annual Review of Sociology* 34 (2008): 55–85.

Gorski, Philip S., and William McMillan. "Barack Obama and American Exceptionalism." *Review of Faith and International Affairs* 20, no. 2 (2012): 41–50.

Goudzwaard, Bob. "Christian Social Thought in the Dutch Neo-Calvinist Tradition." In *Religion, Economics, and Social Thought: Proceedings of an International Conference,* 251–279. Vancouver, BC: Fraser Institute, 1986.

Graphic. "War Artists." December 1890, 643.

Grimsley, Mark. *The Hard Hand of War: Union Policy toward Southern Civilians, 1861–1865.* New York: Cambridge Univ. Press, 1997.

Groupe URD. *L'espace humanitaire en danger.* Plaisians, France: Université d'Automne de l'Humanitaire, 2006.

Groves, Brendan. "Civil-Military Cooperation in Civilian Casualty Investigations: Lessons Learned from the Azizabad Attack." *Air Force Law Review* 65 (2010): 1–50.

Gunn, Michael J., and Hilaire McCoubrey. "Medical Ethics and the Laws of Armed Conflict." *Journal of Armed Conflict Law* 3, no. 2 (1998): 133–162.

Guttmann, Allen. *The Olympics: A History of the Modern Games.* Urbana: Univ. of Illinois Press, 2002.

Hagan, John, and Ron Levi. "Crimes of War and the Force of Law." *Social Forces* 83, no. 4 (2005): 1499–1534.

Hagan, John, Heather Schoenfeld, and Alberto Palloni. "The Science of Human Rights, War Crimes, and Humanitarian Emergencies." *Annual Review of Sociology* 32 (2006): 329–349.

Hall, Timothy L. *Religion in America.* New York: Facts on File, 2007.

Haller, John S. *Battlefield Medicine: A History of the Military Ambulance from the Napoleonic Wars through World War I.* Carbondale: Southern Illinois Univ. Press, 2011.

Hammer, Ringier. "Adhésion à la Convention de Genève." *Bulletin international des sociétés de la Croix-Rouge* 20, no. 78 (1889): 100–101.

Hammond, Philip. "Moral Combat: Advocacy Journalists and the New Humanitarianism." In *Rethinking Human Rights: Critical Approaches to International Politics,* edited by David Chandler, 176–195. Basingstoke: Palgrave Macmillan, 2002.

Hanegraaff, Marcel, Caelesta Braun, Dirk de Bievre, and Jan Beyers. "The Domestic and Global Origins of Transnational Advocacy Explaining Lobbying Presence during WTO Ministerial Conferences." *Comparative Political Studies* 48, no. 12 (2015): 1591–1621.

Hankinson, Alan. *Man of Wars: William Howard Russell of The Times*. London: Heineman, 1982.

Hantos, János. "Centenary of the Hungarian Red Cross." *International Review of the Red Cross* 21, no. 222 (1981): 175–180.

Hartford Courant. "Red Cross Sunday." July 11, 1898, 10.

Harris, Sam. *The End of Faith: Religion, Terror, and the Future of Reason*. New York: W. W. Norton & Co., 2005.

Haskell, Thomas L. "Capitalism and the Origins of the Humanitarian Sensibility, Part I." *American Historical Review* 90, no. 2 (1985): 339–361.

Haskell, Thomas L. "Capitalism and the Origins of the Humanitarian Sensibility, Part II." *American Historical Review* 90, no. 3 (1985): 547–566.

Haynes, Stephen R. *Noah's Curse: The Biblical Justification of American Slavery*. Oxford: Oxford Univ. Press, 2002.

Hermet, Guy. "The Human Rights Challenge to Sovereignty." In *Life, Death, and Aid: The Médecins sans Frontières Report on World Crisis Intervention*, edited by François Jean, 131–137. London: Routledge, 1993.

Hippler, Thomas, and Miloš Vec. *Paradoxes of Peace in Nineteenth Century Europe*. Oxford: Oxford Univ. Press, 2015.

Hirschman, Daniel, and Isaac Ariail Reed. "Formation Stories and Causality in Sociology." *Sociological Theory* 32, no. 4 (2014): 259–282.

Hitchens, Christopher. *God Is Not Great: How Religion Poisons Everything*. New York: Twelve [Hachette, Warner], 2007.

Hochschild, Adam. *King Leopold's Ghost: A Story of Greed, Terror, and Heroism in Colonial Africa*. Boston: Houghton Mifflin, 1999.

Holmes, Richard. *Redcoat: The British Soldier in the Age of Horse and Musket*. London: Harper Collins, 2001.

Horowitz, Richard S. "International Law and State Transformation in China, Siam, and the Ottoman Empire during the Nineteenth Century." *Journal of World History* 15, no. 4 (2004): 445–486.

Howard, Michael. *The Franco-Prussian War: The German Invasion of France, 1870–1871*. London: Routledge, 2001.

Huppatz, Kate. "Reworking Bourdieu's 'Capital': Feminine and Female Capitals in the Field of Paid Caring Work." *Sociology* 43, no. 1 (2009): 45–66.

Huston, James A. *The Sinews of War: Army Logistics, 1775–1953*. Washington, DC: Center of Military History, United States Army, 1988.

Hutchinson, John F. *Champions of Charity: War and the Rise of the Red Cross*. Boulder, CO: Westview Press, 1996.

Hutchinson, John F. "Rethinking the Origins of the Red Cross." *Bulletin of the History of Medicine* 63, no. 4 (1989): 557–578.

IFRC. "Volunteers Lead by Example in the Promotion of Peace." *IFRC*. November 26, 2011. http://www.ifrc.org/fr/nouvelles/nouvelles/common/volunteers-lead-by-example-in -the-promotion-of-peace/ (accessed April 23, 2018).

Ignatieff, Michael. *The Lesser Evil: Political Ethics in an Age of Terror*. Edinburgh: Edinburgh Univ. Press, 2000.

Ignatieff, Michael. "The Stories We Tell: Television and Humanitarian Aid." In *Hard Choices: Moral Dilemmas in Humanitarian Intervention*, edited by Jonathan Moore, 287–302. Lanham, MD: Rowman & Littlefield Publishers, 1998.

Illouz, Eva. "From the Lisbon Disaster to Oprah Winfrey: Suffering as Identity in the Era of Globalization." In *Global America? The Cultural Consequences of Globalization*, edited by Ulrich Beck, Natan Sznaider, and Rainer Winter, 189–205. Liverpool, UK: Liverpool Univ. Press, 2003.

Illouz, Eva. *Hard-Core Romance: Fifty Shades of Grey, Best-Sellers, and Society.* Chicago: Univ. of Chicago Press, 2014.

Illouz, Eva. *Saving the Modern Soul: Therapy, Emotions, and the Culture of Self-Help.* Berkeley: Univ. of California Press, 2008.

International Committee of the Red Cross. "Statutes of the International Committee of the Red Cross." March 10, 2013. https://www.icrc.org/eng/resources/documents/misc /icrc-statutes-080503.htm.

Irwin, Julia. *Making the World Safe: The American Red Cross and a Nation's Humanitarian Awakening.* New York: Oxford Univ. Press, 2013.

Jaeger, Gérard A. *Henry Dunant: l'homme qui inventa le droit humanitaire.* Paris: L'Archipel, 2009.

James, Leighton S. *Witnessing the Revolutionary and Napoleonic Wars in German Central Europe.* New York: Palgrave Macmillan, 2013.

Jean, François, ed. *Life, Death, and Aid: The Médecins sans Frontières Report on World Crisis Intervention.* London: Routledge, 1993.

Jellema, Dirk. "Abraham Kuyper's Attack on Liberalism." *Review of Politics* 19, no. 4 (1957): 472–485.

Jijon, Isabel. "The Universal Kind? Memory, Globalization, and Martin Luther King, Jr." *Sociological Inquiry* 88, no. 1 (2018): 79–105.

Jobe, Kathleen. "Disaster Relief in Post-Earthquake Haiti: Unintended Consequences of Humanitarian Volunteerism." *Travel Medicine and Infectious Disease* 9, no. 1 (2011): 1–5.

Jones, J. *"Una and Her Paupers": Memorials of Agnes Elizabeth Jones.* 2nd ed. New York: G. Routledge and Sons, 1872.

Jones, Marian Moser. *The American Red Cross from Clara Barton to the New Deal.* Baltimore, MD: Johns Hopkins Univ. Press, 2013.

Kahl, Sigrun. "The Religious Roots of Modern Poverty Policy: Catholic, Lutheran, and Reformed Protestant Traditions Compared." *European Journal of Sociology* 46, no. 1 (2005): 91–126.

Kaldor, Mary. "The Idea of Global Civil Society." *International Affairs* 79, no. 3 (2003): 583–593.

Kay, Tamara. "Labor Transnationalism and Global Governance: The Impact of NAFTA on Transnational Labor Relationships in North America." *American Journal of Sociology* 111, no. 3 (2005): 715–756.

Kay, Tamara. "Legal Transnationalism: The Relationship between Transnational Social Movement Building and International Law." *Law and Social Inquiry* 36, no. 2 (2011): 419–454.

Keck, Margaret E., and Kathryn Sikkink. *Activists beyond Borders: Advocacy Networks in International Politics.* Ithaca, NY: Cornell Univ. Press, 1998.

Keck, Margaret E., and Kathryn Sikkink. "Transnational Advocacy Networks in International and Regional Politics." *International Social Science Journal* 51, no. 159 (1999): 89–101.

Kellenberger, Jakob. "Speaking Out or Remaining Silent in Humanitarian Work." *International Review of the Red Cross* 86, no. 855 (2004): 593–609.

Kestnbaum, Meyer. "Mars Revealed: The Entry of Ordinary People into War among States." In *Remaking Modernity: Politics, History, and Sociology*, edited by Julia Adams, Elisabeth S. Clemens, and Ann Shola Orloff, 249–285. Durham, NC: Duke Univ. Press, 2005.

Ketelaar, James Edward. *Of Heretics and Martyrs in Meiji Japan: Buddhism and Its Persecution.* Princeton, NJ: Princeton Univ. Press, 1990.

Kingdon, Robert M. "Calvin and the Establishment of Consistory Discipline in Geneva: The Institution and the Men who Directed It." *Dutch Review of Church History* 70, no. 2 (1990): 158–172.

Koskenniemi, Martti. *The Gentle Civilizer of Nations: The Rise and Fall of International Law 1870–1960.* Cambridge: Cambridge Univ. Press, 2002.

Kouchner, Bernard. "Vive la vie." *Le Monde*, December 11, 1999.

Knack, Stephen. "Aid Dependence and the Quality of Governance: Cross-Country Empirical Tests." *Southern Economic Journal* 68, no. 2 (2001): 310–329.

Krähenbühl, Pierre. "There are no 'Good' or 'Bad' Civilians in Syria—We Must Help All who Need Aid." *Guardian.* March 3, 2013. https://www.theguardian.com/commentisfree/2013/mar/03/red-cross-aid-inside-syria (accessed March 27, 2018).

Krause, Monika. *The Good Project: Humanitarian Relief NGOs and the Fragmentation of Reason.* Chicago: Univ. of Chicago Press, 2014.

Krause, Monika. "Reporting and the Transformations of the Journalistic Field: US News Media, 1890–2000." *Media, Culture, and Society* 33, no. 1 (2011): 89–104.

Kselman, Thomas A. *Death and Afterlife in Modern France.* Princeton, NJ: Princeton Univ. Press, 1993.

Kurasawa, Fuyuki. "L'humanitaire, manifestation du cosmopolitisme?" *Sociologie et sociétés* 44, no. 1 (2012): 217–237.

Kuyper, Abraham. "Calvinism, a Life-System." In *Lectures on Calvinism*, by Abraham Kuyper, 9–40. New York: Cosimo Inc., 2007.

Kuyper, Abraham. "Calvinism and Politics." In *Lectures on Calvinism*, by Abraham Kuyper, 78–109. New York: Cosimo Inc., 2007.

Kuyper, Abraham. *The Problem of Poverty.* Washington, DC: Center for Public Justice; Grand Rapids, MI: Baker Book House, 1991.

Lancet. "Relief of the Wounded in War." February 29, 1896, 592–593.

Laqueur, Walter. *The Terrible Secret: Suppression of the Truth about Hitler's "Final Solution."* Paris: Gallimard, 1981.

Lawson, Melinda. *Patriot Fires: Forging a New American Nationalism in the Civil War North.* Lawrence: Univ. Press of Kansas, 2002.

La Belgique coloniale. "L'Association congolaise et africaine de la Croix-Rouge." *La Belgique coloniale* 2, no. 19 (1896): 220–221.

Lee, Alexandra J. *Resilience by Design: Advance Sciences and Technologies for Security Applications.* Cham, Switzerland: Springer, 2016.

Leeds Mercury. "The War." July 11, 1877, 5.

Lelandais, Renée. "Les Filles de la Charité sur les champs de bataille, 1847–1863." In *Préludes et pionniers: Les précurseurs de la Croix-Rouge, 1840–1860*, edited by Roger Durand and Jacques Meurant, 299–319. Geneva: Société Henry Dunant, 1991.

Lewis, Mark. *The Birth of the New Justice: The Internationalization of Crime and Punishment, 1919–1950.* Oxford: Oxford Univ. Press, 2014.

Leyton, Elliott. *Touched by Fire: Doctors without Borders in a Third World Crisis.* Toronto: McClelland & Stewart Inc., 1998.

Libération. "Le nouvel horizon humanitaire." December 10, 1999.

Livermore, Mary A. *My Story of the War: A Woman's Narrative of Four Years Personal Experience as Nurse in the Union Army, and in Relief Work at Home, in Hospitals, Camps, and at the Front during the War of the Rebellion.* Hartford, CT: A. D. Worthington, 1896.

Liverpool Mercury. "The Geneva Convention." April 26, 1865, 6.

Löwenthal, Zdenko. "Anglo-Yugoslav Medical Relations in Peace and War." *British Medical Journal* 2, no. 5267 (1961): 1634–1637.

Lueder, Charles. *La convention de Genève au point de vue historique, critique, et dogmatique.* Paris: C. Reinwald & C., 1876.

"Lutheran World Relief." *Charity Navigator.* n.d. https://www.charitynavigator.org/index .cfm?bay=search.history&orgid=4031 (accessed April 29, 2018).

Lynch, Cecelia. "Peace Movements, Civil Society, and the Development of International Law." In *The Oxford Handbook of the History of International Law,* edited by Bardo Fassbender and Anne Peters, 198–221. Oxford: Oxford Univ. Press, 2012.

MacGahan, Januarius A., and Eugene Schuyler. *Turkish Atrocities in Bulgaria.* London: Bradbury, Agnew & Co., 1876.

Macleod, David I. *Building Character in the American Boy: The Boy Scouts, YMCA, and Their Forerunners, 1870–1920.* Madison: Univ. of Wisconsin Press, 2004.

Manetsch, Scott M. *Calvin's Company of Pastors: Pastoral Care and the Emerging Reformed Church, 1536–1609.* Oxford: Oxford Univ. Press, 2013.

Mann, Michael. "Have Wars and Violence Declined?" *Theory and Society* 47, no. 1 (2018): 37–60.

Markandya, Polly. "Secular Aid Reaches Those in Most Need." *Guardian.* September 24, 2010. https://www.theguardian.com/commentisfree/belief/2010/sep/24/secular-aid -medecins-sans-frontieres (accessed April 9, 2018).

Maunoir, Théodore. "Note sur l'œuvre des comités de secours aux États-Unis d'Amérique." In *Secours aux blessés: Communication du Comité international faisant suite au compte rendu de la conférence internationale de Genève,* 179–187. Geneva: Imprimerie de Jules-Guillaume Fick, 1864.

"Maurice Rossel's ICRC visit to Theresienstadt and Auschwitz." *United States Holocaust Memorial Museum.* n.d. https://collections.ushmm.org/search/catalog/irn1004374 (accessed March 27, 2018).

Mayrl, Damon. "Fields, Logics, and Social Movements: Prison Abolition and the Social Justice Field." *Sociological Inquiry* 83, no. 2 (2013): 286–309.

Mazower, Mark. *Governing the World: The History of an Idea, 1815 to the Present.* New York: Penguin Books, 2013.

Mazzoni, Gaetano. *La neutralità dei feriti in guerra: Studio storico.* Naples: Croce Rossa Italiana, 1895.

McAllister, Ian. *Sustaining Relief with Development: Strategic Issues for the Red Cross and Red Crescent.* Dordrecht: Martinus Nijhoff Publishers, 1993.

McDonald, Lynn. "War and Militarism," in *Florence Nightingale: An Introduction to Her Life and Family,* vol. 1, edited by Lynn McDonald (Waterloo: Wilfrid Laurier Univ. Press, 2001), 75–79.

McDonnell, Terence E. *Best Laid Plans: Cultural Entropy and the Unraveling of AIDS Media Campaigns.* Chicago: Univ. of Chicago Press, 2016.

McDonnell, Terence E., Christopher A. Bail, and Iddo Tavory. "A Theory of Resonance." *Sociological Theory* 3, no. 1 (2017): 1–14.

Médecins sans Frontières. *2016 Annual Report.* Geneva: MSF International, 2017.

Melucci, Alberto. "Social Movements and the Democratization of Everyday Life." In *Civil Society and the State: New European Perspectives,* edited by John Keane, 245–60. London: Verso, 1988.

Merle d'Aubigné, Jean-Henri. *Discours sur l'étude de l'histoire du christianisme et son utilité pour l'époque actuelle.* Paris: J. J. Risler; Geneva: A. Cherbuliez, 1832.

Merle d'Aubigné, Jean-Henri. *Jean Calvin, un des fondateurs des libertés modernes: Discours prononcé a Genève pour l'inauguration de la Salle de la Réformation, le 26 septembre 1867.* Paris: Grassart, 1868.

Merle d'Aubigné, Jean-Henri. *La pierre sur laquelle l'académie de Genève fut posée en Juin 1559.* Geneva: E. Beroud, 1859.

Merry, Sally Engle. "Transnational Human Rights and Local Activism: Mapping the Middle." *American Anthropologist* 108, no. 1 (2006): 38–51.

Michel, Jean-Baptiste, et al. "Quantitative Analysis of Culture Using Millions of Digitized Books." *Science* 331, no. 6014 (2011): 176–182.

"Military Sanitary Matters, and Statistics." *American Journal of the Medical Sciences* 50, no. 99 (1865): 171–180.

Miller, Ilana D. *Reports from America: William Howard Russell and the Civil War.* Stroud, UK: Sutton, 2001.

Mitchell, Brian R. *International Historical Statistics: Europe, 1750–1993.* 4th ed. New York: Stockton Press, 1998.

Moir, Lindsay. "The Historical Development of the Application of Humanitarian Law in Non-International Armed Conflict to 1949." *International and Comparative Law Quarterly* 47, no. 2 (1998): 337–361.

Moneta, E. T., and E. Caldara. "Letter of the Peace Societies of Europe to the International Conference of the Red Cross Societies, Met in Rome, April, 1892." *American Advocate of Peace* 54, no. 3 (1892): 62–64.

Moniz, Amanda B. *From Empire to Humanity: The American Revolution and the Origins of Humanitarianism.* New York: Oxford Univ. Press, 2016.

Moorehead, Caroline. *Dunant's Dream: War, Switzerland, and the History of the Red Cross.* New York: Carroll & Graf Publishers, 1999.

Morning Post. "Sketches in the Basque Provinces." February 27, 1837: 2.

Morgenstern, Sally. "Henri Dunant and the Red Cross." *Bulletin of the New York Academy of Medicine* 57, no. 4 (1981): 311–326.

Morrison, Larry. "The Religious Defense of American Slavery before 1830." *Journal of Religious Thought* 37, no. 2 (1980): 16–29.

Mostafanezhad, Mary. "Volunteer Tourism and the Popular Humanitarian Gaze." *Geoforum* 54 (July 2014): 111–118.

Moszynski, Peter. "Medical Charity Is Expelled from Darfur." *British Medical Journal* 342, no. 7795 (2011): 464.

Moynier, Gustave. *Ce que c'est que la Croix-Rouge.* Geneva: Imprimerie B. Soullier, 1874.

Moynier, Gustave. "La convention de Genève au point de vue religieux." *Revue Chrétienne* 46, no. 8 (1899): 161–168.

Moynier, Gustave. *La Croix-Rouge: son passé et son avenir.* Paris: Sandoz & Thuillier, 1882.

Moynier, Gustave. *La fondation de l'état indépendant du Congo au point de vue juridique.* Paris: l'Académie des sciences morales et politiques, 1887.

Moynier, Gustave. "Le congrès de Bruxelles et la révision de la Convention de Genève: trentième circulaire à Messieurs les Présidents et les Membres des Comités centraux de secours aux militaires blessés." *Bulletin international des sociétés de secours aux militaires blessés* 4, no. 17 (1873): 197–201.

Moynier, Gustave. "Note sur la création d'une institution judiciaire internationale propre à prévenir et à réprimer les infractions à la convention de Genève." *Bulletin international des sociétés de secours aux militaires blessés* 3, no. 11 (1872): 122–131.

Moynier, Gustave. *Rappel succinct de l'activité déployée par le comité international de la Croix-Rouge à Genève pendant les quarante premières années de son existence (1863 à 1904).* Geneva: Comité international de la Croix-Rouge, 1905.

Moynier, Gustave, and Louis Amédée Appia. *Help for Sick and Wounded: Being a Translation of "La Guerre et la Charité," Together with Other Writings on the Subject by Officers of Her Majesty's Service*. Translated by John Furley. London: J. C. Hotten, 1870.

Moynier, Gustave, and Edouard Odier. "Formation d'une société congolaise et africaine de la Croix-Rouge." *Bulletin international des sociétés de la Croix-Rouge* 20, no. 78 (1889): 76–80.

"MSF Financial Report 2012." *Médecins sans Frontières*. n.d. http://www.msf.org/sites /msf.org/files/msf_financial_report_interactive_2012_final.pdf (accessed March 27, 2018).

"MSF International Activity Report 2012—Syria." *Médecins sans Frontières*. n.d. http://www .msf.org/international-activity-report-2012-syria (accessed March 27, 2018).

Mudge, Stephanie Lee. "What's Left of Leftism? Neoliberal Politics in Western Party Systems, 1945–2004." *Social Science History* 35, no. 3 (2011): 337–380.

Mudge, Stephanie Lee, and Antoine Vauchez. "Building Europe on a Weak Field: Law, Economics, and Scholarly Avatars in Transnational Politics." *American Journal of Sociology* 118, no. 2 (2012): 449–492.

Murdock, Graeme. *Beyond Calvin: The Intellectual, Political, and Cultural World of Europe's Reformed Churches, c. 1540–1620*. Basingstoke, UK: Palgrave Macmillan, 2004.

Neff, Stephen C. "A Short History of International Law." In *International Law*, edited by Malcolm Evans, 29–55. Oxford: Oxford Univ. Press, 2006.

Neier, Aryeh. "War and War Crimes: A Brief History." In *Crimes of War: Guilt and Denial in the Twentieth Century*, edited by Omer Bartov, Atina Grossmann, and Mary Nolan, 1–7. New York: New Press, 2003.

New York Herald. "Foreign Club Talk." July 23, 1883, 5.

New York Herald. "The Red Cross." October 29, 1877: 4.

Nightingale, Florence. *Notes on Nursing: What It Is, and What It Is Not*. Boston: Carter, 1860.

Norgaard, Kari Marie. *Living in Denial: Climate Change, Emotions, and Everyday Life*. Cambridge, MA: MIT Press, 2011.

Nussbaum, Martha C. "Patriotism and Cosmopolitanism." In *For Love of Country: Debating the Limits of Patriotism*, edited by Joshua Cohen, 2–29. Boston: Beacon Press, 1996.

Nyamu-Musembi, Celestine, and Andrea Cornwall. *What Is the "Rights-based Approach" All About?: Perspectives from International Development Agencies*. Brighton: Institute of Development Studies, 2004.

Nye, Joseph S. "Public Diplomacy and Soft Power." *Annals of the American Academy of Political and Social Science* 616, no. 1 (2008): 94–109.

Nye, Joseph S. *Soft Power: The Means to Success in World Politics*. New York: Public Affairs, 2004.

Offe, Claus. "New Social Movements: Challenging the Boundaries of Institutional Politics." *Social Research* 52, no. 4 (1985): 817–868.

Olson, Jeannine E. "Social Welfare and the Transformation of Polity in Geneva." In *The Identity of Geneva: The Christian Commonwealth, 1564–1864*, edited by John B. Roney and Martin I. Klauber, 155–168. Westport, CT: Greenwood Press, 1998.

Ottaviani, Raimonda, Paolo Vanni, M. Grazia Baccolo, Elizabeth Guerin, and Duccio Vanni. "The First Nobel Prize Henry Dunant (Founder of the International Red Cross) and His 'Memoires.'" *Vesalius* 9, no. 1 (2003): 20–27.

Oxfam America. *Annual Report 2017*. Boston, MA: Oxfam America, 2018.

Oxfam International. *Oxfam Annual Report 2015–2016*. Oxford: Oxfam International, 2016.

Palasciano, Ferdinando. *Dritto delle genti lettera su convenzione di Ginevra per neutralità dei feriti*. Naples: Tipografia di Angelo Trani, 1871.

Pall Mall Gazette. "Missionaries of Civilization." August 15, 1876, 10.

Pandolfi, Mariella. "Contract of Mutual (In)difference: Governance and the Humanitarian Apparatus in Contemporary Albania and Kosovo." *India Journal of Global Legal Studies* 10, no. 1 (2003): 369–381.

Paret, Peter. *Understanding War: Essays on Clausewitz and the History of Military Power.* Princeton, NJ: Princeton Univ. Press, 1992.

Parker, Geoffrey. "Early Modern Europe." In *The Laws of War: Constraints on Warfare in the Western World,* edited by Michael Howard, George J. Andreopoulos, and Mark R. Shulman, 40–54. New Haven, CT: Yale Univ. Press, 1994.

Pearson, Emma Maria. "The Anglo-American Ambulance." *Times,* November 4, 1870: 6.

Pearson, Emma Maria. "A Voice from Orleans." *Times,* February 22, 1871: 10.

Pearson, Emma Maria, and Louisa Elisabeth McLaughlin. *Our Adventures During the War of 1870.* London: Richard Bentley and Son, 1871.

Pearson, Emma Maria, and Louisa Elisabeth McLaughlin. *Service in Servia under the Red Cross.* London: Tinsley Brothers, 1877.

Pelling, Margaret. "Nurses and Nursekeepers: Problems of Identification in the Early Modern Period." In *The Common Lot: Sickness, Medical Occupations, and the Urban Poor in Early Modern England,* edited by Margaret Pelling, 179–202. London: Longmans, 1998.

Perouse de Montclos, Marc-Antoine. "Humanitarian Aid and the Biafra War: Lessons Not Learned." *Africa Development* 34, no. 1 (2009): 69–82.

Perroux, Olivier, and Michel Oris. "Religion Affiliations in Early Nineteenth Century Geneva: The Emergence of Catholics in the 'Calvinist Rome.'" *Paper presented at the annual meeting of the Social Science History Association, Baltimore, Maryland, November 13–16, 2003.*

Petzke, Martin. "Taken In by the Numbers Game: The Globalization of a Religious 'Illusio' and 'Doxa' in Nineteenth-Century Evangelical Missions to India." *Sociological Review Monographs* 64, no. 2 (2016): 124–145.

Pfeiffer, James. "International NGOs and Primary Health Care in Mozambique: The Need for a New Model of Collaboration." *Social Science and Medicine* 56, no. 4 (2003): 725–738.

Phelan, Kevin P. Q. "From an Idea to Action: The Evolution of Médecins sans Frontières." In *The New Humanitarians: Inspiration, Innovations, and Blueprints for Visionaries,* edited by Chris E. Stout, 1–30. Westport, CT: Praeger Publishers, 2009.

Pinker, Steven. *The Better Angels of Our Nature: Why Violence Has Declined.* New York: Penguin Books, 2011.

Pinker, Steven. *Enlightenment Now: The Case for Reason, Science, Humanism, and Progress.* New York: Viking, 2018.

Powell, Walter W. "Neither Market nor Hierarchy: Network Forms of Organization." In *Research in Organizational Behavior,* edited by Barry Staw and Larry L. Cummings, 295–336. Greenwich, CT: JAI, 1990.

Pradier, Françoise. "Médecins sans Frontières, au service de la médecine des catastrophes." *Le Quotidien du Médecins,* December 16, 1971: 5.

Price, Richard. "Reversing the Gun Sights: Transnational Civil Society Targets Land Mines." *International Organization* 52, no. 3 (1998): 613–644.

Protocol Additional to the Geneva Conventions of 12 August 1949, and Relating to the Adoption of an Additional Distinctive Emblem (Protocol III). December 8, 2005.

Protocol Additional to the Geneva Conventions of 12 August 1949, and Relating to the Protection of Victims of International Armed Conflicts (Protocol I). June 8, 1977.

Protocols Additional to the Geneva Conventions of 12 August 1949: Resolutions of the Diplomatic Conference: Extracts from the Final Act of the Diplomatic Conference.

"Public Release of Initial MSF Initial Review." *Médecins sans Frontières.* November 5, 2015. http://www.msf.org/sites/msf.org/files/msf_kunduz_review_041115_for_public _release.pdf (accessed November 15, 2018).

Quataert, Jean H. *Staging Philanthropy: Patriotic Women and the National Imagination in Dynastic Germany, 1813–1916.* Ann Arbor: Univ. of Michigan Press, 2001.

Ramachandran, Vijaya, and Julie Walz. "Haiti: Where Has All the Money Gone?" *Journal of Haitian Studies* 21, no. 1 (2015): 26–65.

Ray, Larry, John Lea, Hilary Rose, and Chetan Bhatt. Book review symposium on Steven Pinker, *The Better Angels of Our Nature. Sociology* 47, no. 6 (2013): 1224–1232.

"Red Cross Aid at Siboney." *Journal of the American Medical Association* 32, no. 17 (1898): 995–996.

Redfield, Peter. "Doctors, Borders, and Life in Crisis." *Cultural Anthropology* 20, no. 3 (2005): 328–361.

Redfield, Peter. "A Less Modest Witness." *American Ethnologist* 33, no. 1 (2006): 3–26.

Redfield, Peter. *Life in Crisis: The Ethical Journey of Doctors without Borders.* Berkeley: Univ. of California Press, 2013.

Redfield, Peter. "Secular Humanism and the Value of Life." In *What Matters? Ethnographies of Value in a Not So Secular Age,* edited by Courtney Bender and Ann Taves, 144–178. New York: Columbia Univ. Press, 2012.

"Review of *First Aid to the Injured.* Five Ambulance Lecture. By Dr. Frederick Esmarch." *Glasgow Medical Journal* 19 (January–June 1883): 151–153.

Richardson, Teresa. *In Japanese Hospitals during War-Time: Fifteen Months with the Red Cross Society of Japan.* Edinburgh: W. Blackwood and Sons, 1905.

Rieff, David. *A Bed for the Night: Humanitarianism in Crisis.* New York: Simon & Schuster, 2002.

Rocamora, Agnès. "Fields of Fashion: Critical Insights into Bourdieu's Sociology of Culture." *Journal of Consumer Culture* 2, no. 3 (2002): 341–362.

Rolin-Jaequemyns, Gustave. "Chronique du droit international: Étude complémentaire sur la guerre franco-allemande, dans ses rapports avec le droit international: De la conduite respective des belligérants par rapport aux lois de la guerre." *Revue de droit international et de législation comparée* 3 (1871): 288–384.

Rolin-Jaequemyns, Gustave. "Note sur le projet de M. Moynier, relatif à l'établissement d'une institution judiciaire internationale, protectrice de la Convention, avec lettres de MM. Lieber, Ach, Morin, de Holtzendorff et Westlake." *Revue de droit international et de législation comparée* 4 (1872): 325–347.

Roney, John B. *The Inside of History: Jean-Henri Merle d'Aubigné and Romantic Historiography.* Westport, CT: Greenwood Press, 1996.

Rorty, Richard. "Human Rights, Rationality, and Sentimentality." In *On Human Rights,* edited by Stephen Shute and Susan Hurley, 111–134. New York: Basic Books, 1993.

Russell, William Howard. *Complete History of the Russian War, from Its Commencement to Its Close: Giving a Graphic Picture of the Great Drama of War.* New York: J. G. Wells, 1857.

"Samaritan's Purse." *Charity Navigator.* n.d. https://www.charitynavigator.org/index.cfm ?bay=search.history&orgid=4423 (accessed April 29, 2018).

Santana-Acuña, Alvaro. "How a Literary Work Becomes a Classic: The Case of *One Hundred Years of Solitude.*" *American Journal of Cultural Sociology* 2, no. 1 (2014): 97–149.

Savelsberg, Joachim J. *Representing Mass Violence: Conflicting Responses to Human Rights Violations in Darfur.* Berkeley: Univ. of California Press, 2015.

Scarnecchia, Daniel P., Nathaniel A. Raymond, Faine Greenwood, Caitlin Howarth, and Danielle N. Poole. "A Rights-based Approach to Information in Humanitarian Assistance." *Plos Currents*, September 20, 2017.

Schindler, Dietrich. "J. C. Bluntschli's Contribution to the Law of War." In *Promoting Justice Human Rights and Conflict Resolution through International Law*, edited by Marcelo Kohen, 437–454. Leiden: Brill, 2006.

Schmitt, Eric, and Thom Shanker. "U.S. Report Finds Errors in Afgan Airstrikes." *New York Times*. June 2, 2009. https://www.nytimes.com/2009/06/03/world/asia/03military .html (accessed November 18, 2018).

Schön, Volkmar. "Hamburger Betrachtungen zum Rotkreuzzeichen." *Notizen zur Hamburger Rotkreuzgeschichte* 5 (February 2015): 3.

Schulz, Matthias. "The Guarantee of Humanity: The Concert of Europe and the Origins of the Russo-Ottoman War of 1877." In *Humanitarian Intervention: A History*, edited by Brendan Simms and David J. B. Trim, 184–204. Cambridge: Cambridge Univ. Press, 2011.

Schulz, William F. *In Our Own Best Interest: How Defending Human Rights Benefits Us All*. Boston: Beacon Press, 2001.

Seacole, Mary. *The Wonderful Adventures of Mrs. Seacole in Many Lands*. Oxford: Oxford Univ. Press, 1988 [1857].

Shalizi, Hamid, and Peter Graff. "U.S Strikes Killed 140 Villagers: Afghan Probe." *Reuters*. May 16, 2009. https://www.reuters.com/article/us-afghanistan-civilians -idUSTRE54E22V20090516 (accessed November 18, 2018).

Shani, Liron. *Nationalism between Land and Environment: The Conflict between "Oranges" and "Greens" over Settling in the East Lakhish Area*. Baltimore: Univ. of Maryland Institute for Israel Studies Research Papers Series, 2011.

Shapin, Steven, and Simon Schaffer. *Leviathan and the Air-Pump: Hobbes, Boyle, and the Experimental Life*. Princeton, NJ: Princeton Univ. Press, 1985.

Siamese Red Cross Society. *The Siamese Red Cross Society: Its Origin and Activities*. Bangkok: Siamese Red Cross Society, 1934.

Siméant, Johanna. "What Is Going Global? The Internationalization of French NGOs 'Without Borders'." *Review of International Political Economy* 12, no. 5 (2005): 851–883.

Singer, J. David. *The Wages of War, 1816–1965: A Statistical Handbook*. New York: Wiley, 1972.

Singer, Sandra. "The Protection of Children during Armed Conflict Situations." *International Review of the Red Cross* 26, no. 252 (1986): 133–168.

Singh, Sourabh. "What Is Relational Structure? Introducing History to the Debates on the Relation between Fields and Social Networks." *Sociological Theory* 34, no. 2 (2016): 128–150.

Sire, Henry J. A. *The Knights of Malta*. New Haven, CT: Yale Univ. Press, 1994.

Skeel, David. "How Churches Are Helping Puerto Rico." *Wall Street Journal*. November 9, 2017. https://www.wsj.com/articles/how-churches-are-helping-puerto-rico -1510274035 (accessed April 29, 2018).

Slim, Hugo. "Dissolving the Difference between Humanitarianism and Development: The Mixing of a Rights-based Solution." *Development in Practice* 10, no. 3–4 (2000): 491–494.

Slim, Hugo. "Not Philanthropy but Rights: The Proper Politicisation of Humanitarian Philosophy." *International Journal of Human Rights* 6, no. 2 (2002): 1–22.

Smith, Jackie, and Dawn Wiest. "The Uneven Geography of Global Civil Society: National and Global Influences on Transnational Association." *Social Forces* 84, no. 2005 (2005): 621–651.

Smith, Louis P. "The Medical Department of the Army." *Journal of the American Medical Association* 31, no. 9 (1898): 477–478.

Snay, Mitchell. *Gospel of Disunion: Religion and Separatism in the Antebellum South*. Chapel Hill: Univ. of North Carolina Press, 1997.

Société autrichienne. "Autriche." *Bulletin international des sociétés de secours aux militaires blessés* 2, no. 5 (1870): 27–28.

Société de Baden. "Le secours badois pendant la dernière guerre." *Bulletin international des sociétés de secours aux militaires blessés* 3, no. 12 (1872): 190–194.

Société de secours aux blessés militaires (France). "Bibliographie." *Bulletin de la Société de secours aux blessés militaires des armées de terre et de mer* 1, no. 1 August (1865): 4.

Société française de secours aux blessés militaires. "Assemblée générale de la société française et rapport annuel." *Bulletin International des Sociétés de la Croix-Rouge* 42, no. 168 (1911): 228–229.

Société genevoise d'utilité publique. *Compte-rendu de la Conférence internationale réunie a Genève les 26, 27, 28, 29 Oct. 1863 pour étudier les moyens de pourvoir a l'insuffisance du Service sanitaire dans les Armées en campagne*. Geneva: Imprimerie de Jules-Guillaume Fick, 1863.

Société hessoise. "Programme de la Société hessoise en temps de paix." *Bulletin international des sociétés de secours aux militaires blessés* 1, no. 2 (1870): 91–93.

Société suédoise. "Assemblée générale de la Société suédoise." *Bulletin international des sociétés de secours aux militaires blessés* 1, no. 2 (1870): 99–100.

Sphere. "The Care of the Wounded in the War." May 28, 1904, b2.

Stamatov, Peter. "Activist Religion, Empire, and the Emergence of Modern Long-Distance Advocacy Networks." *American Sociological Review* 75, no. 4 (2010): 607–28.

Stamatov, Peter. *The Origins of Global Humanitarianism: Religion, Empires, and Advocacy*. Cambridge: Cambridge Univ. Press, 2013.

Steinacher, Gerald. *Humanitarians at War: The Red Cross in the Shadow of the Holocaust*. Oxford: Oxford Univ. Press, 2017.

Steinmetz, George. "Bourdieu, Historicity, and Historical Sociology." *Cultural Sociology* 5, no. 1 (2011): 45–66.

Steinmetz, George. "The Colonial State as a Social Field: Ethnographic Capital and Native Policy in the German Overseas Empire before 1914." *American Sociological Review* 73, no. 4 August (2008): 589–612.

Steinmetz, George. *The Devil's Handwriting: Precoloniality and the German Colonial State in Qingdao, Samoa, and Southwest Africa*. Chicago: Univ. of Chicago Press, 2007.

Stewart, Kenneth J. *Restoring the Reformation: British Evangelicalism and the Francophone "Réveil" 1816–1849*. Milton Keynes, UK: Paternoster, 2006.

Stibbe, Matthew. "The Internment of Civilians by Belligerent States during the First World War and the Response of the International Committee of the Red Cross." *Journal of Contemporary History* 41, no. 1 (2006): 5–19.

Stoddard, Abby. "Humanitarian NGOs: Challenges and Trends." *HPG Briefing* 12 (2003): 1–4.

Strand, Michael. "The Genesis and Structure of Moral Universalism: Social Justice in Victorian Britain, 1834–1901." *Theory and Society* 44, no. 6 (2015): 537–573.

Stroup, Sarah S. *Borders among Activists: International NGOs in the United States, Britain, and France*. Ithaca, NY: Cornell Univ Press, 2012.

Stroup, Sarah S., and Amanda Murdie. "There's No Place like Home: Explaining International NGO Advocacy." *Review of International Organizations* 7, no. 2 (2012): 425–448.

Stunt, Timothy C. F. *From Awakening to Secession: Radical Evangelicals in Switzerland and Britain, 1815–35.* Edinburgh: T&T Clark, 2000.

Sulek, Marty. *"The Last Romantic War, the First Modern War: The Crimean War of 1854–1856 and the Genesis of Contemporary Wartime Humanitarian Relief."* Unpublished manuscript, n.d.

Swidler, Ann, and Susan Cotts Watkins. *A Fraught Embrace: The Romance and Reality of AIDS Altruism in Africa.* Princeton, NJ: Princeton Univ. Press, 2017.

Sydow, Rudolf von. *Compte rendu des travaux de la conférence internationale tenue à Berlin du 22 au 27 Avril 1869 par les délégués des gouvernements signataires de la Convention de Genève et des sociétés et associations de secours aux militaires blessés et malades.* Berlin: J. F. Stracke, 1869.

"Syria: Aid Reaches Beleaguered Population in Homs and Harasta (Operational Update No. 14/2012)." *ICRC.* October 25, 2012. www.icrc.org/eng/resources/documents /update/2012/syriaupdate-2012-10-25.htm (accessed March 27, 2018).

"Syria: Assistance Reaches People in Old City of Homs (News Release No. 12/213)." *ICRC.* November 4, 2012. http://www.icrc.org/eng/resources/documents/news-release/2012 /11-04-syria-homs.htm (accessed March 27, 2018).

"Syria: Humanitarian Situation Catastrophic." *ICRC.* February 19, 2013. http://www .icrc.org/eng/resources/documents/press-briefing/2013/02-15-syria-humanitarian -situation.htm. (accessed March 27, 2018).

Taithe, Bertrand. *Defeated Flesh: Welfare, Warfare, and the Making of Modern France.* Manchester: Manchester Univ. Press, 1999.

Terry, Fiona. *Condemned to Repeat? The Paradox of Humanitarian Action.* Ithaca, NY: Cornell Univ. Press, 2002.

Thornton, Arland. *Reading History Sideways: The Fallacy and Enduring Impact of the Developmental Paradigm on Family Life.* Chicago: Univ. of Chicago Press, 2005.

Thornton, Arland, Shawn F. Dorius, and Jeffrey Swindle. "Developmental Idealism: The Cultural Foundations of World Development Programs." *Sociology of Development* 1, no. 2 (2015): 277–320.

Thornton, William H. "Back to Basics: Human Rights and Power Politics in the New Moral Realism." *International Journal of Politics, Culture, and Society* 14, no. 2 (2000): 315–332.

Ticktin, Miriam. "Transnational Humanitarianism." *Annual Review of Anthropology* 43: (2014): 273–289.

Touraine, Alain. "An Introduction to the Study of Social Movements." *Social Research* 52, no. 4 (1985): 749–788.

Towers, Bridget. "Red Cross Organisational Politics, 1918–1922: Relations of Dominance and the Influence of the United States." In *International Health Organisations and Movements: 1918–1939,* edited by Paul Weindling, 36–55. New York: Cambridge Univ. Press, 1995.

Trépardoux, Francis. "Henri Arrault, précurseur de la convention de Genève, promoteur des ambulances volantes et ami de George Sand." *Revue d'histoire de la pharmacie* 94, no. 349 (2006): 61–89.

Trout, Robert J. *Memoirs of the Stuart Horse Artillery Battalion: Moorman's and Hart's Batteries.* Knoxville: Univ. of Tennessee Press, 2008.

Turner, Bryan S. *Vulnerability and Human Rights.* University Park, PA: Pennsylvania State Univ. Press, 2006.

U.S. Navy Dept. Bureau of Medicine and Surgery. *Report on the Russian Medical and Sanitary*

Features of the Russo-Japanese War to the Surgeon-General. Washington, DC: Government Printing Office, 1906.

Uche, Chibuike. "Oil, British Interests, and the Nigerian Civil War." *Journal of African History* 49, no. 1 (2008): 111–135.

Union League Club. *In Memoriam, Henry Whitney Bellows, D.D.* New York: G. P. Putnam's Sons, 1882.

"Updated Death Toll—42 People Killed in the US Airstrikes on Kunduz Hospital." *Médecins sans Frontières.* December 12, 2015. http://www.msf.org/en/article/kunduz -updated-death-toll-%E2%80%93-42-people-killed-us-airstrikes-kunduz-hospital (accessed November 15, 2018).

USIP. *Haiti: A Republic of NGOs?* United States Institute of Peace Briefs, Washington, DC: USIP, 2010.

Uzzi, Brian. "Networks and the Paradox of Embeddedness." *Administrative Science Quarterly* 42 (1990): 35–67.

van Heyningen, Elizabeth. "The South African War as Humanitarian Crisis." *International Review of the Red Cross* 97, no. 900 (2015): 999–1028.

Vidal, Claudine. "Natural Disasters: 'Do Something!' (Interview with Rony Brauman)." In *Humanitarian Negotiations Revealed: The MSF Experience,* edited by Claire Magone, Michaël Neuman, and Fabrice Weissman, 219–238. London: Hurst & Co., 2011.

Viterna, Jocelyn. *Women in War. The Micro-Processes of Mobilization in El Salvador.* New York: Oxford Univ. Press, 2013.

Viterna, Jocelyn, and Cassandra Robertson. "New Directions for the Sociology of Development." *Annual Review of Sociology* 41 (2015): 243–269.

von Itzenplitz, Charlotte. "Association patriotique de dames à Berlin." *Bulletin international des sociétés de secours aux militaires blessés* 1, no. 2 (1870): 68–69.

Walker, Dale L. *Januarius MacGahan: The Life and Campaigns of an American War Correspondent.* Athens: Ohio Univ. Press, 1988.

Wall Street Journal. "Afghan Urges Obama to End Civilian Deaths." November 6, 2008: 11.

Walzer, Michael. *The Revolution of the Saints: A Study in the Origins of Radical Politics.* Cambridge, MA: Harvard Univ. Press, 1965.

War Office. "The Decoration of 'The Royal Red Cross.'" *Illustrated Naval and Military Magazine* 4 (1884): 253.

Warner, Daniel. "Henry Dunant's Imagined Community: Humanitarianism and the Tragic." *Alternatives: Global, Local, Political* 38, no. 1 (2012): 3–28.

Weissman, Fabrice. *Humanitarian Aid and the International Criminal Court: Grounds for Divorce.* Paris: CRASH, 2009.

Weissman, Fabrice. "Silence Heals . . . From the Cold War to the War on Terror, MSF Speaks Out: A Brief History." In *Humanitarian Negotiations Revealed: The MSF Experience,* edited by Claire Magone, Michaël Neuman, and Fabrice Weissman, translated by Nina Friedman, 177–198. London: Hurst & Co., 2011.

Wetzel, David. *A Duel of Nations: Germany, France, and the Diplomacy of the War of 1870–1871.* Madison: Univ. of Wisconsin Press, 2012.

Williams, Leslie. "Irish Identity and the Illustrated London News, 1846–1851." In *Representing Ireland: Gender, Class Nationality,* edited by Susan S. Sailer, 59–93. Gainesville: Univ. Press of Florida, 1997.

Wilson, Andrew N. *The Victorians.* New York: Norton, 2003.

Winter, Jay. *Sites of Memory, Sites of Mourning: The Great War in European Cultural History.* Cambridge: Cambridge Univ. Press, 1995.

Witt, John Fabian. "Two Conceptions of Suffering in War." In *Knowing the Suffering of*

Others: Legal Perspectives on Pain and its Meanings, edited by Austin Sarat, 129–157. Tuscaloosa: Univ. of Alabama Press, 2014.

Wolfe, Timothy W., and Clifton D. Bryant. "'Full Military Honors': Ceremonial Interment as Sacred Compact." In *Handbook of Death and Dying*, edited by Clifton D. Bryant, 159–172. Thousand Oaks, CA: Sage Publications, 2003.

Woodward, Susan L. *Balkan Tragedy: Chaos and Dissolution after the Cold War*. Washington, DC: Brookings Institution, 1995.

Wu, Yiyang. "Pinker: No Scientific Evidence for God." *Harvard Crimson*. April 11, 2004. http://www.thecrimson.com/article/2004/4/21/pinker-no-scientific-evidence-for-god/ (accessed April 9, 2018).

Young, Michael P. *Bearing Witness against Sin: The Evangelical Birth of the American Social Movement*. Chicago: Univ. of Chicago Press, 2006.

Young, Michael P. "Religious Minorities and Resistance to Genocide: The Collective Rescue of Jews in the Netherlands during the Holocaust." *American Political Science Review* 110, no. 1 (2016): 127–147.

Zubrzycki, Geneviève. *Beheading the Saint: Nationalism, Religion, and Secularism in Quebec*. Chicago: Univ. of Chicago Press, 2016.

Zubrzycki, Geneviève. "History and the National Sensorium: Making Sense of Polish Mythology." *Qualitative Sociology* 34, no. 1 (2011): 21–57.

INDEX

Note: Italicized page locators refer to figures and illustrations.

Academy of Geneva, 41; Calvin and founding of, 39; organization of, 40

accountability: calls for reform of humanitarian NGO work and, 137; faith-based organizations and, 135; "upward" vs. "bottom-up," 179n17

Action Internationale Contre la Faim (AICF), 129

activism: abolitionist, 6, 10; contemporary long-distance, radicalized religious actors and, 60. *See also* social activism

actors: affiliation with humanitarian agents and, 13; fields populated by, 11

Ador, Gustave, 75, 119; tenure at ICRC, 118; tenure with the National Council, 122

Afghanistan: noncombatant death tolls tied to deadly incidents in, vii–viii

Africa: Red Cross and the Scramble for, 82–85

After the Battle of Gravelotte (1870/1871), *frontispiece*; depiction of humanitarian space on a battlefield, 3–4

AICF (Action Internationale Contre la Faim), 129

aid agencies and societies: empowerment issues and, 6; journalists and, 105–6; neutrality of humanitarians and beneficiaries and, 55–59; NRCs and, 64. *See also* relief organizations; women's aid societies

AIDS organizations: religious organizations and, 178n12

Alabama Claims: Moynier inspired by successful arbitration of, 102, 172

Alcott, Louisa May: on her work as army nurse in Civil War, 26

Alexander I (czar of Russia), 43

Alexander II (czar of Russia), 113

Algeria: ICRC interventions in, 122

Alice of Hesse, 96

ambulances: neutrality of, 55, 56, 112

American Friends Service Committee, 136

American National Red Cross (ANRC): Barton and reconstitution of, 75; Boardman's tenure at, 118; in Cuba, 92; famine relief in Russia and Asia and, 66; founder of, 54, 157n48; Ohio River rise (1884), the press, and, 105–6; primacy of ICRC challenged by, 173n6; Spanish-American War and, 161n25; U.S. blood bank and, 166n112

Amnesty International, 138

Amsterdam: MSF operational center in, 124

Andrássy, Gyula, Count, 107

Anglo-American Ambulance, 100

ANRC. *See* American National Red Cross (ANRC)

Appia, Louis, 15, 20, 33, 37, 40, 45, 53

aristocratic women: endowments and, 96; Red Cross linkage between nationalism and charity and, 72; women's aid societies and patronage of, 95; women's societies in each German state and patronage of, 96

Armenian massacre of 1896: Barton commenting on Red Cross intervention in, 72
Arneth, Franz von, 73
Arrault, Henri, 18, 21
Articles organiques des cultes protestants (French Consulate), 40
Associated Press, 106
atheists, "new," 133
atrocities: in Biafra, French doctors bear witness to, 124; MSF on impartiality and bearing witness to, 117
Augusta (empress of Prussia): as avid supporter of the Red Cross, 95, 96, 97; nursing award created by, 100
Auschwitz: invoking memory of, Biafra's breaking point and, 125–26; Rossel heads Red Cross delegation to, 120, 174n21
Austria: NRCs, Second Schleswig War, and, 64; Red Cross activists in, 62
Austrian Red Cross, 79
Austro-Prussian War (1866), 64
autonomy: of the humanitarian field, 89; interconnectedness balanced with, 115; NGOs and, 2, 3. See also impartiality; neutrality; permanence; universality
Avocats sans Frontières, 173n3
awards and honors for nurses, and new systems of, 98, 100

baby boom–generation French physicians: influx of, into humanitarian NGOs, 122
Baden: active NRCs in, 65; Geneva Convention articles and military instructions in, 110–11
Balibar, Étienne, 7
Balkan Wars of the 1870s: aid societies and success of, 50; Geneva Convention, journalistic discourse, and, 57; reports of humanitarian crises in, 106–7
Barcelona: MSF operational center in, 124
Barnett, Michael, 6
Barton, Clara, 57, 118, 157n48; advocacy struggle over Geneva Convention, 163n61; American National Red Cross reconstituted by, 75; clashes between competitor humanitarian organizations in U.S. and, 163n66; on ethical concerns about volunteers, 58; on future of transnational humanitarianism, 71–72; on

media and Red Cross relationship, 101, 102; praised for her efforts in Spanish-American War, 106; reporting about Red Cross activities, 102, 103; response to pacifists, 58–59; on Russian famine, 105; on Spanish-American War experiences, 54; on women in Red Cross movement and fitness for nursing, 93, 97
Basel: economic development in, 38; population in 1798, 155n10
Bashir, Omar al-: indicted for war crimes, 130
Basting, J. H. C., 56
battlefield(s): aid societies and improving medical care on, 8; ambivalent stance toward, in A Memory of Solferino, 25–27, 33; autobiographic accounts on excitement of, 26; emerging presence of nurses on, 95; hygiene on, increased attention to, 98; medical aid, humanitarian space, and, 3; neutrality of humanitarians and beneficiaries on, 55–59; new humanitarian movements and condemnation of practices on, 116; Red Cross and journalists on frontlines of, 105–6; Red Cross nurses as active caregivers beyond, 98, 99; Rolin-Jaequemyns on preventing abuses in, 113; South African, Second Boer War and, 117
battlefield relief in the nineteenth century, 17–24; faith-based groups and, 19–20; legislating neutrality and, 20–22; nurses and military medical facilities and, 18–19; peace societies and, 22–23
Battle of Gravelotte, 100
Battle of Solferino, 15. See also Memory of Solferino, A (Dunant)
Baudelaire, Charles, 11
Baumberger, Georg, 34
Bavaria: active NRCs in, 65; Geneva Convention articles and military instructions in, 110–11
bearing witness to human rights abuses: témoignage principle and, 124
Belgian Congo: Congo Free State converted into, 84
Belgian Red Cross, 8
Belgium: competing aid societies in, 81
Bellevue Hospital School of Nursing (New York): establishment of, 94
Bellows, Henry Whitney, 19, 74, 75, 91, 92

Benthall, Jonathan, 134
bereaved survivors: consoling, 65. See also
   families
Berlin: population in 1860, 38; Red Cross
   periodical resembling the Bulletin in, 67
Berlin International Statistical Congress, 33
Bern: population in 1798, 155n10; popu-
   lation in 1850, 155n9
Best, Geoffrey, 8
Better Angels of Our Nature, The (Pinker), 133
Biafra: emergence of new humanitarianism
   and French doctors in, 122–25, 176n51
Bickerdyke, Mary Ann, 19
Bluntschli, Johann Caspar, 112
Boardman, Mabel, 118, 160n16
Born, Friedrich, 120
Bost, Ami, 41
"bottom-up" accountability: "upward" ac-
   countability vs., 179n17
Bourdieu, Pierre, 11, 12, 148–49n55,
   149n56, 173n7; examples of field open-
   ness, 167n1; skepticism toward trans-
   national fields, 166n117
Bourdieusian field analysis: interpretation
   of historical findings and, x
Bowles, Charles S. P., 111
Brauman, Rony, 2, 122, 125, 129, 130, 131
Britain: copycat Red Cross societies in, 81
British evangelicalism: the Réveil and
   radical factions within, 43
British National Red Cross: Darmstadt hos-
   pital established by, 96
Brussels: MSF operational center in, 124
Brussels Declaration, 113, 114
Brussels Protestant Church, 42
Bulletin international des sociétés de la Croix-
   Rouge, 179n1
Bulletin international des sociétés de secours
   aux militaires blessés, 141–42; cohesive-
   ness of Red Cross network demon-
   strated in, 68; establishment and pur-
   pose of, 66–67; Red Cross periodicals
   resembling, 67
Bullinger, Heinrich, 39
burials: battlefield, Dunant on, in A
   Memory of Solferino, 30, 33; practices in
   nineteenth-century militaries, 154n54

Calvin, John: arrives in Geneva, 38; Institutes of the Christian Religion, 39; Réveil
   ministers on writings of, 43

Calvinism: communal ecclesiastical disciplinary bodies and Calvinist polities,
   44; Dunant's personal movement away
   from, 157n53; Geneva as theological
   center of, 38–40; Genevan Consistory
   and spread of, 39; Red Cross emergence
   and Calvinist revival, 36; reinvigoration of social activism and, 44, 45; the
   Réveil's objections to modernizing Calvinist theology, 43
Calvinists: internationalism of Reformed
   Protestantism and, 63. See also Réveil
Cambodia: Malhuret advocates interventionist stance toward Khmer Rouge in, 126,
   129; MSF initiative and famine in, 129
capital: field-specific, 11
CARE International, 2
Caritas Puerto Rico, 135
casualties lists: in newspapers, 105
Catholic Charities International, 135
Catholic minority: Geneva Canton and, 40
Catholic priests: expelled from Geneva, 38
Catholic Relief Services, 135
censorship: war journalism in transition
   and, 104
Central Europe: aid societies and success of
   wars in, 1860s–1870s, 50
chaplains: neutrality of actors on battlefield
   and, 55
charity: on the battlefield, Dunant on
   natural human zeal for, 32–33; permanence of, Red Cross founding conferences and, 47–51; Red Cross linkage
   between nationalism and, 72
Charity Navigator, 135
cholera, 18
Christian charity: Red Cross project and
   revitalization of, 5
Christian ethic: transnational humanitarianism under aegis of, 36, 37
Christian interpretations of the Red Cross,
   popular, 92–93
Christian world: expanding reach of transnational humanitarian field beyond, 90
Christian X (king of Denmark), 120
churches: Puerto Rican, mobilized in wake
   of Hurricane Maria, 135; in support of
   the Red Cross, 91–92
Church of Geneva, 44–45; under Napoleonic rule, 41
Church of the Augsburg Confession, 40

civilians: incorporation of, into battlefield humanitarian efforts, 158n76

Civil War (U.S.): endorsement of patriotism and model of, 71; faith-based groups and, 20; heroic death notion and news reports from the front, 29; search for prisoners of war and, 98; U.S. Sanitary Commission's work during, 73

clergy: Geneva Convention and inclusion of, 91

Cold War: American Friends Service Committee and advocacy against, 136

Columbia (feminine personification of the U.S.): Red Cross in national imagery and, 76–77, 76

Committee for the Wounded of the Evangelical Society of Geneva, 45

Committee of Five, formation of, 15–16

Company of Pastors: Calvin and organization of, 39

compassion between militaries: lack of, in A Memory of Solferino, 27, 29

competition: local, rising prestige of NRCs and breeding of, 79–82, 115

concentration camps, Nazi: ICRC's lack of systematic policy with regard to, 120; initial reports of, 119

Concert of Europe, 20

"confessional state" vision, 156n33

conflict zones: autonomy for NGOs and, 2. See also battlefield(s); war

Congo, Free State of: annexation of, 84; converted into Belgian Congo, 84; formal establishment of, 83; "humanitarian colonialism" and, 82–84; Institut de droit international and, 83

Congo Red Cross, 82, 83; becomes full member of Red Cross movement, 83; controversy over King Leopold's brutal regime and, 84; on future aspirations of, 83–84

Congress of Paris, 22

Congress of Vienna, 40

Constantinople: Geneva Convention ratified by, 65; Society for Assistance to the Wounded and Disabled in Action established in, 78

Convention Relative to the Protection of Civilian Persons in Time of War: ICRC and, 121

Crimean War, 18, 19, 20, 22; news reports

of, 104; number of casualties in, 64; pioneering group of battlefield nurses in, 95; Seacole's account of, 26

cross-national identity, shared: ICRC and creation of, 66–68, 69

Cuba: American National Red Cross in, 92

cultural origins of humanitarian NGOs, 14–34; battlefield relief in the nineteenth century, 17–24; impact and success of A Memory of Solferino, 16, 33–34; in A Memory of Solferino, 24–33; promotion of A Memory of Solferino, 15

culture: field emergence and, 133; genesis and mass expansion of humanitarian field and, 132–33. See also humanitarian culture, spread of, across borders; humanitarian field, reconsidering culture of

Dachau: ICRC visits to, 120

Daily News: massacre as a term adopted by, 107

Danish Red Cross, 120

Darfur: Médecins du Monde expelled from, 130

Davey, Eleanor, 175n40

Davison, Henry Pomeroy, 119

Dawkins, Richard, 133

Deacon House of Duisburg, 20

death: senseless, portrayed in A Memory of Solferino, 29–31, 33

decentralization: American National Red Cross and, 75; ICRC and maintenance of, 69–70; vision for the Red Cross and, 62–63

de las Casas, Bartolomé, 10

Delcourt, Marcel, 123

Demidov, Anatoli, 19

Denmark: Nigerian Civil War and Red Cross society of, 123; NRCs, Second Schleswig War and, 64

Dennett, Daniel, 133

de Swaan, Abram, 6

de Waal, Alex, 88

Dickens, Charles, 33

dignity of dead and wounded soldiers: loss of, in A Memory of Solferino, 31

diplomatic front: women and, 95

disarmament initiatives: activist groups advocating for, 35

discipline, communal: Calvinist law and, 44, 45

Doctors without Borders. *See* Médecins sans Frontières (MSF)
domestic caregiving: nursing rapidly dissociated from, 93
Drummond, Henry, 43
Dufour, Guillaume Henri, 15, 33, 48
Dunant, Henry (Jean-Henri), 46, 55, 60, 91, 92, 107, 114, 117, 136, 150n5; birth and early life of, 14; Bluntschli's codification and, 112; central role of, in Red Cross movement, 15–16, 34, 35; death of, 34; declares bankruptcy, 34; evangelism of the Réveil and, 45; *A Memory of Solferino*, 15, 16, 21, 24–34; on neutrality, and push to include issue in 1863 conference, 20, 56; permanence of charity and role of, 47; personal files of, 141; receives Nobel Peace Prize (1901), 34; on spiritual influences and calling from God, 46, 156n39; war abolition mission of, 157n53; wartime relief initiatives pursued by, 34
Durham, Edith, 119

East Pakistan (later Bangladesh): physicians and journalists direct attention to conflict in, 124
Écoles sans Frontières, 173n3
ecumenicism: revival movements and, 41
El Salvador: Oxfam and fight against predatory mining in, 137
"emergency imaginary" position, 130
Emmanuelli, Xavier, 123
Empaytaz, Henri-Louis: the Réveil's influence and role of, 43; treatise on Christ's divinity, 41–42
endowments: aristocratic women and, 96
English Puritans: in Geneva, 39
Enlightenment, 6
environmental field: national dynamics and, 87
Esmarch, Friedrich von, 98
ethical code: humanitarian work and, ix
ethics: competing views on humanitarian aid and, 6; of humanitarian field, emergence of, 17; international aid, x; intervention, humanitarian NGOs and, 5–6; predominant framework for humanitarian NGOs and, 136
Ethiopia: humanitarian NGO intervention in, 1; MSF expelled from, 128–29

Eugénie (empress of France), 96
European armies: mass conscription schemes of, 16
Evangelical Society of Geneva: Committee for the Wounded of, 45; Merle d'Aubigné speaking to, 43

faith-based organizations, 152n25; battlefield relief in nineteenth century and, 19–20; contemporary humanitarian aid sector and, 135; nonreligious NGOs and, 134
families: bereaved, Dunant's laments on senseless death in *A Memory of Solferino* and, 29, 31; casualties lists in newspapers and, 105; ICRC and communications with, 98
famine, 2; Nigerian Civil War and, 123; in Russia, Barton on, 105
Fassin, Didier, 7, 88
Faust, Drew Gilpin, 29
Federal Bureau of Investigation: American Friends Service Committee scrutinized by, 136
Ferdinand II (king), 21
field(s): autonomy of, 89; definition of, 11; new, genesis of, 11
field boundaries: porosity of, 89, 172n110
field emergence: addressing, in two different ways, 148–49n55; culture's key role in, 133
field openness: Bourdieu's examples of, 167n1
field-specific capital, 11
field theory: Bourdieu's intention and view on, 149n56; relationship between transnational and local fields and, 160n10
Finland: Nigerian Civil War and Red Cross society of, 123
Finnemore, Martha, 36
first aid: Samaritan Society and, 98
First Carlist War: Basque women nurses in, 93
Flaubert, Gustave, 11
Forbes, Archibald, 106
Forsythe, David, 61
France: casualties during Franco-Prussian War, 64; copycat Red Cross societies in, 81; doctor job market saturated in (mid-1960s), 122; Nigerian oil extraction and, 123; Red Cross activists in, 62

Franco-Prussian War (1870–1871), 34, 50, 53, 55, 57, 61, 77, 112; American women volunteering in, 92; Belgian Baroness de Crombrugghe's battlefront reports, 79; charitable activities during, 96; devastating toll of, 64–65; French pastors and, 91; Geneva Convention and local jurists in aftermath of, 111; Geneva Convention and neutrality for humanitarian agents in, 107; legalistic claims for national superiority and, 73; Militär-Sanitäts-Kreuz decoration award and, 101; mutual praise within Red Cross network after, 68; NRCs and, 64; Red Cross name mentioned in aftermath of, 67; report of ICRC activities during, 69–70

"free churches": history behind, 40

French avant-garde literature: field of, 11

French Consulate: *Articles organiques des cultes protestants* published by, 40

French Directory: annexation of Geneva and, 39

French doctors in Biafra: glorifying *sans-frontiérisme* and, 126–27; memory of Auschwitz returns, 125–26; new humanitarianism emerges, 122–25, 176n51; Nigerian Civil War and, 123

French intellectual currents: *sans-frontiérisme* and, 116

French National Red Cross: Joan of Arc as patron saint of, 77

French Protestants: as refugees in Geneva, 39

French Red Cross societies, 162n40; antecedent of, 152n24; mission to Biafra, future MSF founders, and, 123; Vicomte de Melun quoted in 1871 report, 70

French Reformed Church: organization of, 40

French Revolution, 10

French Wars of Religion, 39

Friedrich Karl (prince of Prussia), 15

fundraising: for American Red Cross in Cuba, 92; churches and, 92–93; ICRC and MSF and, 124–25; MSF's nonhierarchical organizational structure and, 128; Nigerian Civil War and, 123; Puerto Rico in wake of Hurricane Maria and, 135

Gaussen, François Louis, 155n20; key influence of, on Red Cross, 42; sermons and letters of, 45, 142

Geneva: annexed to France, 1798, 39; Calvinist majority/Catholic minority relations in, 42; as Calvinist theological center, 36, 38–40; MSF operational center in, 124; Napoleonic rule and, 39–40, 155n15; population in 1798, 155n10; population in 1860, 38; Reformed institutions in, 39

Geneva Bible, 39

Geneva Company of the Swiss Colonies of Sétif, 15

Geneva Convention, ix, 70, 86, 92, 96, 118; Bluntschli and establishing status of, 112; clergy included in, 91; Congo Free State and ratification of, 83; Constantinople ratifies in 1865, 65; forbears of, 21; Franco-Prussian War, legalistic claims for national superiority, and, 73; ICRC as a legal agent and, 110–11; international lawyers and, 111–12; Ottoman government, war correspondent's accounts, and, 107; Paris Declaration Respecting Maritime Law and, 21; as symbol of neutrality, 114–15; unenforceability of, 112–14; wide-scale ratification of, 61

Geneva Convention of 1864, 7, 13, 54; neutralization as main concern of, 55, 56, 57; Red Cross and widespread ratification of, 3, 8–9, 56, 64; signing of, 47

Geneva Convention of 1906: militaries' freedom of action and, 159n78

Geneva Convention of 1949: Convention Relative to the Protection of Civilian Persons in Time of War adopted by, 121; ICRC activities and, 160n11; ICRC as sole INGO mentioned by, 108–9

Genevan Consistory: Calvin and organization of, 39

Geneva Society for Public Utility, 16

Geneva Society for Public Welfare: concerns of, 46

genocide: ICRC's preference for confidential diplomacy over speaking out against, 121–22, 125; shortcomings of ICRC in addressing, 120, 121, 122

German Civil War (Austro-Prussian War of 1866), 64

Germanic Confederation: charitable "patriotic societies" within, 96

German Red Cross: modeling new nationhood through humanitarian activism

and, 77; national imagery of, 77; Nazi
nationalization of, 119, 120; unified
women's aid societies and, 97
German Unification Wars of the 1860s, 20
Germany: Arianizing eugenics promoted
across, 119; casualties during Franco-
Prussian War, 64; Samaritan schools
in, 98
Gilby, Anthony, 39
GIMCU (Groupe d'intervention médico-
chirurgicale d'urgence—Group for
Medical and Surgical Emergency Inter-
vention): formation of, 124
global action: national sentiments as me-
diators of, 85–87
God Is Not Great (Hitchens), 133
Goncourt brothers, 33
Governing the World (Mazower), 20
Grand Council of Geneva, 38, 39
Graphic, The, 105
Great Britain: copycat Red Cross societies
in, 81
Great Eastern Crisis of 1875–1878: Euro-
pean NRCs and, 65
Greece: ICRC interventions in, 122
Groen van Prinsterer, Guillaume, 42
Groupe d'intervention médico-chirurgicale
d'urgence—Group for Medical and Sur-
gical Emergency Intervention (GIMCU):
formation of, 124
Guers, Émile, 41

Hague, The: Omar al-Bashir indicted for
war crimes by, 130; Permanent Court of
Arbitration in, 115
Hague Convention of 1899: Lieber Code
and, 22
Haiti: humanitarian policy conversa-
tions and difficult questions arising
from, 138; NGOs working in, 1; post-
earthquake, disaster relief in, 144n4
Haldane, Robert, 42, 43
Harris, Sam, 133
Hartford Courant: "Red Cross Sundays" re-
ported by, 91–92
Haskell, Thomas, 6
Hermet, Guy, 127
Hesse: active NRCs in, 65
Hitchens, Christopher, 133
Holocaust: Biafra's breaking point and
Kouchner's potent metaphor of, 125–

26; ICRC's relative silence on, 120, 121,
122, 125
Holocaust Memorial Museum: ICRC's
World War II files released to, 121
Holy Roman Empire: international lawyers
and dissolution of, 109
Honduras: MSF and guerilla factions' use of
cover of neutrality in, 128
"hospitaller" orders, 20
Houdetot, Count: Geneva Convention and,
107
House of Savoy, 38
Huber, Max, 119
Hugo, Victor, 33
Huguenot rebellions (1620s), 39
humanitarian action: uses of emergency
discourse in, 144n8
humanitarian activism: modeling new nationhood through, 77–79
humanitarian aid societies: Dunant's advocacy for, 17, 34
humanitarian character: creating, 66–68
"humanitarian colonialism": Red Cross, the
Scramble for Africa, and, 82–85
humanitarian community, foundational
assumption of, 5
humanitarian culture, spread of, across
borders, 61–87; creating a humanitarian
character, 66–68; expansion from a
movement to a transnational field, 63–
66; making transnational humanitarianism into a national mission, 69–79;
national sentiments as mediators of
global action, 85–87; Red Cross and
the Scramble for Africa, 82–85; rising
prestige and breeding of local competition, 79–82
"humanitarian emergency": newsreaders
introduced to notion of, 104; politicians
and use of term, 88; Western donors
and notion of, 144n8
humanitarian field, 11–13; appearance of
MSF and existence of, 173n6; autonomous pole of, ICRC and MSF and, 131;
culture and genesis and mass expansion
of, 132–33; emerging ethics of, 17; exer-
tion of belief on "noncultural" realms
and, 60; ongoing tensions in, 130–31;
permanence established as key logic of,
47; the Réveil and the origins of the logics of, 37–46; uniqueness of, 9

humanitarian field, reconsidering culture of, 132–38; central arguments related to, 132–33; religion and humanitarian work reconsidered, 133–36; rethinking mission of humanitarianism, 136–38

humanitarian governance approach, 145n17

humanitarian INGOs: nationalism, cultural frameworks, and, 87

humanitarianism: independence of, Red Cross founding conferences and, 47, 51–55; *A Memory of Solferino* dedicated to, 24; religion and, 9–10; rethinking mission of, 136–38; rights-based, 138. *See also* "new humanitarianism"; transnational humanitarianism

humanitarian language: journalistic field and adoption of, 106–8

humanitarian logics, spread of into new domains, 88–115; balancing interconnectedness and autonomy, 115; international law, 108–15; journalism, 88, 101–2, *103*, 104–8, 115; professional nursing, 88, 93–98, *99*, 100–101, 115; religious field, 89–93, 115

humanitarian NGO model: battle over acceptance of, 3

humanitarian NGO policies: history of transnational humanitarian field and implications for, 13

humanitarian NGOs: autonomy of, 35; global community and enduring trust in, 6; impossible dilemmas faced by, 132; influx of baby boom–generation French physicians into, 122; international success and virtuous work of, 4; nonreligious, 134; original Red Cross template and twentieth-century paradigm for, 147n41; war economy and, 128. *See also* cultural origins of humanitarian NGOs

humanitarian norms: transnational spread of, 62

humanitarians and beneficiaries: neutrality of, 47, 55–59

humanitarian sector: defined, 4; emergence of, 6–9; impact of nineteenth-century origins of, 4–5

humanitarian societies: ideal, Red Cross founders and depiction of, 35; transatlantic, 144n9

humanitarian space, 1–13; on a battlefield, 3; divergence on nature of humanitarian NGOs, 2–4; emergence of the humanitarian sector, 6–9; humanitarian field and, 11–13; religion and humanitarianism, 9–10; ubiquity of humanitarian NGOs in, 1

humanitarian work: ethical underpinnings of, ix; historicizing current beliefs about, x

human rights: compromised, MSF's "duty to interfere" and, 124

"human-rights approach": to humanitarian action, ethics questions tied to, 5–6

human rights organizations, 138

Human Rights Watch, 138

Hungary: copycat Red Cross society in, 81; ICRC interventions in, 122; national revival of, within Austro-Hungary, 78

Hurricane Maria, 135

Hussein, Zeid Ra'ad Al, vii

Hutchinson, John, 36, 62, 118

hygiene: increased attention to, on the battlefield, 98

ICRC. *See* International Committee of the Red Cross (ICRC)

identity work: ICRC and, 67–68

IFRC. *See* International Federation of the Red Cross (IFRC)

Ignatieff, Michael, 4

Illustrated London News: Red Cross in action accounts in, 106

impartiality, 12, 132; best humanitarian organizations and, 11; disputes in national chapters of Red Cross movement and, 87; humanitarian NGOs and, viii, ix, 2, 5, 144n9; of humanitarian work, 89; international law profession and, 110; as marker of authority in humanitarian field, 137; MSF's and ICRC's shared underlying belief in, 131; MSF vs. Red Cross views on, 117; World War II, revisiting question of, 121–22. *See also* autonomy; neutrality; permanence; universality

imperialism: emergence of humanitarianism linked to, 6

Imperial Medical Society (Constantinople), 78

independence, 38, 89, 132; of humanitarianism, Red Cross founding conferences and, 47, 51–55; as marker of authority in humanitarian field, 137; MSF's and ICRC's shared underlying belief in, 131

INGOs. *See* international NGOs (INGOs)

Institut de droit international (Ghent): Congo Free State and, 83; establishment of, 110

Institute of International Law: study of Brussels Declaration and, 114

Institutes of the Christian Religion (Calvin), 39

inter arma caritas ("in war, charity"): roots of ICRC enshrined in motto of, 14

International African Association: establishment of, 82

International Aid Committee for Wounded Soldiers: creation of, 8

international aid ethics, x

International Christian Peace Fellowship, 23

International Committee for Aid to the Wounded: early endeavors of, 15, 16. *See also* International Committee of the Red Cross (ICRC)

International Committee for Relief to the Wounded, 47

International Committee of the Red Cross (ICRC), viii, 9, 51, 88, 95, 101; acceptance of humanitarian NGO model and, 3; achievements during World War II, 120–21; activities aimed at building a shared identity, 67–68; adoption of name for, 67, 145n10; appeal to national cultures and international success of, 62; archives of, 141; background of, 16; challenges to its authority faced by, 118; control of recognition of the official NRC in each state and, 79–81; diplomatic work of, 63; diversification of Red Cross, 65, 66; founding members of, 37; Geneva Convention and, ix; Geneva Conventions of 1949 and mention of, 108–9; humanitarian field and founding role of, 59; humanitarian organizations challenging primacy of, 173n6; impartial aid societies and, 47; international conferences and, 157n41; international meetings organized for NRC representatives, 67–68; International Prisoners-of-War Agency established by, 118; as a legal agent, 110–11;

letter from War Office in London to, 52; maintenance of decentralization and, 69–70; major tasks performed by, 2; model of volunteer humanitarianism advocated by, 61; motto, additional, acknowledged by, 150n1; motto of, longstanding, 14; Moynier's tenure at, 118; neutrality and religious convictions of members of, 56; "new humanitarianism" and departure from norms of, 116; Nigerian Civil War and limited initial means of, 123; note on name, x; ongoing tensions in humanitarian field and, 130–31; permanence of charity and, 47, 48; powers of patriotism espoused by, 70; prisoners of war and, 98; question of World War II impartiality revisited, 121–22; recognition as an NRC, advantages of, 80–81; relative silence of, on matter of the Holocaust, 120, 121, 122, 125; on remoteness of the New York Committee, 74; working relationship with MSF, 125; in World War II, 119–21. *See also* national Red Cross societies (NRCs); Red Cross

international conferences: ICRC: and importance of, 157n41

International Court for the Settlement of Investment Disputes: at World Bank, 137

International Criminal Court, The Hague: Omar al-Bashir indicted for war crimes by, 130

International Federation of the Red Cross (IFRC): history behind, 119; motto used by, 150n1; primacy of ICRC challenged by, 173n6

international law, 108–15; depoliticization of profession of, 110; emergence of field of, 109–10, 171n90; emergence of transnational humanitarian field and, 13; Geneva Convention of 1864 and growing appeal of, 47; ICRC as a legal agent, 110–11; spread of humanitarian logics into, 89, 108–15; state-centered rather than universalistic basis of, 110; unenforceability of Geneva Convention, 112–14

International Law Association (Brussels), 110

international lawyers: Geneva Convention and, 111–12

International Monetary Fund, 138
international NGOs (INGOs): accountability and, 137; ethics of, questions
related to, 6; international conferences
and, 157n41; scope and operational
reach of, 1–2; "upward" accountability
vs. "bottom-up" accountability and,
179n17. *See also* nongovernmental organizations (NGOs)
International Prisoners-of-War Agency: establishment of, 118
International Red Cross, viii, 7. *See also*
International Committee of the Red
Cross (ICRC)
International Rescue Committee (IRC),
viii, 129
International Review of the Red Cross, 124,
130, 131
International Shipwreck Society, 7
international treaties, 20
intervention ethics: humanitarian organiza-
tions and, 5–6
Iranian national society: Red Lion with Sun
symbol used by, 167–68n5
Iran-Iraq War, 2
Iraq, 2
IRC. *See* International Rescue Committee
(IRC)
Irish Potato Famine, 17; critical long-
distance reporting on, 16; war journal-
ism in transition and news reports
about, 104
Irving, Edward, 43
Italian States: 1848 revolutions in, 21

Japanese Red Cross, 78; Chinese war of
1894–1895 and, 79; depiction of volunteers at work in Russo-Japanese War,
73–74, *74*; military focus of, 75; news
accounts of, 106; nurses in, assisting
army surgeons caring for a Russian soldier, *80*; rapid growth of, 90, 96
Jews: alarming reports of deportations of,
120. *See also* Holocaust
Joan of Arc: as patron saint of French
NRC, 77
John of Saxony (king), 15, 33
Jones, Agnes, 45, 94, 168n24
journalism: emergence of transnational humanitarian field and, 13; humanitarian
language adopted by journalistic field,

106–8; spread of humanitarian logics
into, 101–2, 104–8, 115; war journalism
in transition, 102, 104–5
journalists: humanitarianism of Red Cross
and, 5

Kaiserswerth: Nightingale and Lutheran
deaconess motherhouse in, 94
Kellenberger, Jakob, 121
Khmer Rouge Cambodia: Malhuret advo-
cates interventionist stance toward, 126,
129
Ki-moon, Ban, vii
Knights Hospitaller, 19
Knox, John, 39
Kouchner, Bernard, 122, 123, 124, 125,
126, 129, 130
Krause, Monika, 131
Krüdener, Madame de, 43
Kunduz Trauma Centre, Afghanistan, viii;
international outrage over U.S. airstrikes
on, vii, viii
Kuyper, Abraham, 44, 45, 156n29

Lake Chad basin, 2
Lanzmann, Claude, 174n21
lawyers: international, humanitarianism of
Red Cross and, 5. *See also* international
law
League of French Women, 109
League of Nations, 118
League of Red Cross Societies, 119; split and
orientation of, 174n15. *See also* Interna-
tional Federation of the Red Cross (IFRC)
Lebanon: MSF operations in, 128
left-wing movements: cohort of new French
physicians and, 122
Le Monde: French doctors in Biafra publish
articles in, 123–24
Leopold II (king of Belgium): Red Cross,
the Scramble for Africa, and Congo, Free
State of, 82, 83, 84
Leo XIII (pope), 91
Le Petit Journal: Red Cross in action
accounts in, 106
Le Petit Parisien: Red Cross in action
accounts in, 106
Library of Geneva, 141
Libya: humanitarian policy conversations
and difficult questions arising from, 138
Lieber, Francis, 22, 111, 112, 113

Lieber Code, 22
Ligue internationale et permanente de la paix, 49
Lincoln, Abraham, 22
literary field(s): Bourdieusian analysis and, 154n56; new type of capital, elites, and emergence of, 11
Livermore, Mary, 19
Liverpool Workhouse Infirmary, 94
Lombardo-Venetian Kingdom, 14
Lombardy: Dunant reports on experience in, 15
London: population in 1860, 38
London Peace Society (Society for the Promotion of Universal and Permanent Peace), 22–23
Louis (prince of Ligne): Congo Red Cross and, 84
Louise (princess), 95
Lutheran Church–Missouri Synod: Nigerian Civil War and, 123
Lutherans and Lutheranism, 44; conventicles and, 40; Geneva's conversion to, 38; revival of orders of Lutheran deaconesses, in 1830s, 94
Lutheran World Relief, 135

MacGahan, Januarius, 16, 106, 107, 171n74
machine gun: introduction of, 17
MacLaughlin, Louisa Elisabeth, 100–101, 105
Madrid: Red Cross periodical resembling the Bulletin in, 67
magazines, illustrated: Red Cross in action accounts in, 106
Magdeburg provincial society: nationalism and statute declaration of, 71
Magyar society (Budapest): establishment of, 78
Malan, César, 42, 43
Malhuret, Claude: advocates interventionist stance toward Khmer Rouge Cambodia, 126; elected president of MSF, 129
Manual of the Laws and Customs of War: adoption of, 114
Maria Feodorovna (empress of Russia), 96
Markandya, Polly, 134
Martyr, Pierre, 39
Mary I (queen of England), 39
massacre: adoption of term, by newspapers, 107

Maunoir, Théodore, 15, 33, 46
Mazower, Mark, 20
McKinley, William, 92
MDM (Médecins du Monde), 126, 130
meaning systems: national definition of, 63
Médecins du Monde (MDM), 126, 130
Médecins sans Frontières (MSF), 2, 9, 13, 136–37; centrality of témoignage principle to identity of, 124; establishment of, 116; forming of, history behind, 123–24; founders of, 123; founding declaration of, 124; French preoccupation with the Third World and emergence of, 175n40; growth into multinational federated INGO, 124; Kunduz hospital airstrike and, viii; media celebrates founders of, 126; national sovereigns and outspoken nature of, 128–29; ongoing tensions in humanitarian field and, 130–31; operational centers of, 124, 173n5; parallels between rise of the Red Cross and rise of, 130; reconsideration of témoignage and, 128–30; Redfield's description of, 134; sources, existing historiographies, and, 142; troubled institutionalization and hard lessons learned by, 127–30; working relationship with ICRC, 125
media: relationship with Red Cross, 101. See also journalism; newspapers
medical welfare on the battlefield: A Memory of Solferino and discourse on, 26, 33
Melucci, Alberto, 122
Memory of Solferino, A (Dunant): from glory to misery in, 24–27, 33; impact on humanitarian work, 24; inefficiency of existing arrangements in, 27–29, 33; promotion of, 15; publishing of, 15; role of the volunteer in, 31–33; senseless death in, 29–31, 33; success of, 33–34, 60; themes in, 15, 33; three sections of, 24
Merle d'Aubigné, Jean-Henri, 42, 43, 45; on scourge of war, 43–44; sermons and letters of, 142
Messina: 1848 revolutions in Italian States and, 21
Methodists: conventicles and, 40
"militarization of charity," 118
Militär-Sanitäts-Kreuz decoration, 101

military codes of conduct: international law and, 109
military establishment: reporters gain independence from, 104
military medical facilities: Dunant's criticisms of, in *A Memory of Solferino*, 27–28, 29, 33; nurses and, 18–19
military nursing: Nightingale and establishment of, 19
military relief work: calls for reform of, 18, 23
missing persons: searching for, 98
missing soldiers: locating, 65
Moniz, Amanda B., 144n9
Montauban Academy, 40, 155n15
Montenegrin-Ottoman War (1876–1878): European NRCs and, 65
Montenegro: establishing of NRC by, as declaration of self-determination, 77
morale building: cohesiveness of Red Cross network and, 68
Moravian evangelists: Société des Amis and, 41
Moynier, Gustave, 15, 33, 40, 46, 47, 48, 49, 55, 56, 75, 90, 115, 117, 136, 150n5; advocates for Society for Assistance to the Wounded and Disabled in Action in Constantinople, 78; Bluntschli's codification and, 112; international arbitration tribunal proposal and, 112–13; on international success of the Red Cross, 61; lifelong interest in international law, 108; private files of, 141; on Red Cross as fruit of Christianity, 49; on role of the aid societies, 52–53; Scramble for Africa and, 82, 83; successful arbitration of Alabama Claims and, 102, 172; on Swiss origins of humanitarian initiatives, 72; tenure at ICRC, 118; treatise for national relief societies, 37; on use of term "international," 69
MSF. *See* Médecins sans Frontières (MSF)
mythical national figures: national Red Cross societies represented by, 76–77, 76

Napoleon Bonaparte, 17; Geneva and rule of, 39–40, 155n15
Napoleonic Wars, 17
Napoleon III, 14, 15; censorship under, 170n55

national exceptionalism: stances taken by, 87
National Health Society (Britain), 100
national humanitarian projects: varieties of, 72–75
national imagery: Red Cross in, 75–77, 76
nationalism, 61, 154n7; intermingling of universality and, 85; Red Cross linkage between charity and, 72
national Red Cross societies (NRCs): adoption of Red Cross name and, 67, 68; country-level focus of, 62; endorsements of patriotism and, 71–72; enter concentration camps and administer aid to survivors, 121; ICRC as a legal agent and communications with, 110, 111; movement to a transnational field and, 64; "new humanitarianism" and departure from norms of, 116; rapid professionalization of, 118; relations with local news outlets, 79; rising prestige of, and breeding of local competition, 79–82; Second Boer War and, 117; types of claims made for national superiority and, 73. *See also* International Committee of the Red Cross (ICRC); Red Cross
national sensoriums: resilience and potency of, 163–64n71
national sentiments: as mediators of global action, 85–87
national settings: prominent role of, in transnational humanitarian field, 110
"national sin": religious reformers and notion of, 10
National Society for Aid to the Sick and Wounded in War, 100
national sovereigns: outspoken nature of MSF and, 128–29
nationhood: new, modeling through humanitarian activism, 77–79
nation-states: emerging, Red Cross modeling of nationhood through humanitarian activism and, 77–79
natural disasters: American National Red Cross and relief work, 75; in Haiti, 1
natural law: international law and movement away from, 109–10
Nazi concentration camps: ICRC's lack of systematic policy with regard to, 120; initial reports of, 119
Neo-Calvinism, 156n29

Netherlands, the: Geneva Convention articles and military instructions in, 110–11; Nigerian Civil War and Red Cross society of, 123

neutrality, 12, 23, 38, 64, 109, 132; of ambulances, 55, 56, 112; clergy and, 91; Geneva Convention and problem of, 8, 9; Geneva Convention as a symbol of, 114–15; humanitarian NGOs and, viii, ix, 2, 5, 144n9; of humanitarians and beneficiaries, 55–59; of humanitarian work, 89; legislating, 20–22; as marker of authority in humanitarian field, 137; of medical facilities on the battlefield, ratification of Geneva Convention of 1864 and, 47; MSF's and ICRC's shared underlying belief in, 131; nonreligious humanitarian NGOs and, 134; of NRC volunteers, 70; Palasciano's addresses on, 152n35; Palasciano's precedence over Dunant in advocating for, 153n37. See also autonomy; impartiality; permanence; universality

neutral "space": NGOs and, 2

"never again" commitment, 116

"new atheists," 133

"new humanitarianism": evolution of, as a new social movement, 122; French doctors in Biafra and emergence of, 122–25; sans-frontiérisme and rise of, 116–31

news outlets: Barton's special relations with, 102; local, NRCs and close relations with, 79

newspapers: casualties lists in, 105; glorification of battle victories in, 26; on government compliance with Red Cross proposals, 107–8; Red Cross in action accounts in, 106

NGOs. See nongovernmental organizations (NGOs)

Nigerian Civil War (1967–1970): as first destination for physicians, 123

Nigerian Red Cross Society, 123

Nightingale, Florence, 19, 45, 51; commissioning of, 104; Crimean War and, 95; Notes on Nursing, 94

nongovernmental organizations (NGOs): humanitarian, ubiquity of, 1; impartial, independent, and neutral values of, viii,

ix, 2, 5, 144n9. See also cultural origins of humanitarian NGOs; humanitarian NGOs; international NGOs (INGOs)

North Cyprus Red Crescent Society, 164n87

North Korea: dilemmas faced by MSF in, 128

Norway: Nigerian Civil War and Red Cross society of, 123

Notes on Nursing (Nightingale), 94

NRCs. See national Red Cross societies (NRCs)

nuns: battlefield tasks performed by, 95

nurses: as active caregivers beyond battlefield, 98, 99; empowerment of, in the public sphere, 100–101; humanitarianism of Red Cross and, 5; humorous portrayal of, 101, 102; military medical facilities and, 18–19; neutrality of actors on battlefield and, 55; peacetime activities and, 98, 99; pioneer, 45; in the service of the Red Cross, 97–98

nursing: emergence of transnational humanitarian field and, 13; emerging profession of, 93–95; new systems of reward in, 98, 100; role of "femaleness" in, 169n26; spread of humanitarian logics into, 89, 93–101, 115; women's aid societies and the Red Cross, 95–97

nursing schools: establishment of, 94

Offe, Claus, 122

Olympic movement: intermingling of nationalism and universality and, 85

Order of St. John of Jerusalem (Prussian), 19, 20, 109

orthodoxy: adamant, Calvinist law and, 44, 45

Ottoman Empire: Red Cross and expansion into, 78–79; weak NRCs in, 81

Ottoman government: Geneva Convention and, 107

Oxfam International, viii, 2; El Salvador's fight against predatory mining and, 137; Nigerian Civil War and, 123

pacifism: American Friends Service Committee and, 136

Pakistan: MSF and guerilla factions' use of cover of neutrality in, 128

Palasciano, Ferdinando, 18–19, 21

Paris: MSF operational center in, 124; population in 1860, 38

Paris Commune, 64; Paris-based NRC and view of, 69

Paris Declaration Respecting Maritime Law, 21

Passy, Frédéric, 34, 49

Patriotic Aid Society for Wounded Soldiers (Austria), 77

"patriotic societies": within Germanic Confederation, 96

patriotism: powers of, 70–72

peace activists: nineteenth-century, volunteer battlefield relief work denounced by, 3; Pentagon surveillance of, 179n15

peace congresses, 23

peace movements: in nineteenth-century Europe, 153n40

peace societies: agendas of, 35; battlefield relief in the nineteenth century and, 22–23

peacetime activities: Red Cross and, 98, 99

Pearson, Emma, 100–101, 105, 115

permanence, 12, 38. See also autonomy; impartiality; neutrality; universality

Permanent Court of Arbitration, in The Hague, 115

philanthropic mission: Christian ethic and, 37

philanthropists: early Red Cross activists, 46; linkage between nationalism and charity and, 72

philanthropy: popularity of, in late nineteenth century, 54. See also fundraising

physicians: neutrality of actors on battlefield and, 55. See also French doctors in Biafra

Pilkington, James, 39

Pinker, Steven, 6, 133

population displacement, mass: in Haiti, 1

positive law: international law and move toward, 109

power holders: humanitarian NGOs and, 4

predestination, 44

press. See journalism

prisoners of war: ICRC during World War I and, 118; notifying families of, 65; searching for, 98; World War II, ICRC humanitarian relief to, 120

privateering, 22

Protestant Christianity: core elements in, 42

Protestant Ethic and the Spirit of Capitalism, The (Weber), 148n47

Protestantism: Geneva's conversion to, 38; revival movements, invigorated Christian doctrine, and, 40–41. See also Calvinism; Lutherans and Lutheranism; Quakers; Reformed Protestantism; Swiss Reformed Protestants

Prussia: active NRCs in, 65; Geneva Convention and military instructions in, 111; NRCs, Second Schleswig War, and, 64

Prussian Red Cross: cooperation between myriad religious aid societies and, 91

public protest: news of war carnage and, 104, 105

Puerto Rico: humanitarian response to 2017 crisis in, 135; NGO intervention in, 1

Quakers, 136; abolitionist activism and, 10; disarmament initiatives and, 35; peace advocacy and, 22, 23

Quataert, Jean, 97

Radoman, Vladan, 123

railroads: mobility of news through, 104

Rauhe Haus: Field Deacons of, 20; Foundation, archive of, 141

rebel nonstate actors: MSF and inadvertent alignment with, 128, 131

Recamier, Max, 123

red crescent emblem: Ottoman government and use of, 78–79, 89

Red Crescent movement, viii, 7, 174n16

Red Cross: autonomy of humanitarian work established by, 35; balancing interconnectedness and autonomy, 115; Calvinist heritage and organizational logics of, 132; centuries-spanning influence on transnational humanitarian activism field, 131; churches in support of, 91–92; comparison of early Japanese and U.S. societies and humanitarian relief of, 73–75; connection between humanitarian and international law fields and, 108–9; considering alternatives to paradigm of, 138; copycat societies, 81; cross-denominational appeal of, 90–91; decentralization and overall vision for, 62–63; delegation to Theresienstadt concentration camp, 120; diplomatic level and spread of, across borders, 62; dissemination of new cultural structure and role of, 7–9; diversification of, 65–66; early advocates of, 12, 20; empowerment of nurses in the public sphere and, 100–101; ethical criticism of, 3–4; expansion into U.S., Bellows on, 91; expositions dedicated to work of, 67; flag of, 75–76, 114, 167n3; Geneva as birthplace of, 36; illustrated magazines and, 106; influence of *A Memory of Solferino* on, 24; journalists on the front and, 105–6; late nineteenth-century expansion of, 61; linkage between nationalism and charity, 72; local competition and rising prestige of, 79–82, 115; name, gradual adoption of, 67; nascent, competition for public attention faced by, 3; in national imagery, 75–77, 76; nurses as active caregivers beyond battlefield, 98, 99; nurses in service of, 97–98; papal approval of, 91; parallels between rise of MSF and rise of, 130; peacetime activities and, 98, 99, 119; popular Christian interpretation of, 92–93; redefines humanitarianism as a social field, 146n33; from religious values to a nascent social field, 59–60; the Réveil and inspiration for, 43–46; societies, growth of, 9; sources, 141, 142; state leaders and appeal of, 62; true success of, reasons behind, 35–36; violent first decade of, 64–65; war correspondents and, 105; women's aid societies and, 95–97. *See also* American National Red Cross (ANRC); International Committee of the Red Cross (ICRC); national Red Cross societies (NRCs); Red Cross movement

"Red Cross," mention of terms related to, in publications, 1850–1900, 67, *68*

Red Cross founding conferences of 1863–1864, 46–59; genesis of transnational field and, 46; independence of humanitarianism and, 47, 51–55; neutrality of humanitarians and beneficiaries and, 47, 55–59; organization and success of, 46; permanence of charity and, 47–51

Red Cross movement: Dunant's central role in establishment of, 15–16, 34, 35; journalism and interrelationship

with, 101–2; "militarization of charity" criticism and, 118–19; nascent, doctrinal points of the Réveil and, 43–46; religious affiliation of, downplaying, 89–90; Second Boer War and, 117; support for humanitarian NGOs and, ix

Red Cross societies: *A Memory of Solferino* and organizing principles of, 15; proliferation of, history behind, 3. *See also* national Red Cross societies (NRCs)

Red Cross Society of the Republic of China (Taipei-based), 164n87

"Red Cross Sundays," 91–92

Redfield, Peter, 134

Reformed Christianity: Geneva and expansion of, 39, 40

Reformed institutions: in Geneva, 39

Reformed Protestantism: contemporary NGOs and imprint of, 5; internationalism of, 63; role differentiation between church and state and, 45

Reformed Protestant world: Geneva's significance in, 38

refugees: post–World War II, ICRC and, 121; Syrian, 2

relief organizations: in Haiti, 1. *See also* humanitarian NGOs; nongovernmental organizations (NGOs)

religion: emergence of transnational humanitarian field and, 13; humanitarianism and, 9–10; impartial humanitarianism and role of, 59; reconsideration of humanitarian work and, 133–36; role of, in shaping civil society organization, ix

religious beliefs: rise of social institutions and, 36–37

religious field: churches in support of the Red Cross, 91–92; popular Christian interpretation of the Red Cross, 92–93; spread of humanitarian logics into, 89–93, 115

Religious Rejections of the World and Their Directions (Weber), 148n47

Renan, Ernest, 33

reporters: gain independence from the military, 104. *See also* journalism; newspapers

Reporters without Borders, 173n3

Republic of Biafra, 123

Réveil, the, 11, 59, 63; doctrinal points of, and nascent Red Cross movement, 43–46; Dutch offshoot of, 42; emergence of, 10; humanitarian sector and ethical principles inherited from, 10; ICRC founders and, ix; inspiration for the Red Cross and, 40–46; origins of, 41–43; origins of the logics of humanitarian field and, 37–46; prominent members of, 41, 45; Red Cross organizational model and theology of, 5

Revue de Droit International et de Législation Comparée: establishment of, 113

Revue international de la Croix-Rouge, 179n1

Richards, Linda, 94

rights-based humanitarianism: criticisms of, 138; proponents of, 137

Rolin-Jaequemyns, Gustave, 113

Romania: establishment of NRC as declaration of self-determination, 77; Red Cross societies in, 62

Rossel, Maurice: ICRC visit to Theresienstadt and Auschwitz headed by, 120, 174n21

royal houses: leverage attached to rising prestige of NRCs and attention of, 81. *See also* aristocratic women

Royal Red Cross award: establishment of, 98

Russell, William Howard: reporting from Crimean War, 104–5

Russia: Barton on famine in, 105; Geneva Convention articles and military instructions in, 111

Russo-Japanese War (1905), 78; Japanese woodblock print depicting Red Cross volunteers at work in, 73–74, 74

Russo-Turkish War, 78

Rwanda: NGO intervention in, 1

Salvation Army: Nigerian Civil War and, 123

Samaritan Society: founding of, 98

Samaritan's Purse, 135

San Francisco Call, The: Barton on Red Cross in Cuba feature, 103

sans-frontiérisme: French preoccupation with the Third World and emergence of, 175n40; glorifying, 126–27; rise of "new humanitarianism" and, 116–31

SARC (Syrian Arab Red Crescent), 131

Save the Children: Nigerian Civil War and, 123

Saxony: active NRCs in, 65

scandals, within humanitarian community, 2

Schleswig War of 1864, 53

School of Nursing and Midwifery (London): Nightingale and establishment of, 94

Scouting movement: intermingling of nationalism and universality and, 85

Scramble for Africa: Red Cross and, 82–85

Seacole, Mary, 26

Sebastopol Sketches (Tolstoy), 20

Second Boer War, 54, 117

Second Great Awakening, 10

Second Helvetic Confession: republishing of, 43

Second Italian War of Independence (1859), 14

Second Schleswig War (1864), 95; Geneva Convention and local jurists in aftermath of, 111; NRCs on both sides of, 64

Secours médical français—French Medical Relief (SMF): formation of, 124

secular humanitarian organizations: faith-based humanitarian NGOs and, 135

sensational internationalism, 79

sensational stories: Red Cross coverage and, 106, 108

senseless death: portrayed in Dunant's *A Memory of Solferino*, 29–31, 33

Serbia: establishment of NRC as declaration of self-determination, 77; Red Cross societies in, 62

Serbian Red Cross, 105

Serbo-Bulgarian War (1885), 54, 79, 101

Serbo-Turkish War (1876–1878), 65, 105

Seven Weeks War (Austro-Prussian War, 1866), 64

Shōken (empress of Japan), 96

Siam: NRC of, modeled after Japanese chapter, 78

Siege of Paris, 64

sinfulness: Calvinist belief in nature of, 49

Sisters of Mercy, 19, 20, 93, 94, 152n28

slaveholding: "national sin" notion and, 10

slavery: Scramble for Africa and, 82, 83

SMF (Secours médical français—French Medical Relief): formation of, 124 social activism: engaged, Réveil theologians call for return of, 44; reformist, religious movements and, 41

social institutions: rise of, religious beliefs and, 36–37

socialist pacifist circles: agendas of, 35

socialists: peace societies and, 23

social reforms: revival movements and, 41

social suffering: depoliticizing of, criticism leveled at, 5–6

Société des Amis, 41, 42

Société de secours aux blessés militaires: Sanitary Commission and, 152n24

Société nationale belge de la Croix-Rouge (copycat society), 81

Society for Assistance to the Wounded and Disabled in Action (Constantinople), 78

Society for Public Utility (Geneva), 46

Society for the Amelioration of the Condition of Prisoners of War, 107

Society for the Promotion of Universal and Permanent Peace (London Peace Society), 22–23

Society of Friends. See Quakers

Society of May Second: Spanish Red Cross and, 71

Society of the Holy Cross: Spanish Red Cross and, 71

sources and methodology, 141–42

South Sudan: Médecins du Monde expelled from Darfur, 130

Sovereign Military Order of Malta, 20

Sovereign Order of St. John, 20

Spanish-American War, 54, 161n25; criticism of Red Cross efficiency during, 106

Spanish Red Cross: endorsements of patriotism and, 71; height of popularity of, 161n25; on humanitarian mission, 50; Third Carlist War and, 57, 161n25

Speak Truth to Power, 179n15

Sphere, The: Japanese Red Cross nurses depicted in, 80; Red Cross in action accounts in, 106

sphere differentiation (Weber), 148n47

Srebrenica: humanitarian policy conversations and difficult questions arising from, 138

Stamatov, Peter, 10, 60

Standing Commission of the Red Cross: establishment of, 174n16

state and unchecked power: the Réveil's suspicious view of, 45

state interest "pollution": ICRC's susceptibility to, 131

state leaders: appeal of Red Cross to, 62; growing legitimacy of Red Cross societies and, 72–73; Red Cross linkage between nationalism and charity and, 72

state sovereignty: MSF and rising suspicion of, 127

sterilization: new knowledge about importance of, 97–98

St. John Ambulance (Britain), 98

Stockholm: Red Cross periodical resembling the Bulletin in, 67

St. Petersburg: Red Cross periodical resembling the Bulletin in, 67

Strong Program in Cultural Sociology, x; field analysis conjoined with, 149n58

student movements of the 1960s: "new social movements" and, 122

Sweden: Nigerian Civil War and Red Cross society of, 123

Swiss Confederation, 118; Geneva as twenty-second canton within, 40

Swiss Federal Council, 121

Swiss National Council, 118

Swiss Red Cross: Nigerian Civil War and, 123

Swiss Reformation: reinvigorated Calvinist social activism and, 45

Swiss Reformed Church, 10, 43

Swiss Reformed Protestants: language and imagery of Red Cross movement and, 5

Switzerland: internationally recognized neutral status of, 118; recognition of Red Cross flag and armband in, 110

Sydow, Rudolf von, 50

Syria, 2, 177n77; differences between ICRC and MSF responses to crisis in, 130–31; MSF and hospitals in, 125

Syrian Arab Red Crescent (SARC), 131

technological innovations: mid-nineteenth-century battlefield and, 17

Télécoms sans Frontières, 173n3

telegraph: mobility of news and introduction of, 104

témoignage: declaration for MSF and meaning of, 124; reconsideration of, 128–30

Thailand: MSF and guerilla factions' use of cover of neutrality in, 128

Theresienstadt concentration camp: Rossel heads Red Cross delegation to, 120, 174n21

Third Carlist War: endeavors of Spanish NRC during, 111; mention of Red Cross name with, 67; Red Cross and, 65

Third World: French doctors turn to relief work in, 123

Times, The: massacre as a term adopted by, 107

Tolstoy, Leo, 20

transnational advocacy networks: early, 10

transnational empathy, 6

transnational fields: Bourdieu's skepticism toward, 166n117; humanitarian norms and formation of, 86

transnational humanism: Christian ethic and, 36, 37

transnational humanitarian activism: scholarship on, 7

transnational humanitarian field: adjacent fields impacted by, 13; national settings in, 110; persisting affinity to religious field sentiments and, 92–93; present-day humanitarian NGO policies and, 13

transnational humanitarianism: Barton on future of, 71–72; expansion of Red Cross movement and, 85; nurses' involvement in, 94

transnational humanitarianism, making into a national mission, 69–79; modeling new nationhood through humanitarian activism, 77–79; powers of patriotism, 70–72; Red Cross in national imagery, 75–77, 76; sensational internationalism, 79; varieties of national humanitarian projects, 72–75

transnational humanitarian work: religious beliefs in generating field of, x

transparency: faith-based organizations and, 135. See also accountability

Treaty of Turin (1816), 40

typhus, 18

United Kingdom: Nigerian oil extraction and, 123

United States: Bellows on expansion of Red Cross into, 91; Nigerian Civil War and Red Cross society of, 123; peace societies in, 23; ratifies Geneva Convention (1882), 163n61; Second Great Awakening in, 10

United States Christian Society, 20

United States Sanitary Commission, 19, 37, 73

Universal Declaration of Human Rights (1949), 116

universality, 132; humanitarian NGOs and, viii, ix, 2; intermingling of nationalism and, 85. See also autonomy; impartiality; neutrality; permanence

"upward" accountability: "bottom-up" accountability vs., 179n17

Venerable Company, 39, 42

Victor Emmanuel II, 14

Victoria (empress consort of Germany), 96

Victoria (queen of England), 95; on Ottoman soldiers, 105; Royal Red Cross award established by, 98, 100

Vienna: population in 1860, 38

Vietnam: MSF's operations in, 128; MSF's unapproved mission to, 129–30

volunteers: controversy related to volunteer movements, 3; Dunant's depiction of, in A Memory of Solferino, 28–29, 33; glorifying sans-frontiérisme and, 126–27; leverage attached to rising prestige of NRCs and attention of, 81; national sentiments expressed by, 72; neutrality of actors on battlefield and, 55, 56–57; Nigerian Civil War and, 123; popularity of Red Cross with, 62

volunteer societies: Red Cross founding conferences and movement toward, 52

"voluntourism": exploitation of local distress and, 137

Walzer, Michael, 44

war: American Friends Service Committee and advocacy against, 136; Calvinist view of human sinfulness and, 49; Dunant's work and two opposing views of, 26–27; Merle d'Aubigné on scourge of, 43–44; neutral "space" for NGOs and, 2; positivist international law and legal evaluation of, 110. See also individual wars

war casualties: mass burial of, in nineteenth century, 31

war correspondents: Crimean War and, 104; Red Cross and, 105; reprimands for breaches of Geneva Convention and, 107

war economy: humanitarian NGOs and, 128

war journalism: in transition, 102, 104–5

war practices: mid-nineteenth-century, details on, 151n15

Wasserführ, August, 19

Way, Lewis, 43

Weber, Max: notion of sphere differentiation, 148n47

Wilhelm I (emperor of Germany), 77

William II (crown prince of the Netherlands), 42

women: participation in Red Cross movement, 93. *See also* nuns; nurses; nursing

women's aid societies, 20; Red Cross and, 95–97

women's philanthropic associations: relief provided by, 54

Wonderful Adventures of Mrs. Seacole in Many Lands, The (Seacole), 26

World Bank: International Court for the Settlement of Investment Disputes at, 137

World Council of Churches: Nigerian Civil War and, 123

World Health Organization, 129, 138

World Vision, 2

World War I, 30; ICRC and coordination of humanitarian activities during, 118;

NRCs and communication with families during, 98

World War II: humanitarian NGOs and historical arc of recovery from, 4; ICRC in, 119–21

wounded soldiers: Dunant's depiction of, in *A Memory of Solferino*, 24–25, 28; enemy, ratification of Geneva Convention and treatment of, 47; neutrality of, 47, 55–59; neutrality of actors on battlefield and, 55–59; volunteer aid societies and, 8

Württemberg: active NRCs in, 65; Geneva Convention articles and military instructions in, 111

xenophobia, 61, 63, 159n2

Yemen: ICRC interventions in, 122

Yugoslavia: Nigerian Civil War and Red Cross society of, 123

Yugoslav wars: ICRC and, 2

Zaire: MSF and guerilla factions' use of cover of neutrality in, 128

Zubrzycki, Geneviève: on national sensoriums, 163–64n71

Zurich: economic development in, 38; population in 1798, 155n10; population in 1850, 155n9; Red Cross periodical resembling the *Bulletin* in, 67